*From Bended Knee
to a New Republic*

## About the Author

Brendan Ogle is Ireland's Education, Politics & Development Organiser for the union Unite and one of the founders of the Right2Water and Right2Change campaigns. He is the author of *Off the Rails: The Story of the ILDA.*

# From Bended Knee to a New Republic

*How the Fight for Water is Changing Ireland*

Brendan Ogle

The Liffey Press

Published by
The Liffey Press Ltd.
Raheny Shopping Centre, Second Floor
Raheny, Dublin 5, Ireland
www.theliffeypress.com


© 2016 Brendan Ogle


A catalogue record of this book is
available from the British Library.


ISBN 978-1-908308-95-5

Printed in Ireland by SPRINT-print Ltd.

# Contents

Acknowledgements                                                vii

Preface                                                           1

*Chapter 1*
A Life Changed While a Nation Breaks                              5

*Chapter 2*
It Begins with Water …                                           20

*Chapter 3*
Neoliberalism                                                    30

*Chapter 4*
The Labour Party – From Democratic Socialism
    to Social Democracy                      40

*Chapter 5*
From Horseback to Hope Back                                      57

*Chapter 6*
Off Our Knees – Right2Water Hits the Streets                     64

*Chapter 7*
Right2Water Day 3: Added Tensions
    and Meeting Russell Brand                 96

*Chapter 8*
Damaged Media = Damaged Democracy                    113

*Chapter 9*
Now Let's Build – Early 2015 …                       126

*Chapter 10*
Policies First                                       156

*Chapter 11*
ICTU Conference Victory – 'No Way, We Won't Pay'     188

*Chapter 12*
Right2Water Day 5 – 29 August 2015                   195

*Chapter 13*
Be a Big Part of Something Small, or a
      Small Part of Something Big?                   200

*Chapter 14*
Building towards Election 2016                       214

*Chapter 15*
Elections Results and the Aftermath –
      All Is Changed, Changed Utterly                231

*Chapter 16*
17 September 2016 – 'Abolition Not Suspension'       243

*Chapter 17*
So Where Will Our Progressive Government
      Come From?                                     262

Index                                                270

# Acknowledgements

The journey set out in this book is not one that anyone can embark upon alone. Throughout it I have always felt that I have been among literally hundreds of thousands of our citizens who crave a better nation. They all have stories equally as important as this one. I just hope that my story does justice to theirs.

Of that mass of people literally hundreds of them are in regular contact with me in one way or another. These people, who I have come to know through the water charges movement, have lifted and propelled this campaign in the hours and days when, without them, it would have stumbled and fallen. It could so easily have been just another failed campaign in a failed Republic which cherishes none of its children equally. They know who they are and I thank them for being so strong for us all, and for future generations too.

There are people without whom none of the events in this book, let alone my role in them, would have been possible. Two in particular stick out. Jimmy Kelly is my 'boss' in Unite but that is just his job title. In reality he is a friend and comrade without whom I doubt I would be even in the trade union movement at this point. Jimmy, and his partner Mary, have stood with me, backed me, supported me and even held me up on occasion when I have needed it most in all sorts of ways, professional and personal. I am never afraid of taking anything on but that sometimes leads to a mistake here and there and a chance for the enemies our positions create to take their opportunity. But you can't make an omelette without breaking eggs and on those occasions it is people like Jimmy Kelly you need at your back. He will never know how grateful I am for his support, guidance, experience, solidarity and friendship. Maybe this will help.

Dave Gibney could have written this book too. But Dave is a perfectionist and this book is far from perfect – so I did it. But without Dave Gibney there would be no Right2Water and no book. Nobody I have met has Dave's expertise with how to use media and internet tools to build a campaign such as this. In addition, his skill with words and people is not just 'part of the job'. It is reflective of an inner decency and empathy he has with the people of our country who have been exposed to the worst excesses of austerity and inequality. Put those skills, knowledge, heart and empathy together and you have the real driver of the Right2Water campaign behind the scenes, and that is exactly what Dave has been. We have become deep and close friends even if the 'bro-mance' has cooled somewhat (thanks Lucia!), and whatever happens from here on in I am clear about this – wherever there are people who are suffering from deprivation or exclusion Dave Gibney will always be in their corner. Thanks comrade.

I also want to thank all at Unite and the Right2Water unions who have supported this campaign so valiantly. In addition to our own Executive the campaign has posed challenges for all the Executives of Mandate, the Communications Workers Union, the Civil and Public Services Union, OPATSI and the TEEU who came on board later and had to get over some difficult barriers to do so. I believe the people of Ireland owe them all a debt. To John, Stevie, Des, Billy, Cormac and all others who have worked so hard to hold this campaign together a special word of acknowledgement for their unity and hard work. And Moira's artwork and support has been brilliant. And for all the hard work you can bet your life that with this lot you are going to have some right laughs along the way too.

I also want to acknowledge the photographic work of all who have contributed to this book but, in particular, Siobhan Walsh and Derek and to thank them for their patience. And thanks also to Neil Michaels for help with photographs. Also thank you to Sinead Stewart for her help in trying to make sense of, and collating, some of my Facebook blogs and thoughts. Some task!

Artists have played a massive part in the campaign and have brought their immense talents to bear throughout, and without personal gain. They are acknowledged in the book and here I want to thank Stephen Murphy whose poem 'It Isn't Just About the Water' completes this book. Stephen is a true genius with the written and spoken word but, not only that, he speaks from a soul which feels the pain of those he speaks about. Stephen's work is not about empty words, it is about capturing the spirit of a broken, but now rising nation. Everybody should access his work, listen, learn and be inspired. Thank you Stephen for inspiring me.

Inspiration comes from further afield too. As you are about to read the fight to save our water from commodification and corporate greed is a global fight. I have learned so much from the wonderful Maude Barlow, the planet's foremost 'water warrior' and her colleagues Meera and Brent at the Blue Planet Project. Future generations owe these people a debt they might never know. And so too our friends in the European Water Movement who lit the fuse in Europe with their citizen's initiative gathering over 2 million signatures to have water declared a human right by the European Union. Their support and help are invaluable. Thank you Pablo, David, Elizabeth and Yiorgos and others who have been in touch with support and guidance.

Stevie and Mel at Trademark and Jim at Unite Education in London deserve thanks for supporting me throughout as do all my colleagues on the 'Ed Orgs' team along with Lenny, Andrew and Tony. Other people are mentioned throughout the book but the work of Noelle Whelan in the Unite Office in Dublin has been outstanding. Noelle has often kept the vital administration side of things together when it looked like it might come apart at the seams. She has given fantastic support to the movement, Unite and myself, and she even found the publisher for this book when I might have given up on it.

And so to David Givens of The Liffey Press. From the moment we sent him the plan for the book he cut straight to the chase and set challenging deadlines that were hard to meet but necessary. Once he started reading the book his advice was vital and I hope he thinks I took at least some of it on board. I am very grateful to him because in a small book market like Ireland I could not have funded or finished this project myself. I hope the book is worthy of a great publishing house.

Family is everything really, however it is defined in the modern era. Some of the events in this book record painful experiences and without the support of Mum, my late Father, Briege, John, Anne and the rest of the gang none of this could have happened. Since I last wrote a book 13 years ago my 'kids', Dara and Kate, are barely kids at all now and I hope in time they will find stories, experiences and direction in these events that will help them on the difficult path all young people are faced with in an Ireland now constructed on a most unequal and unfair basis. Especially for our youth. I also want to thank Pauline for being their Mum, and a super one at that.

I also want to give my heartfelt thanks to Ann Kirwan for helping me in ways that are not the subject matter of this book, but in ways that are nonetheless vital and worthy of the sincerest acknowledgement and thanks.

# Acknowledgements

I'm nearly fifty now and as I approach that landmark in my life I think it is time to settle down again and try to find fulfilment on a personal, as well as a professional level. That has been elusive for many years but this water journey also brought Mandy in to my life at a time when it was a struggle and I could see little light at the end of the tunnel. Things now look immeasurably brighter and more positive and her care, support, principle, talent and humour have led me through the toughest times. I hope I will be worthy of such support and love in the times ahead.

If I manage to do so it will be down to so many people helping me along the road that it would take another book to do justice to them. The 13 years since *Off the Rails* was published have been challenging from every perspective but, as I say elsewhere, I have been very lucky indeed. This country has broken many people and I believe the reasons why, and the mechanisms of how, are captured in this book.

For all who shared the journey so far, and all who may commit to a future journey to change it for the better, thank you and enjoy the book.

Brendan Ogle
September 2016

# Preface

You won't read about this story anywhere else. You won't see it on your TV stations and it won't be turning up in future editions of *Reeling in the Years*. That is why this book has been written.

This book will take you on a journey. It is at first a dark and despairing journey through the travails of a nation broken, sold and left in penury. The story outlines how a promised Republic that would cherish all of the children of the nation equally, an egalitarian oasis, was stolen and then destroyed first by the whims of the gombeen and, now, by the evils of global neoliberalism.

The terms will be explained and assessed later, but first let me be clear about the subject matter of this book. It is about people and their human right to life, a right which is intrinsically linked and inseparable to their right to water. If you think that statement is overly dramatic then tell it to the people of Flint, Michigan and their neighbours in Detroit. On 10 December 2014, Right2Water held its third national protest. Unlike the first two massive outpourings, this one would be different. This one was not held on a Saturday but in the middle of the week, in the middle of the winter, outside our parliament. We had visitors that day: 'Shu', Justin, Meeko and 'AtPeace' had been touring Ireland with us meeting the water warriors of Edenmore and Dublin North, of Crumlin and Dublin South, of

Cobh and Cork, of Tallaght and Jobstown and, ultimately, of my home town Dundalk. Everywhere they went they brought such sincerity and, as 'Shu' would put it, 'peace and love' that they were adored. I think every single person they met that week fell in love with these wonderful Americans. This was all very strange because they were actually ghosts.

As we approached Christmas 2014, our Fine Gael/Labour Government was busy putting in place the hardware for water commodification. Meters were being installed, veritable toll booths on our human right to water. Consultants were hired, a massive public relations campaign was launched, offices procured, a bonus culture for the chosen leaders of Irish Water was embedded and billing systems were built while the threat by our European Commissioner Phil Hogan that non-payers would 'have their water pressure turned down to a trickle for basic human health reasons and obviously that won't be too attractive for them' still rang in our ears. Even as he headed off to Brussels to earn €336,446.65 a year as well as expenses.

And amid all of this we had, right in our midst, the Detroit Water Brigade, the 'ghosts of Christmas future'. The future they foretold was terrifying. The once great industrial city of Detroit had been laid bare of its automotive heritage as globalisation moved real jobs elsewhere and replaced them with financial capital. For some this model of de-industrialisation was a highway to super riches, but to many it was a slow and painful road into unemployment, early retirement and social and economic inequality. And so water meters became a new source of revenue to a city starved of the taxes of working people. Water bills, low and seemingly inconsequential at first, rose higher and higher until many impoverished people simply could not afford to pay them.

And then the shut-offs came.

By mid-July 2014, just as we in Ireland were beginning our slow and painful journey to water privatisation, 16,000 Detroit residents had their water shut off entirely. There would be no showering, cooking, washing or flushing for these people in districts such as Highland Park, where drugs and gun crime were already major problems tormenting parents trying to raise their children. This, added to the problems already faced by such parents as one resident, Valerie Blakely, whose water bill was over $1,000 pointed out: 'As far as I am concerned, what the city is doing is illegal activity. You're not going to come and put us in a life-or-death situation and not have us act like we are fighting for our own survival.'

Life or death. Survival. Water.

'Shu' and 'AtPeace' know all about life and death and survival. As they outlined their personal stories they implored meetings all over Ireland: 'Don't let them put the meters in, this is where it starts. We are your ghosts of Christmas future, learn from us Ireland, do not let them do it.' Then, on 10 December 2014, and in temperatures more normal for Detroit than Dublin, they got onto a stage in front of 80,000 souls and told them the same. And then they danced a jig with us on stage to the brilliant music of the Rolling Tav Revue and we all linked arms and hugged and pledged that they will not do it to us. And they will not!

My life changed that day, and I am not the only one. Justin Wedes, one of the visitors and a veteran of 'Occupy Wall Street', put it in context for me in McGrattan's bar afterwards. He explained that in terms of numbers the demonstration that he had just attended was, pro rata, bigger than anything America had ever seen. Martin Luther King Jr.'s famous 'I Have a Dream' speech at the Lincoln Memorial was witnessed by 250,000 people. Justin pointed out that the population of the USA was 319 million, and he had just gotten off a stage in front of 80,000 people in a country of only 4.5 million. Incredible.

We have now, in Ireland, the biggest (per capita) and most peaceful protest movement for social change anywhere in the world. If you haven't been told that, if it hasn't been recorded anywhere else, it will be recorded here.

This is a people's movement and this is their book, this is their story and this is their cause. We are loud, we are proud and we are not going anywhere. All together now...

'From Dublin to Detroit – Water is a Human Right'

# 1

# A Life Changed While
# a Nation Breaks

This is my second, and by far the more difficult, book that I have written. While my first book was essentially a story about 114 workers and their struggle, this one has much wider import. The events set out in this book affect everybody in this country in one way or another, and others beyond it. But it is in essence an account of a movement and how it has evolved through a single set of eyes, ears and experiences. As such it is subjective – it couldn't be anything else.

What it is, however, is an honest, sometimes brutally so, account of my involvement in that movement. All the views and experiences are mine and all the opinions I give are honestly held. Many who have been involved, particularly those with a certain political mindset or agenda, will see in this book criticisms or shortcomings. This is unavoidable.

I believe that Ireland is a broken nation, an unequal nation, and that it is manifestly so. I believe it is that way for a reason. Whether that reason is the policies and behaviour of those who have governed us to date, or the failures of those who have not yet governed us through their inability to build a progressive alternative, honest analysis is all that I have. In a country as broken, as inequitable, as indebted as ours, some honest analysis challenging the all-consuming 'consensus' might not be the worst thing to offer.

It has been thirteen years since I wrote my first book, *Off The Rails: The Story of ILDA*, published by the good people of Currach Press, which has sadly just gone into liquidation. Thirteen years ago – unlucky for some, but for whom?

The cover of that book included the words of then *Sunday Independent* journalist John Drennan who stated boldly: 'For anyone who wants to know how modern Ireland works, this book is absolutely essential.' I was grateful to John then for those words, along with kind tributes from other journalists, authors, documentary makers and academics, but the truth is that that book sets out only a fleeting glimpse of how our broken Republic actually operates. I didn't know it then, but in the years that have followed I have seen and learned so much more about how a nation that started as a proclaimed egalitarian Republic, cherishing all of the children equally, has evolved into one of the most unequal nations in the European Union today.

That inequality, and a nation's fight back against it, is the subject matter of this book. For this author these thirteen years have been ones of massive upheaval personally and professionally. In 2003 I was a train driver living in Athlone, but now in 2016 I have been a trade union official for over a decade and have found myself at the forefront of industrial campaigns in ESB and, latterly, in the water charges and change movements as encapsulated by the Right2Water and Right2Change campaigns.

Personal details are not the main focus here, but for the benefit of readers I am, since 2005, a separated father of two beautiful daughters, Dara and Kate. I have lived in Dublin since in various accommodations and these past years have been life-changing ones where I have fought not just the battles outlined in this book but other ones too. These included the pain of losing my family, my home, my father and struggling with demons that came in both my head and in a glass at times.

In fact, they often came in both simultaneously. Life is a journey, but I am aware that on this journey I am relatively lucky. For all the difficulties I have had, I have been fortunate to be in continuous and satisfying employment and am not one of the 37 per cent of Irish citizens suffering multiple deprivation. Unlike many, I haven't been driven out of our country by unemployment or had to sleep on streets or in emergency state-sponsored accommodation.

The Republic of Ireland in 2016, a century after the reading of the Proclamation, is a broken one that not only does not treat all of its children equally, but treats many of them disgracefully. It is a nation whose citizens were launched into a period of national collective trauma in 2009 when we lost or economic independence and sovereignty. That we lost it by our own collective hand through tolerating and facilitating decades of mismanagement, corruption and gombeenism, only to then surrender to economic imperialism, helped to leave us reeling and unable to fight back. But now the fight back has not only begun, but it has entered an emergent phase of developing a more participative and representative democracy. The parties of the 'old civil war politics' are struggling to keep up with the demand for change as new protests, ideas and networks develop to reclaim our Republic.

If the role of the wider trade union movement in collaborating with the policies that wrecked a nation (so-called 'social partnership' from 1987 to 2009) was shameful, it is also true that there were those within the movement who not only resisted that lazy partnership consensus, but who are now trying to forge a new model of community and workplace-based 'lifelong trade unionism'. This model seeks to assist citizens acting 'in union' through campaigns and a developing movement that has those citizens fighting back at last. The enemy that attacks our living standards and the futures of our children and grandchildren does so inside and outside the workplace, and it does so throughout every aspect of our lives. Only by acting in solidarity will we continue to challenge and maybe even defeat that enemy.

I was born in a working class housing estate in Dundalk into a family of eight children and a father who worked in a single income household. I left – emigrated seems a funny word to use now for moving to London – but it was emigration in 1987. I left, along with many others, at a time when Charles Haughey was telling us to 'tighten our belts' as he and his ilk fattened their bellies. After a year on building sites I found myself working for London Underground Limited and then British Rail. I was in my first union, the National Union of Railwaymen (NUR), just in time for Thatcher's privatisation agenda and the strikes and struggles that it unleashed. This was a multicultural environment then too, and even as the IRA planted bombs in London I was treated by all with decency and respect. And it was as a member of the NUR, and later the RMT, that I closed my signal boxes and stood proudly with workers of all backgrounds and ages while we fought, over and over, Thatcher's attacks on us and her efforts – ultimately 'successful' – of privatising 'our' national rail system.

Thatcher won her battle to privatise the railways, the electricity system, the telecommunications sector, the gas network and the rest of the transport system. She turned housing from a 'need' into a 'commodity' and shut down the mining industry and much of the steel industry. Thatcher won, and the people lost. And then she privatised water too, and people are still losing as a result in the United Kingdom. The next time somebody turns up on *Liveline* to tell Joe Duffy about how they pay domestic water charges in the United Kingdom – as if that meant it was written on a tablet of stone – remember that they only do so because of Thatcher. Fortunately it would seem that most Irish people don't support Thatcherite policies. Why would they?

## Why Water? Inequality, Deprivation and a United Nations Resolution in 2010

I have been asked many times 'why water?' by commentators, interviewers, academics, students and even opponents of the campaign. There is a chapter dedicated to that later, but at first glance it seems a strange issue on which the Irish people would take their first and biggest real stand against austerity. At first glance!

Of course, the fact that one in six of those born in Ireland now live abroad – most having left out of economic necessity – should be the cause of grave political concern. Indeed, 300,000 emigrated during the reign of the Fine Gael/Labour coalition from 2011–2016. Add to that the following facts that are accurate at the time of writing (April 2016):

- More than 10 per cent of our people suffer from food poverty

- 36 per cent of children experience multiple deprivation

- We have the second highest prevalence of low pay in the OECD

- We have the second highest prevalence of under-employment in the original EU 15

- We have real unemployment, when 'job activation' schemes like Jobsbridge and Gateway are discounted, of over 12 per cent

- Lone parents – who are the most deprived group in the state with 63 per cent already experiencing multiple deprivation – are having their supports cut

- And it is clear that we are in a situation where inequality and deprivation affect so many people, and at so many different levels, that each area on its own is worthy of massive campaigns to bring about social change.

Before addressing the specific issue of 'why water?' there are two specific areas of social inequality that deserve special focus. The first is our broken health service. One of the things we all need, from the cradle to the grave, is decent healthcare. There is no doubt that in Ireland we have a two tier health service where the best health cover is only available based on means, not need. In a country that purports to be a civilised republic, people routinely suffer and die for the want of healthcare available to fellow citizens who are richer. Think about that.

## Healthcare

I have long felt that the best way to ensure that we all enjoyed the best healthcare available was to have a single tier healthcare system. Put bluntly, if the most privileged people in Ireland had to endure the same hospital conditions as the poorest we would have the best healthcare system in the world. Well, apart from Cuba anyway. Why do I say this? Well Cuba, with its wonderful and resilient people, should probably be the subject of another book. Maybe later. But for now suffice it to remind readers that this little Caribbean island with a similar land mass to Ireland, but three times the population, has been subjected to an illegal economic blockade for over 50 years. The blockade has been enforced by the United States, the world's sole remaining 'superpower' (at least in the traditional sense) whose southernmost tip on Key West lies just 84 miles away across the Straits of Florida. The blockade has prevented any real growth or development of the Cuban economy and stunted the nation's Gross Domestic Product (GDP) to such an extent that for many years Cuba resembled a third world country to the naked eye. To some it still does.

Not when it comes to healthcare though! Cuba's brand of universal healthcare is based on a delivery of primary healthcare to every citizen – most Cubans live in remote rural communities – delivered by regular compulsory health checks provided by skilled practitioners operating on horseback around hills and mountains, and the tobacco and citrus farms where many Cubans make a living. This model is allied to ground breaking research and development (R&D) in healthcare that Cuba uses to address cancers, transplants and their citizens' general well-being and that leads to Cubans enjoying a life expectancy four years *higher* than in the neighbouring United States (trumpeted as the most developed economy in the world). Cuba is rightly regarded as having one of the best healthcare systems in the world, universal in nature throughout.

So what of Ireland? As mentioned earlier, if the richest in our society had to use the same facilities, queues, waiting lists, trolleys and accident and emergency provision as the poorest many of our health service issues would be addressed overnight.

I had the misfortune on a few occasions to have to accompany people to the accident and emergency department of one of Dublin's largest hospitals, St. James. On each occasion it happened to be on a Friday night and the wait from triage to treatment lasted hours, on one occasion nine hours! While I sat there ambulances would regularly arrive with other patients, in many cases ones who had fallen victim to the weekend, some call it a lifestyle choice, others to the culture of excess drinking and drug use. Fights had broken out, beatings and stabbings had taken place, and the staff struggled to treat what were increasingly volatile and, in more than one case, violent new 'patients' while an 83-year-old man sat waiting and hoping for the sanctuary of a trolley. It is not an exaggeration to say that as you sit there on the plastic seats hour after hour looking at some of the worst excesses of human self-harm you could imagine, a trolley down a corridor behind locked doors stops being 'poor service provision' and increasingly becomes a refuge, even an oasis.

There are others, however, who don't go through any of this. Those fortunate enough to be able to afford private health insurance have a variety of options available to them depending on what they can afford. Did that sentence slip by you?

Those with money can get better healthcare based on their income, or wealth, as opposed to need, while those in more need with no income will wait, linger, and in many cases die prematurely or in unnecessary pain for lack of money to pay for available treatments. It is obscene.

And that's not all. Private healthcare is substantially subsidised by the taxpayer, even those taxpayers who will suffer from the inequality it delivers. The fact is that we all pay for the training of doctors, that private healthcare is generally provided from publicly-funded hospitals, that consultants draw a substantial public salary while making what they consider the 'real money' from their private practice on the side. Yes, the situation is obscene.

We all like to think that, sudden death apart, we will die in peace and dignity. But I have been in a public hospital ward, a ward full of sick and elderly patients and their visiting families, as a thin plain curtain was pulled around a neighbouring bed behind which a priest said prayers over a dying man while his family cried and comforted him and themselves in a complete absence of privacy or dignity. Scandalous.

Universal healthcare which ensures that all assets can be directed into a system that provides top quality care based solely on need are essential in a relatively prosperous republic.

But as I write this (April 2016), it has been confirmed that waits for public patients in Ireland are 25 times longer than for private patients – 25 times! 'Sick' indeed.

## Homelessness

There has always been some homelessness in society. In all societies, as far as I can see. But the situation in Ireland has changed utterly and for the worse. There have always been those who have fallen on unfortunate life circumstances, or who may suffer from mental health or addiction problems, who have found themselves living on our streets or relying on some of the fantastic charities that exist to help in such circumstances. That has always been the case.

I was born in the 1960s and grew up in Marian Park in Dundalk. There are 158 houses in Marian Park which was a housing scheme built in the 1950s. The houses are brick, solid, pass all fire standards and are pyrite-free. They stand as solid now as they did the year they were built. They were built by the local council and my home housed nine children and my parents. The house on my left had seven children and parents, another had six, another nine, and streets and neighbouring fields were packed with children playing. The neighbouring estate is Cox's Demesne, a sprawling estate where many school friends grew up and which later spawned Ashling Park. Close by are O'Hanlon Park, Father Murray Park and Fatima Park and Drive. All were built by the local council with labour directly employed on a 'not for profit' basis. Sustainable jobs and housing provided by the state. And guess what? It worked!

Most homes in those estates housed large families – at least by modern standards – and most were, in my time, single income households. My father was an extremely hard worker but for many years while the children were small our home, like so many, had only his modest weekly wage to survive on. The home we lived in was paid for through a rent controlled and collected by the local authority (I am old enough to remember the council-employed 'rent man' calling every Friday). The rent was a relatively modest percentage (I have calculated it at one memorable point at 7 per cent) of my father's wage, and that pattern was repeated in literally thousands of houses in Dundalk which was then a vibrant town teeming with heavy manufacturing industries, shoe factories, two breweries and a major cigarette factory.

The private sector was present too. Within a short walking distance of Marian Park lies Ard Easmainn, Newtownbalregan and 'the back of the wall', where privately owned houses stand for those who want, and are able, to provide their own housing needs in locations of their choosing. And good luck to them. From those areas too came, generally, large families of children attending school with us, playing on the same football teams and sharing the same communities and experiences as us. And that is just one town, my home town, Dundalk.

All over Ireland it was the same. Social housing was not only owned but built and controlled by local authorities making up the bulk of the state's housing stock and living cheek by jowl with private housing schemes. Those social housing schemes brought with them a virtuous cycle of house building leading to employment, then house provision and sustainable living with income left over after 'rent' to rear children and support what would now be called the 'local economy'. The Dundalk and Ireland I describe had a fully functioning 'economy' made up of manufacturing and local businesses like grocers, barber shops, bars, butchers, shoe shops and drapers, many of whose wares were sourced or manufactured locally. The main streets of the town were busy, active, alive. Where did it all go wrong?

It went wrong with Margaret Thatcher and an Irish politic unable to think for itself, blindly following what has turned out to be a dreadful prescription of 'Torynomics' imported from Britain and, ultimately, the Chicago School Economics of Milton Friedman, about which I will expound further. I actually remember the day Margaret Thatcher's philosophy first found its way into my life. My Mam and Dad were having a discussion. The local council had come up with a plan. Those who had hitherto lived in social housing and paid rents for properties owned by the state were to be offered a chance to buy their houses off the local authorities, 'on the purchase' as it was called. I can't recall the figures but I do recall it was the early 1980s and Mam and Dad were considering whether to take the house we lived in 'on the purchase'. It would require a modest increase in what was then 'rent', but over time they would own their home. It was all the rage in the 1980s, this home ownership lark.

What it was of course was the state selling off its housing stock for very little. Was this justified? Well, look at its results 35 years on. It should go without saying that this sell-off was accompanied by the local authorities gradually exiting the stage as 'house builder and employer of construction workers'. I remember the men, Dad's friends, who worked for the Council. There were brickies, sparks, spreads, painters and decorators. There used to be bin men too, and lighting engineers responsible for street lighting. And road sweepers. Remember them? It was a functioning, organic and self-perpetuating economy, a 'society' even, that those in power just decided to pick apart bit by bit. What we as a nation did then was nothing less than to hand the provision of the basic human need for shelter, for housing, entirely to the private sector. We removed the 'competition' that the private sector trumpets so much but actually despises in its grand pursuit of exploitative 'private monopolies'. The 'competition' for the private housing sector then was the public housing sector, and once we, as a nation, took the policy decision to exit the provision of publicly-built housing the current homelessness crisis was not just possible, it was inevitable. So do we have a 'homelessness crisis'? No, what we have had since the 1980s is a 'homelessness policy', followed blindly by every party that has entered Government in the intervening years, with the current inevitable disaster.

By the time I was buying my first home in 1994 the only option was the private sector, but the prices then were modest by modern standards. My first house when I moved to Athlone as a train driver cost IR£45,000, but by the time I moved again in 2002 the price had almost doubled. By now my household was double income and we were paying about one-third of our joint incomes on providing the roof over our heads. I'm not sure if I would have wanted nine children like my Mam and Dad, but it never really felt like a realistic option anyway. We had two. And so it was all around the nation. Some rural dwellers got planning permission to build one-off units that blight much of the landscape and add costs to infrastructure, whether in terms of roads, energy provision or other utilities, but in the towns and cities new houses were routinely being bought off plans all over the state as the property bubble was created and inflated. They called it the 'Celtic Tiger'. It wasn't, tigers are clever animals. This was utter stupidity.

The Government of course fell over themselves to provide massive tax breaks for the builders who made property development and speculation a multibillion euro sector and, in return, those grateful developers pushed funds into the political system and also the mainstream media in terms of massive advertising. Who paid for all this? Well, people buying homes whose values were massively inflated above construction costs paid for it, as did the taxpayer in the end.

## 2008 and the Day the Property Roof Fell in (Literally)

I had to begin to rent myself when my marriage broke up in 2005 and the landlord, a decent skin, kept encouraging me to buy one of the apartments myself. But I just knew that the figures he gave me were 'monopoly money' that bore little relation to my income and ability to pay. This couldn't last. This was highlighted to me in a shocking way on 10 August 2008. I remember the date well. Kerry were playing Galway in the All Ireland Football Quarterfinal in Croke Park. It was a Saturday afternoon and I was watching the game in my modern, way-too-expensive rented duplex apartment in Royal Canal Park. As I watched the game the rain was literally chucking it down and the small balcony, barely wide enough to stand up on, was taking a battering from the deluge which quickly burst a drain above. The players in Croke Park, just a few miles away, were barely able to see each other in the deluge which seemed like it would never end. It got so bad the floodlights had to go on – for an afternoon match in August! As I watched Galway's excellent Michael Meenan take on the Kingdom almost on his own, moving towards goal, crash … the roof literally fell in. From below I heard gushing water and ran down the stairs to find the centre of the ceiling lying on the bed with rain rushing in the hole from the balcony above. The apartment, newly built in a new complex, was uninhabitable in an instant and when I found a new one not far away I remember it was so badly built I didn't need an alarm clock, so regular were my upstairs neighbour's bathroom habits at 7:30 am, seven days a week!

I have often reflected on the fact that my first experience as a renter in the Irish property bubble in 2008 resulted in the ceiling literally falling in, just as the roof on our economy was collapsing all around us and sending the entire country over a cliff.

You now know the rest.

We the citizenry ended up picking up the tab for mismanagement, recklessness and the complete failure of governance while the chancers who caused it, at least the highest net wealth ones, got bailed out to the tune of at least €65 billion. The sad reality is that our children and grandchildren will be paying for this until – at current estimates – 2053. Yes, through atrocious political mismanagement, not only of the causes of the crisis but of the crisis itself, Ireland with less than 1 per cent of the population of the European Union is now foisted with an astronomical 41 per cent of its total banking debt.

And that's just the devastating financial cost. The human cost is horrendous. Rampant unemployment and under-employment has coincided with the forced emigration of

300,000 Irish economic migrants. And it gets worse. Suicide, especially among males, is at crisis levels, and on every inequality measurement Ireland currently sits either at, or near, the top of Eurozone league tables. And then there is the homelessness. There are families being made homeless in Ireland now for the first time since the famine. Entire families. 'Homes' are now considered 'assets', and while we all picked up the tab for the banking debt, those banks are rewarding us by kicking out ever increasing numbers from their homes to make more and more profit. They are also now profiteering on mortgage rates while paying merely interest on deposits. Same old banks!

Even homelessness itself is now seen as yet another 'thing' to be profited from as Councils like Dublin City Council build what they call 'modular housing' (glorified chalets to me and you) initially planned at a cost of a massive €99,000, but even that astronomical price has now doubled to €200,000 per unit. Property speculators are now 'investing' in the provision of emergency accommodation to make profits from a human tragedy. Simultaneously, hoteliers are renting out entire floors of hotels whose rooms masquerade as 'homes' for families, with little children walking through hotel lobbies in mornings with schoolbags on their backs while business groups huddle around coffee tables preparing to use those very hotels for their meetings.

And if you thought it couldn't get any worse, in a classic case of turning public suffering into private profit, the Government are not providing cheap or free homes to desperate families, but are giving free land to building developers! Instead of learning the lessons of our homelessness crisis, instead of learning that it was the handing over of housing provision in its entirety to the private sector that led to the crisis, Fine Gael Minister Simon Coveney is now going to make it worse. He has announced that land banks owned by the state, that is 'us', will be handed over 'free gratis' to the very same construction sector whose corruption and profiteering wrecked the nation to begin with. Instead of using the land that we own, and the homes that we found ourselves as a state owning when the gamblers crashed the nation, those assets are now just to be handed over to the same sector, and usually the very same people, again. Will we ever learn?

And now they want our water too. Well they aren't getting it. This book begins, and the stealth of our nation ends, with the fight for our life-giving Right2Water.

# 2

# It Begins with Water ...

It is not by accident that the social movement that is evolving in Ireland, and whose birth is set out in these pages, has its genesis as a water protest movement. All life begins with water and without water there is no life. And without a water movement there would have been no chance of breathing life into a small nation surrounded by water, but which has been ravaged by corruption, gombeenism and an austerity agenda that left a once proud people reeling. And it was the European Central Bank (ECB) and International Monetary Fund (IMF) who combined to force one of the European Union's smallest nations to pay a horrendously disproportionate price for their own fiscal and political failures.

That the resistance that eventually emerged arrived in the guise of a populace revolting about the attempted commodifying of their water and sanitation is not surprising. At least it is not surprising to those who understand what is being done to our planet's water supply to generate profit for the already super-rich. But the fact that many of you may be hearing about this for the first time in these few pages illustrates that, for all that has been written and said about water charges in Ireland since 2014, we have never had an honest national discussion about what is planned for our water and sanitation services, and why. It is long past time that we cut through the spin and 'got real'.

First, let me establish something. The earth is running out of water. We may have been educated to believe that the 'hydrologic cycle' is eternal which means that we can never run out of water, but that is simply not correct. Yes, between water vapour and precipitation water may still exist on the planet somewhere, but global birth rates allied to our consumption patterns, incorporating ruinous models of industrialisation, agriculture and food production, results in the human race wrecking the planet's water resources through pollution and displacement. Let's look at the demand side. It is estimated that the world's population will rise to between 9 and 10 billion by 2050. Today the population is just short of 7.5 billion and 2.5 times more people are being born every day than are dying. There are nearly 400,000 births in the world per day. Pretty impressive 'growth' figures! In the next twenty years China plans to build 500 new cities with more than 100,000 people in each. India will add 600 million to the world's population by 2050. India and China are the most populated nations on the planet, but across the board populations are rising everywhere except for very small drops, typically a fraction of a single per cent point, in some European states. Ireland's population is now growing by 0.54 per cent annually, net of emigration.

Dr. Peter Gleick, who has just stood down as President and Co-founder of the Pacific Institute, has studied the science of how the world's population changes affect our water supply for over three decades. At home in California, Gleick published a report in 2003 that showed how farmers there could save a massive 15 per cent of water by simply improving irrigation in a state where agriculture accounts for four-fifths of the water. Globally, agriculture and industry use around 90 per cent of our water. As Gleick points out, although populations grow accessible water is finite and population growth allied to poor use at a time of global warming can only lead to crisis. He recently wrote:

As populations and economies grow, peak water pressure on existing renewable water resources also tend to grow up to the point that natural scarcity begins to constrain the options of water planners and managers. At this point, the effects of natural fluctuations in water availability in the form of extreme weather events become even more potentially disruptive than normal. In particular, droughts begin to bite deeply into human well-being.

In their book *Out of Water*, Colin Chartres and Samyuktha Varma demonstrate that by including the massive amount of water used to grow our food a person who consumes 2,500 calories a day will account for 2,500 litres of water. When those figures are extrapolated globally, to meet population growth by 2050 the authors point out that there is simply not enough water available in the areas of population growth to produce food. Across Africa 'desertification' is advancing apace through a combination of global warming and the over-extraction of rivers and groundwater. As Maude Barlow points out in *Blue Future*, Lake Chad was once the sixth largest lake in the world but today 90 per cent of it has disappeared, putting millions of lives at risk. Elsewhere massive swathes of Mexico and Brazil suffer from desertification and the western side of North America is seeing its biggest period of drought in over 800 years. Across the planet, from Asia to Argentina, the story is the same. Climate change, industrialisation and globalisation are displacing and ruining the world's water supplies. If you live in a slum in India, or a favela in Brazil, or a de-industrialised area of Detroit, or within the poisoned area of Flint, Michigan, this means health worries, misery and even death. But to others it means opportunity to profit from that misery. And so the global commodification of our water has begun.

Back to India. Renowned Indian movie director Shekhar Kapur encapsulated the inequality manifest in water as a commodity when he wrote in his book *Whose Water Is It Anyway*:

> In Mumbai. Just across the road from JuHu Vile Parle Scheme, all the beautiful people and film stars live opposite a slum called Nehru Nagar. Once a day, or maybe even less, water arrives in tankers run by the local 'water mafia' and their goons. Women and children wait in line for a bucket of water, and fights break out as the tankers begin to run dry.
>
> Yet, literally across the road, the 'stars' after their workouts in the gym or a day on a film set can stay in the shower for hours. The water will not stop flowing. Often at less than half the cost that the slum dwellers pay for a single bucket of water.

If you think this is just too far away to affect us here in Ireland, think again. I don't expect many will listen to what a trade unionist has to say on how to make money in the financial markets from water, so listen to Citi's top economist Willem Buiter instead. Willem is paid a lot of money to know about these things, and here is what he was predicting a full five years ago:

> I expect to see in the near future a massive expansion in the water sector, including in the production of fresh, clean water from other sources (desalination, purification), storage, shipping and transportation of water. I expect to see pipeline networks that will exceed those for oil and gas today. I see fleets of water tankers (single-hulled) and storage facilities that will dwarf those we currently have for oil, gas and LNG…

Buiter went on to share his vision of new canals being dug linking massive rivers and other means of transporting water to where it is needed. But before we all applaud this man of vision for the massive efforts Citi and other finance houses will put in to saving the world's population from drought, let's see what the motivation is:

> I expect to see a globally integrated market for fresh water within 25 to 30 years. Once the spot markets for water are integrated futures markets and other derivative water-based financial instruments – puts, calls swaps, both exchange-traded and OTC will follow. There will be different grades and types of fresh water, just the way we have light, sweet and heavy sour crude oil today. Water as an asset class will, in my view, become eventually the single most important physical-commodity-based asset class, dwarfing oil, copper, agriculture commodities and precious metals.

Well, I suppose we can just about live without oil, copper, agriculture commodities and precious metals. But live without water? Not a chance. These vultures who are in the process of using every other finite resource as a plaything for their 'financial instruments', while killing our very planet, are now moving in for the final 'kill', the commodification of our life-giving water resources. And is it going well for them? You can bet your life it is. Let's look close to home for evidence of how the quest to profit from our life-giving water is going. Let's look across the Irish Sea to our nearest neighbour and largest trading partner. Britain, you see, has a fully privatised water 'market' and has had since the late 1980s. That gives us plenty of time to look at what it is costing, who is profiting and how the investment that we hear so much about is going.

The first thing to get straight is this argument that meters are being installed not as 'toll booths' on our water but because they aid conservation. Well the United Kingdom has meters for almost 30 years now and (without accounting for food production) a citizen there uses 68,505 litres of water per annum. Here in Ireland we have never had meters, until the recently failed Irish Water project, so given that these meters save so much water we must be using a lot more than that right? Wrong! Without meters we Irish use 54,750 litres per person per annum, about 20 per cent less.

But it gets even more interesting when we delve into official UK Government OFWAT (Office of Water Services) figures to see what is going on. How are Mr. Buiter's predictions working out in practice there? Well, surprise surprise, he is bang on. In fact, official figures show that water is producing twice the operating surplus and paying twice the dividends to shareholders in water firms as any other class of investment other than financial services. Further analysis shows why. Fully privatised and allowed to do what they like, these investors have pushed water bills in the UK up at twice the rate of the Retail Price Index (RPI) every year from 1991 to 2013. This pattern is so ingrained that it would seem that all providers do to set prices is look at the RPI and double it and that the methods never change. But if the methods of the companies never change the ownership patterns of them do.

In 1989 over half of the UK's water company shares were owned by stock market-listed companies with the remainder split between private UK companies and multinational corporations. But from 2002 a new beast began to buy up these companies, slowly at first, but now well over half of the stocks in companies that must provide British citizens with their water are held by 'private equity consortiums'. This private equity is then used to buy out public ownership to ensure the delisting of the public equity. It attracts massive fees and commissions, is solely profit-driven and divested of all public interest. In the US at the beginning of 2015, a call was issued for more transparency in the private equity industry, due largely to the amount of income, earnings and sky-high salaries earned by employees at nearly all private equity firms.

Maybe this is what ensures that these companies are simply not investing in the United Kingdom's water and sanitation network. 'Retained profit' is the amount of profit a company will hold back before issuing a dividend for investment. The Water Services Regulation Authority (OFWAT) shows that while retained profit for other companies averages about 2.5 per cent, for water companies it is showing close to 0 per cent, as the private equity consortiums make their money. And what money they are making! In 2013 water companies in Britain made €2.81 billion in profits and paid €2.55 billion of this out in dividends to shareholders. So much for investment! And as to tax? Well these massive profits generated just €101 million in taxes with seven of the companies paying no corporation taxes at all. Any investment carried out is used to write down taxes, so the taxpayer pays anyway.

I hope the picture is becoming clear now. Globally, water resources are being stretched and demand will soon outstrip supply. In many parts of the globe it has been doing so for years. Rather than deal with this crisis on a humanitarian 'not for profit' basis, water is being commodified as an asset and where it is privatised bills are going through the roof and profits are going the same way. The taxpayer is subsidising the investment while the capital is all going to the top. Water is literally the new oil.

In Ireland the debate on our water has been conducted as if none of this affects us at all, even as if it isn't happening. In fact, there hasn't been any real debate at all. Without any evidence whatsoever Irish citizens have been dubbed 'water wasters' and freeloaders who won't pay their way. That fact that taxation is the most progressive way of paying for our water, and that it is a method which eliminates the massive waste of meter and billing systems, is simply swept aside as the usual suspects are given free rein on the national airwaves to perpetuate the privatisation agenda behind a veil of reality denial.

## Right2Water

That is why our campaign is called 'Right2Water Ireland'. As Maude Barlow pointed out to me when visiting in 2015, water was not included in the 1948 Universal Declaration of Human Rights because less than 70 years ago nobody could even conceive of a world lacking in clean water. But all has changed, changed utterly, and in 2010 the United Nations recognised water and sanitation as a fundamental human right. A total of 122 nations endorsed this historic vote while over 40 (including Ireland with a Green minister responsible) abstained. Nobody voted against.

The vote followed two decades of campaigning where opponents of water as a 'right', and not just a 'need', included some of the most industrialised First World nations. The reason for this opposition is the obvious neoliberal one: a human 'right' cannot be traded, sold or denied to anyone on the basis of their inability to pay for it. It follows that this boosts the argument for public ownership of our water and sanitation, and it most certainly negates the ability of water companies to shut off people's water or hold them to ransom for inability to pay bills. It also seems that Ireland's model of paying for water through progressive general taxation is tailor made for water and sanitation being held as a human right. Maude Barlow points out that it is important to note that the countries who argued most strongly against this rights-based categorisation of water and sanitation are those who hold most rigidly to the unregulated free market system – Canada, the UK, the US, Australia and New Zealand – and that they all already have a form of water commodification in place. They are also countries that promote extensive global trade and investment rights for corporations over the interests of the citizens of sovereign states in what I describe as an era of 'post-democracy', where the rights of citizens to decide how to run and fund their own nations through democratic processes are surrendered through treaties to corporations and investors in secretive trade deals like TTIP and CETA.

That these nations consider water a 'market good' as opposed to a human right is something that is encapsulated in the view of the European Commission and their reaction to the EU-wide citizens' initiative to have the Right2Water extended into the European Union. I will look at this in more detail later, but for now the objective of the EU Commission for our water is encapsulated in a letter written in Brussels on 26 September 2012. To anybody who believes that water privatisation is not at the core of what we have been fighting since 2014, and to anybody who does not understand the extent to which the privatisation agenda has completely usurped what was once a 'social Europe' project, the text is chilling:

> As you know, privatisation of public companies contributes to the reduction of public debt, as well as to the reduction of subsidies, other transfers or state guarantees to state owned enterprises. It also has the potential of increasing the efficiency of companies and, by extension, the competitiveness of the economy as a whole, while attracting foreign direct investment.

> The Commission believes that the privatisation of public utilities, including water supply firms, can deliver benefits to the society when carefully made. To this end, privatisation should take place once the appropriate regulatory framework has been prepared to avoid abuses by private monopolies. At the same time, public access to basic goods must be ensured. This is why it is important to find balance between equal and fair access to public utilities (water, gas, electricity) good quality of services and a financially sustainable supply.

> The Commission will check that the privatisation process of water companies guarantees full access to water for all citizens.

In February 2016, and despite not being afforded a proper debate on the water privatisation agenda whether in Europe of globally, Irish citizens voted in a general election for many candidates who wanted Irish Water abolished. They did so even while being lied to by some politicians and commentators that water privatisation was not on the agenda. It clearly is not only on the agenda. It is the agenda.

The people who form this water movement, this movement for change, see through the lies and the spin. But we are all subject to a global economic model which has been absorbed into every aspect of our lives and that is aggressively working to push all that we own into the hands of the few, while forcing the financial gambling debts of the reckless on to the heads of us all. It works to redistribute wealth upwards while redistributing debt and burden downwards.

# 3

# Neoliberalism

Writing in *The Guardian* in April, George Monbiot asked us to 'Imagine if the people of the Soviet Union had never heard of communism. The ideology that dominates our lives has, for most of us, no name. Mention it in conversation and you'll be rewarded with a shrug…. Its anonymity is both a symptom and cause of its power.'

I am not an economist and not pretending to be one, but I do believe that we need to have a basic understanding of the dominant economic model that shapes all of our lives, how it operates and who it benefits.

Neoliberalism technically refers to the rebirth, or renewal, of laissez-faire 'liberal' free market economics. This economic model places 'competition' among us as our defining characteristic. It redefines 'citizens' as 'consumers' and the 'market' as the supreme arbiter of good and bad, success or failure, worth or worthlessness. Within its confines to be 'free', or to have 'liberty', is to be free of regulation, government interference or 'big government'. It denotes a veritable survival of the fittest culture with the market as the battle ground upon which we stand or fall like modern day gladiators – but competing with goods and money as our weapons.

These notions are not new of course. They stem from the old eighteenth century notion that the market set free, without regulation or Government intervention, will solve all problems by incentivising businesses and allowing capital to grow, and that this growth would trickle down providing basic needs even to those not equipped or able to succeed. The belief holds that if wealth is unregulated it will provide perpetual growth and create the conditions of full employment to the benefit of all. This lack of regulation and government intervention also extends to a low tax economy with particularly low taxes needed to 'incentivise' capital to invest and grow, although it results in an unfortunate lack of investment in public services such as health, housing, education, utilities and transport. Of course, if you have sufficient wealth, you don't need these services to be publicly provided as you can simply buy them privately in the 'marketplace'. Gladiators ready!

But capital is a 'thing' not a person and it has no emotion or moral conscience. So set completely free laissez-faire capitalism has always wreaked havoc. The Great Depression (1929–1939) arose as a result of the complete failure of laissez-faire economics. It began when an ordinary depression led by a drop in consumer spending resulted in goods backing up and a consequent slowing in production. But the unregulated stock market continued to soar and by the end of 1929 stock prices had reached levels that could not be sustained by anticipated future earnings. This was where the phrase 'stock market bubble' was coined, and a bubble is only going to do one thing. When it burst it did so spectacularly. On 24 October 1929 (Black Thursday), 12.9 million shares were trading in panic selling and five days later this rose to 16 million shares as panic spread. Millions of shares ended up worthless, especially those that had been bought with what was then called 'on margin', or borrowed money. These got wiped out completely. The crisis deepened further as the stock market crash damaged confidence in 'the real economy'; further reduced spending and consequently production lead to massive unemployment. The crisis continued in fact until World War II had ended when most realised that only massive investment in public projects (intervention) could create the conditions of employment and confidence necessary to kick start the economy.

John Maynard Keynes addressed the inherent flaws in laissez-faire economics by advocating a more interventionist approach. He developed this while trying to understand the Great Depression. In essence, Keynes held that full employment and price stability could best be delivered not through complete market liberalism, but through Government intervention with policies that held a nation's output as the key dynamic to be considered rather than an individual's. Keynes, you see, believed in 'society'.

Margaret Thatcher did not believe in 'society'. Here is a direct quote from Thatcher in 1987:

> I think we've been through a period where too many people have been given to understand that if they have a problem, it's the government's job to cope with it. 'I have a problem, I'll get a grant.' 'I'm homeless, the government must house me.' They're casting their problem on society. And, you know, there is no such thing as society. There are individual men and women, and there are families.

This is an interesting viewpoint from a British political leader because after World War II Britain and much of Europe lay in ruins. As a result, people were looking for something that they could believe in again and Keynesian policies effectively encouraged the development of the welfare state. This was expressed through massive rebuilding projects, including ones on social housing, transport infrastructure, and the creation of the National Health Service (NHS). This both provided the required rebuilding of Britain (mirrored in Europe) and created much needed employment schemes. A 'win–win'.

That was the thinking from the late 1940s on, but by 1979 Thatcher was in power and she held that we are individual consumers above all else. There should be no 'state', or 'society', let alone a welfare one. She was opposed to people coming together to their mutual advantage, which is why she so disliked, and set out to destroy, trade unions. Thatcher was an architect of neoliberalism in practice.

As was her counterpart in the White House at the time, Ronald Reagan. And so was their friend in Chile, the fascist dictator Augusto Pinochet. All three, and many leaders who have followed, were advocates of an economic doctrine developed in the Chicago School of Economics under the direction of Milton Friedman, who developed an updated model of unregulated free market economic theory which was 'laissez-faire' reborn. Their economic textbook became known as 'El Ladrillo' (the brick) and was given a Spanish name because its first testing ground was Chile in 1973. Friedman believed that all state assets should be privatised and that if the people through their Governments would not do so (that is, by electing right-wing Governments) that these Governments needed to be removed if the opportunity arose. Capital was not there to advance the wealth of states and their people; rather, nations existed to be agents of capital and help to move all state assets to the rich, what we know today as the 1 per cent.

And so in 1973 the popular democratic Government of Salvador Allende was overthrown by a CIA-sponsored coup in Chile and Augusto Pinochet was installed as a puppet leader. Pinochet was only a natural leader in the military sense and had no political or economic training to run a state. While his blood lust was given full rein against his own people, Friedman and his Chicago School disciples sat in his Ministerial offices directly dictating the privatising of state assets, the moving of wealth from the masses to the wealthy. Friedman later claimed that he had only done so at the invitation of Pinochet, but in whatever manner it happened Friedman personally gave instruction in Santiago about how to enforce the Chicago School prescriptions. While this was going on Pinochet built a right wing military dictatorship that lasted 16 years and killed or 'disappeared' 3,000 Chilean 'leftists'. That was just the start.

In South Africa when apartheid fell, or in the Soviet Union when communism bit the dust, or even in Ireland when our economy fell in 2009, every seismic economic shift is seen as an opportunity to adapt Friedman's model of cutting investment in or even privatising public services, and changing to 'low tax' economies with particularly low taxes for wealth and capital. Naomi Klein refers to this tactic of waiting for the opportune moment for intervention to arise through natural or economic disasters as 'disaster capitalism'. It's happened in Portugal and there are spectacular examples in Cyprus and Greece where the neoliberals, having taken all traditional 'assets', are now even privatising Greek islands!

The International Monetary Fund (IMF) is a key vehicle of this economic theory. The IMF approach is simple. They wait until a country is in trouble, they hold the money back, and then at a time of crisis they offer the money (bailout) in return for the troubled country adopting the neoliberal prescription of privatisation (as we've seen, water is a favourite profit-making resource of the neoliberal these days), welfare state destruction and Government subservience to their prescriptions and low tax dictates. Keep with the programme and reshape your economy to one of systemic inequality and the life support of the 'bailout' will continue. But if a sovereign Government decides it is too much, or it has no mandate for their actions, then the money supply gets switched off or, as Jean-Claude Trichet put it in Ireland's case, 'a bomb will go off in Dublin'.

The results of these policies are all around us. They are there in our homeless crisis where the state not only will not build houses, but won't even house homeless people in the properties it already owns by virtue of the failure of capitalism in 2008. In true 'El Ladrillo' textbook style, our Government has now decided the solution to the homelessness crisis caused by leaving house building entirely to 'the market' is to give state land free to the very builders, the very housing market that caused the crisis. Friedman would have approved.

Neoliberalism can be seen in our tax regime – high taxes for the majority of us on low and medium incomes and low taxes on real wealth and capital. This deliberately contracted tax base inevitably leads to cuts for education, health, transport infrastructure and welfare. And make no mistake about it, neoliberalism is behind the ideological attempt to take publicly owned and funded water and sanitation and hand it over to the private sector for commodification and profit.

We have looked at homelessness, tax and health care, but for now be assured of this: The spirit of Milton Friedman and Margaret Thatcher are alive and well in Irish Government buildings, as they are in the European Commission and the European Central Bank. I will try not to constantly refer to neoliberalism throughout this book, but we must be fully aware that it is the dominant economic model that affects all of our lives.

But for now I will leave the subject with a short case study of how it works, how the demands of 'the market' can become so all pervasive that they almost led to 6,000 Irish workers losing their defined benefit pension scheme.

## The ESB Pension Crisis – Neoliberalism in Action

I was a representative of electricity workers in Ireland from 2004 to 2014. For seven of those years I had the privilege of representing the biggest single block of unionised electricity workers in the state, members of the then Amalgamated Transport & General Workers Unions (ATGWU), now Unite. For the rest of the time I was even more privileged to have been Secretary of the group of unions operating in Ireland's state-owned electricity utility company, the Electricity Supply Board (ESB).

Before turning to neoliberalism and the pension crisis, first a few words about ESB, which in general is the sort of company of which Ireland can be enormously proud. From 1927 to 2002, ESB was a state-owned monopoly in electricity generation, distribution and supply. It brought power and light to every corner of Ireland with a rural electrification project powered from a massive (by the standards of the time) hydro-electric-generating scheme at Ardnacrusha. From then on ESB was there to help bring Ireland out of the dark ages, literally, and looked after the state, customers and staff alike very well.

Then came the demands of the market. In 2002, Ireland had the cheapest electricity prices of the then EU 15, but the economic model adopted by the European Union demanded de-regulation, market opening, competition. The adjectives may be different but the meaning is the same. ESB was required to change from a company that was about electricity, customer service and decent employment to one that was predominant-ly about assisting the energy market to make profits for the rich. In a nutshell, this was done by an Energy Regulator being imposed to encourage competition. But how do you encour-age competition in a tiny market of just 5,000 megawatts stuck out on the edge of Europe? You drive up prices, that's how.

And so in the years from 2002 to 2009 ESB was prevented from competing on prices and building new plants while com-panies such as Airtricity, Endesa and Scottish and Southern Electricity were invited into the Irish electricity market. To achieve this, the market was regulated in a way which fa-voured the newbies while overall prices rose inexorably. Hav-ing been among the lowest electricity prices anywhere, Irish consumers, including business, would soon be screaming about the rising cost of energy. Money was being moved from consumers' pockets into those of the energy giants. And the ideological quest for privatisation was also introduced. First many power stations were effectively privatised, and then so too were the supply companies. ESB was even forced to change its name to Electric Ireland because of the Regulator's fear that Irish customers were so fond of the ESB brand that they might show some loyalty to it and not move to the private companies entering the market. They would have privatised ESB Networks as well, except the unions had an iron grip on the system and we repeatedly fought, successfully, to keep 'the national grid' in public hands.

So what of the workers? Well, ESB has always been a good company with relatively stable employment and decent terms and conditions. ESB workers with seniority are members of the company's defined benefit pension scheme, and so integral was the company seen to the functioning of state that the pension scheme was constructed in a way which meant employees had no state pension entitlement. In other words, they pay their pension contributions, and when they retire they get an ESB pension but no state pension. Confused? Well, for the purposes of this book, let me try to demystify pensions in simple terms. There are basically two types of pension scheme to consider – defined benefit (DB) and defined contribution (DC) – and both do exactly what they say on the tin.

A defined benefit pension scheme is one that workers and employers pay into and the benefits are defined by the rules of the scheme. Typically, the defined benefit is a proportion of final salary (1/80 being the proportion in this case) for every year of service up to a maximum of 40 years (40/80ths), which is half the final salary.

Conversely, a defined contribution scheme does the opposite. Both workers and employers may pay in but the benefit is not defined. All that is defined is what is paid in, the contribution, hence the name. These contributions are then typically invested and can rise or fall as the stocks in which they are invested rise and fall, and the person's pension is whatever is in the pot when they retire. In this case, the 'pension risk' is carried 100 per cent by the members, whereas in the defined benefit case the risk, because the benefit is defined, is carried by someone or something else. In a DB scheme risk becomes an issue when there are insufficient assets to meet the defined benefits. Somebody must plug that gap.

And so back to ESB. Traditionally their workers were in the defined benefit type scheme and, because it became a requirement for companies to record their pension schemes on their annual reports, any shortfall in the DB-type scheme could appear, to the 'markets', like an employer liability. Employers, quite reasonably, do not like such liabilities on their accounts because they affect how the market views that company. It may affect a company's credit rating if the accounts show a large pension liability, and this in turn will affect the cost of borrowing for that company, often for necessary investment and growth.

Still with me? Well when you are an employer with the largest funded DB scheme in the state, a scheme with almost €5 billion in benefits tied up in it, with matching pension assets of just two-thirds of that, there is a problem. As Ireland went from Celtic Tiger 'AAA' to 'junk' status after the 2008 crash, even good companies like ESB were getting extremely icy stares from 'the markets' and their rating agencies. These stares turned icier still when the pension scheme came under analysis. And then the ESB Group of Unions was asked by ESB management to do something rather extraordinary: we were asked to agree that in the 2012 Annual Report ESB could claim that their €5 billion defined benefit (DB) pension scheme was a defined contribution (DC) scheme, thereby transferring all risk to the workers.

The unions, who had helped to resolve several funding crises and were well-versed in pension matters, immediately refused, but under seemingly enormous pressure the board of ESB went ahead and re-designated the scheme in their accounts anyway. Once the unions discovered the problem the issue then came down to education and organising. It was extremely difficult, and it took almost a year, to get through to ESB employees what had been done and how exposed they now were, how they were now potentially on the hook for their own €5 billion pension scheme. The unions worked tirelessly behind the scenes to resolve the growing crises, both with management and the Minister who had signed off on the change, Labour's Pat Rabbitte, while simultaneously alerting the staff to the problem and organising a fight back unless the matter was corrected. Eventually, and only when faced with a legal challenge in the High Court and the potential for the first all-out electricity strike in Ireland since 1991, the Labour Relations Commission intervened with days to go and ordered ESB to again account for their scheme as a defined benefit scheme from then on.

This book is not about the details of that dispute and all that went with it. But for me the issue goes way beyond ESB and their pension scheme. ESB is a company with dedicated and skilled workers and a management who care about the company and the country. It was the furthest thing from a careless, selfish, vulgar, profit-driven monster that there was in the Irish labour market, and certainly in the energy sector.

The lesson I have taken, however, is that if the demands of the neoliberal market can make one of the so-called 'good guys' embark on such a potentially disastrous course, what kind of actions can we expect from the bad guys, the people and the corporations who actually don't give a toss about 'society' but crave only more and more profit with the resulting inequality?

# 4

# The Labour Party – From Democratic Socialism to Social Democracy

If we live at a time where the dominant economic model is so aggressively targeting methods of moving wealth and assets upwards, what have been the political responses to it here in Ireland? Throughout this book politics, in all of its guises, plays a part, but it is important that I set out at the beginning my analysis of the Irish Labour Party and their role in our broken state. I do so because while the founders of the party could not have foreseen the exact political manifestations that would emerge 100 years after the reading of the proclamation, they certainly knew that those with power and capital would seek ways to hold on to and keep our citizens relatively impoverished. The Labour Party was created by these men of vision to counteract those efforts and to pursue an egalitarian Republic.

The role of the Labour Party in the water debate, and in fact in our society in general, strikes at the heart of the subject matter of this book. But not in a good way. The Labour Party is now led by Brendan Howlin and the days since he took control following a vote of their 11-person parliamentary party have seen him all over the airwaves. Brendan Howlin, and his varying roles and positions, encapsulates perfectly the wider quagmire the Labour Party has gotten itself into and from which it may never re-emerge.

My view is that, at least under the current personnel and direction, not only does the Irish Labour Party not deserve to survive, but it is an obstacle to progress towards a more equal Ireland. It is in fact an enabler of neoliberal inequality.

A quick history. Labour was established in Britain by the trade unions to give them, and the workers they represented, a voice in parliament. They were to be the political wing of an industrial movement, and the Irish Labour Party was later founded in 1912 by James Connolly, Jim Larkin and William O'Brien. When the Irish Trade Union Congress National Executive decided to establish a political arm over 100 years ago, it stated that: 'In any parliament to be elected in Ireland Labour must be represented as a separate and independent entity, having no connection with any other party.' This directive could not be clearer, and yet the reverse has been the case for the greater part of the Labour Party's existence.

It is described in its constitution as a 'democratic socialist' party, but in recent days Brendan Howlin has been describing it only as a 'social democratic' party. Previous leaders such as Joan Burton, Eamon Gilmore and Pat Rabbitte routinely described the party as a social democratic party, as if the concept of social democracy was interchangeable with the concept of democratic socialism. It is not.

The Labour party has a unique history in Irish politics in the sense that its origins do not derive from the fractious civil way which spawned Fine Gael (and their predecessors) and Fianna Fáil. These two right of centre parties are ostensibly mirror images of the British Tory party. If Fianna Fáil describes itself as having a broader base than the landlord class that spawned Fine Gael, that is probably true, but the reality of their economic policies is that very little, at least up to now, has divided these two parties for decades. Former Taoiseach John Bruton conceded as much when he said in December 2015:

> FG and FF have complemented each other through
> Irish history. In Ireland we have had consensus about
> major long-term policies largely because we haven't
> had a sharp left/right or ideological divide. We have
> had differences, but they are differences about other
> things, not economics, and that has served the country
> very well.

Labour, on the other hand, began life as a socialist party.
That the brand of socialism was moderate and could never at
any point in the post-partition era have been described as radical is arguably inevitable in a socially conservative Ireland. It
is hard to be a radical democratic socialist in a state controlled
in large part by the Catholic church, especially since the 1937
Constitution gave that church a 'special place' until change occurred in the 1990s. The power and influence of the Catholic
Church had been left untouched by successive national revolutions. It was strengthened by the long counter-revolution begun by Cumann na nGaedheal and continued by Fianna Fáil.
Parish pump concerns, combined with red scares, ensured
that the Church's privileged position went unchecked by the
Labour Party.

For example, it was only in 1995 that the Constitutional
prohibition on divorce was removed from Bunreacht Na
h'Eireann by a vote carried by a margin of just 9,114 votes out
of a valid poll of 1,628,728. This followed a bitter campaign
characterised by slogans such as 'Hello Divorce, Goodbye
Daddy'. In the years that followed the scale of church abuse,
rape, effective kidnapping and violence towards generations
of children began to become clear in church scandal after
scandal. Finally, Ireland began to emerge from under the bish-
op's garments into something resembling maturity, at least on
social issues.

We have never yet reached a stage of having an informed
and mature discussion on economic issues. It has been the job

of the Labour Party to lead such a national debate. That is not just my opinion, that is their duty under their own rules and it is a task which they entirely abandoned.

From at least the mid-1990s an opportunity has opened up for the Labour Party to at last engage with the Irish electorate in a manner that was about grown up, as opposed to juvenile civil war, politics. The politics of right and left, of tax or spend, of public or private, of equality or inequality have been available for Labour to engage in free of Catholic dogma for at least two decades. They have not done so. They have done the opposite.

I believe I understand democratic socialism, and I believe I also understand social democracy. I am a democratic socialist, but I am most certainly not a social democrat. How do I explain this, and is it just jargon?

Not at all. The difference between these political concepts, constructs even, goes to the very heart of the inequality we face today across the globe, and its root causes. Or, to be more precise, the difference between being a democratic socialist or a social democrat is, in my view, the difference between those who seek to oppose social, economic and political inequality and those who seek to kidnap the flag of the 'left' and to abuse the ethos handed to us by Connolly and Larkin which actually helps to enable social, economic and political inequality.

James Connolly believed in a workers' Republic which cherished all of the children of the nation equally and was egalitarian in nature. There is a plaque in my office with possibly his most famous quote, certainly my favourite, which is: 'Our demands most moderate are ... we only want the earth'.

Another longer quote from Connolly best provides the measuring stick by which I measure all of our political parties, but particularly the Labour Party which he co-founded. It is this:

Ireland, as distinct from her people, is nothing to me; and the man that is bubbling over with love and enthusiasm for 'Ireland' yet can pass unmoved through our streets and witness all the wrong and the suffering, shame and degradation wrought upon the people – yea, wrought by Irishmen upon Irish men and women, without burning to end it is, in my opinion, a fraud and a liar in his heart, no matter how he loves that combination of chemical elements he is pleased to call Ireland.

In this centenary year of the reading of a Proclamation declaring an egalitarian Republic, can anybody claim that we have a nation that cherishes all of its children equally? I will go further: can anybody even say that, as a state, we have ever even tried?

As a nation we are not trying and never have. There has never been a Government in this state that hasn't been led by either Fine Gael or Fianna Fáil, and there has never been a Government that made redistribution of wealth downwards its number one priority. That is, or should have been, the key role of the Labour Party.

When I became an Official with the then ATGWU Trade union in 2004, the union was affiliated to the Labour Party. The union then had a strategic position as to how to build a true workers' movement called 'The Third Way'. The position advocated that Labour should declare that as a matter of policy it would never again go into coalition with Fine Gael or Fianna Fáil. By this time, Labour had entered into coalition with either of the mainstream parties on seven different occasions, suffering electorally and rendering itself increasingly unattractive to large sections of the working class.

By doing so, the view, which I agreed with, was that it was unlikely that either Fine Gael of Fianna Fáil would ever have an overall majority to form a Government and by removing themselves as a mudguard for the right, Labour would force the two civil war parties together, thereby opening up a space for a truly progressive Democratic Socialist and independent Labour Party and movement. That was 12 years ago and whatever the compelling logic, in my view, of that approach, once an election is held and Labour has a chance to get into ministerial office the opportunity to re-shape a better Ireland has always been squandered.

These decisions are explained away as 'social democrats' doing their 'duty' to 'act in the national interest'.

A few words about 'social democracy'. I believe social democracy is a compromise with capitalism which its advocates, perhaps sincerely and perhaps not, believe is the best that they can ever achieve. The social democratic models that emerged in Britain and other parts of Europe in the aftermath of World War II could be viewed as: a) a result of social struggles and a shift in the balance of power globally from capital to labour; b) a compromise of interests in specific historical conditions that cannot be recreated; or c) a legitimate strategy for working towards socialism. However, this tactical compromise became the end goal and 'third way' responses complemented the neoliberal offensive. There has been a slow change in the nature of social democratic parties and social democracy itself.

There is nothing 'fighting back' about social democracy, there is nothing 'radical' and there certainly is nothing 'revolutionary' about social democracy. The first real social democrat in this sense was probably Mikhail Gorbachev who, faced with massive corruption and unrest within the Soviet Union, felt the best thing to do was to work to collapse the state and do a deal with that nice Mr Bush (Snr.) in the White House. From the vantage of a tottering Kremlin, Gorbachev came to believe that 'benevolent capitalism' existed elsewhere and was seduced into believing that by working with the likes of Bush he could bring 'democracy' to what was soon to be the former Soviet Union, and that he could deliver a whole range of personal freedoms which the citizens of his country and the rest of Eastern Europe seemed to crave.

On its own this may have worked but, unfortunately for Russia's dispossessed people (dispossessed of their national wealth by oligarchs that is), Bush had not only swallowed the entire Milton Friedman 'brick' but was also in hock to 'democrats' such as the beheading Saudis, the oil rich Kuwaitis and an arms industry with an insatiable thirst for perpetual war to drive its profit machine. So we got 'glasnost' and 'perestroika' and the result is that Russians now have freedoms that they didn't have. They have freedom to watch Hollywood movies and eat Big Macs, they have freedom to drink non-fat caramel macchiatos from Starbucks, they have freedom to borrow and accrue personal debts, they have freedom to have their assets stolen by oligarchs and used to buy football clubs in London and elsewhere, and they have freedom to be slaves to financial capital as the 1 per cent take over Russia as surely as they have taken over the rest of us.

What has that got to do with Ireland and the Labour Party you ask? Well, by the time Ireland was maturing from a backward, conservative, church-controlled state in the mid-1990s it was already clear that any pact between social democracy and aggressive capitalism would not result in any kind of halfway house 'third way' solution where the more excessive elements of extreme right and left wing ideology would work together to deliver a moderate economic model of growth allied to investment in public services. Instead, it was already clear that Milton Friedman had succeeded in persuading leaders such as Thatcher and Reagan to unleash a new wave of super aggressive capitalism, manifest through unregulated finance capital, increasingly reckless speculation, privatisation, globalisation and a destruction of public services that would see a massive redistribution of wealth upwards. The only thing that would 'trickle down' from this economic monster would be inequality, social exclusion and the ending of any real democracy (I assess the quality and nature of our democracy elsewhere).

Tony Blair was – is – a social democrat. I'm just going to let that sentence sit there for a second.

Blair came to power in 1997 with 'New Labour'. In giving the old party of the working class a 'New' label to denote the final move from Democratic Socialism to Social Democracy at least there was a semblance of honesty in the New Labour motif. According to Blair the social democrat, Thatcherism hadn't been all that bad after all. Globalisation wasn't really that bad either. Privatisation of water, electricity, gas and transport weren't bad and so bloody what if previously vibrant communities like Durham, in terms of mining, or Motherwell/Lanarkshire, in terms of steel works, were now full of retired or unemployed people on premature pensions or social welfare? So what if the hearts had been ripped out of previously working communities all over Britain and the jobs were now in China, Taiwan and Indonesia? So what if the cars that used to be made in the midlands were now made in Japan and famous British brands such as Rover were now to be owned by Germany's BMW?

New Labour, almost as a badge of honour, would not reverse any of it and would not invest in manufacturing or rebuilding Britain. New Labour would not do anything to try to recreate the 'society' that Thatcher had decreed did not even exist. No. What New Labour would do would be to compromise with neoliberalism and, ultimately, under Blair's leadership would actually become its champion and embrace the economic imperialism of war.

Here we have the true nature of social democracy. It describes its own evisceration by aggressive neoliberal capitalism as a 'compromise'.

New Labour would also go on to enter or invent wars based on false premises and information to achieve the twin aims of stealing assets from the Middle East and keeping the profit-driven war machine ticking over. Sir John Chilcot has now outlined in massive detail just how crooked, evil even, the New Labour project of warmongering was. So what if it all cost some working class lives on both sides of the Atlantic, not to mention those on the other side? That was just collateral damage in the pursuit of neoliberal nirvana. And don't even get me started about how all the unnecessary consumption driven solely to keep up with the need for perpetual 'growth' has impacted on a dying planet.

Blair certainly helped achieve peace in Northern Ireland, and for that he and Bill Clinton deserve praise. But that praise-worthy endeavour did not deserve the unquestioning near idolatry his New Labour project got from the Irish Labour Party that Connolly had founded in Ireland. This is especially true given that the party had within its grasp the chance to force Fianna Fáil and Fine Gael together at last and create a strong democratic socialist alternative. Instead, what we got from Irish Labour was exactly what the British got from New Labour – a social democratic sell-out.

Nothing makes this choice made by the Irish Labour Party, and its impacts, clearer than their position before election 2011 and the choices the party made afterwards. In my view, Election 2011 was the second last chance (we'll come to the last later which occurred in November 2014) that Labour had to make the breakthrough that they, and all who want a fairer and more equal Ireland, need so badly.

## The Background to Election 2011

Lest we forget, Election 2011 was fought against a background where the nation had lost its economic sovereignty due to years of mismanagement of the state by bankers, building developers, financial regulators and governments. Fianna Fáil in particular were culpable in this regard, more than any other party, since it was in office and engaged in cronyism and corruption that enabled the breaking of a nation.

Fianna Fáil, however, had never seized power in any way other than through the polls and the Irish people themselves had, for too long, voted in known chancers and charlatans interested only in personal enrichment and status. From Haughey to Ahern, from Burke to Lawlor and many more besides, the Irish people routinely voted in spoofers and then wondered how it all went wrong. Well it went so wrong in 2008 and 2009 that we got a Troika bailout package as we surrendered the economic sovereignty we had for so long sought. 'We' created the crisis and the archangels of disaster capitalism arrived to enslave us in return.

Labour was furious and talked a great game. When the bailout went to a vote in the Dáil in December 2010 it was passed by 81 votes to 75 with both Labour and Fine Gael, then in opposition, opposing it. But this opposition was not really about the fundamentals of the bailout. What Labour and Fine Gael opposed was not the bailout itself but the terms on which it was negotiated. It seemed they all agreed that, fundamentally, the taxpaying public would be forced to pay the bills as the banks were rescued and the bondholders paid. While the gamblers should have lost their shirts at the altar of financial capital speculation, instead they left with their pockets bursting, filled by low and middle income earners in taxes and cuts to public services and wages.

Labour only opposed the terms of the loans paid by the Troika, and promised to re-negotiate these terms if voted in after the next election. It is often forgotten that what was described as a 'bailout' was in fact the enforced acceptance by the state of some of the most expensive loans it had ever taken out, rammed down our necks by our so-called friends in Europe and the IMF at a time when we were most in need of real help. With friends like Jean-Claude Trichet, who needs enemies!

When the 30th Dáil fell on 1 February 2011, it triggered an election that took place on 25 February of that year. At that point Fianna Fáil had brought the country to ruin and were nearly in ruin themselves. Two former Taoisaigh, Bertie Ahern and Brian Cowen, had been forced from office and the 'soldiers of destiny' had angered the population to such an extent that their destiny was an almighty kicking from the people in the upcoming election, a kicking that was duly delivered.

Fine Gael had been in opposition and hadn't been within a whiff of power since being routed under Michael Noonan's leadership in 2002 when it lost 23 seats. So bad was the loss that Noonan was forced to resign the leadership immediately and was replaced by Enda Kenny, who had sat on the back seats of the Dáil longer than any other TD without ever getting a sniff of ministerial office. Kenny was a survivor, but if he was a leader his leadership qualities had been well hidden for a very long time. Between 2002 and 2011 he had done a reasonable job rebuilding Fine Gael to within touching distance of getting the support back of its traditional upper class, moneyed and land-owning base, but he was hardly a heavyweight. So with Fianna Fáil on the ropes and losing, and Fine Gael having just survived an existential crisis, this was the perfect backdrop for Labour to blow both away in 2011.

## Labour's Way or Frankfurt's Way

Labour Party leader Eamon Gilmore certainly seemed to 'get it'. When launching the Labour Party election manifesto on 3 February 2011, flanked by Joan Burton and key Labour strategists, he set out the party's position clearly, concisely and rather impressively. The position addressed a fuming public anger at how our European 'friends', particularly the ECB, had battered us in terms of the 'bailout' loans while also taking over our decision making processes. This is what he said in full:

The first choice that the Irish voters are going to have to make in this election is whether our budgets are decided in Frankfurt or whether they are decided by the democratically elected Government of the Irish people. Let's be very clear about this, the bad deal that Fianna Fáil made with the EU and the IMF effectively writes the budgets for the next four years.

Fianna Fáil are prepared to follow these budgetary straight-jackets that have been laid down by the EU and IMF. That's Fianna Fáil's manifesto, they'll will take the shilling and follow the drum, and it appears to us that Fine Gael are essentially taking the same approach because they accept the €9 billion target (budgetary cuts) that is in the prescription.

Let's be clear too, if as a country we accept the budget based on the EU/IMF deal, if will mean more of the same that we got in December [a vicious austerity budget that had effectively been dictated by the EU/IMF and implemented by the previous Government just before leaving office]. It'll be more taxes, more cuts, high unemployment and no recovery.

This election therefore is effectively a choice to be made by the Irish people about whether our budgets and our financial affairs are going to be done Frankfurt's way, or the way that the Labour Party is proposing.

And that choice comes down between the choice of the €9 billion which has been accepted on a consensus basis by both Fianna Fáil and Fine Gael, or the package of measures that the Labour Party is proposing here today and that Joan [Burton, then Labour Finance Spokesperson] will outline to you in a few minutes.

There are essentially three things we are saying here. Firstly the deal with the EU and IMF must be renegotiated, Labour is putting forward the basis for its renegotiation and we are asking every single voter in the country to support us on this. Frankfurt's way or Labour's way.

It would be easy now to look back on this as the ramblings of a man drunk on the hope of power on the campaign trail. Indeed, such was the mess Fianna Fáil was in, with Fine Gael not much better, that 'Gilmore for Taoiseach' calls were being loudly heard from within the party and, allegedly, posters with this demand were on call. In fact, in June 2010 an MRBI poll in *The Irish Times* had projected that Labour were the most popular party in Ireland for the first time ever at 32 per cent.

By the time the election actually came around, however, support had dropped to just over 19 per cent, which was still impressive and certainly a strong platform to build upon. But events since, namely the choices Labour made to enter Government and how they behaved while there, have now led to a situation where most of what remains of the party simply cringe when reminded of the 'Labour's way or Frankfurt's way' moment. But I do not believe it was loose talk or unscripted exaggeration by the then leader at all.

Firstly, Eamon Gilmore, accurately in my view, sets out in the address the correct critique and the proper questions at hand at the time for that campaign. The question was absolutely about whether we in Ireland would decide our budgets or not, and who would be made to pay for the disaster that had occurred, and at what cost? Gilmore also, entirely correctly, links the Fianna Fáil position inextricably with Fine Gael's on those questions, and rightly opens up the debate (as I have tried to here) on the opportunity to at last develop a real progressive alternative to the two conservative civil war parties.

At this remove, of course, Labour may point to the fact that once elected, the crisis was so bad, so endemic, that for all of Gilmore's well-meant words this opportunity was not realistic at that time. I fundamentally disagree with that view. If Milton Friedman can design a 'disaster capitalism' model whereby a crisis such as this poses the opportunity for the systematic overthrow of freely-elected democracies and the redistribution of assets and wealth upwards, then there is absolutely no reason why such a crisis does not also offer an equal opportunity to restructure society in a fair and more equitable manner – a society that not only ensures no repeat of the lunacy that caused the crisis in the first place, but one that enforces an economic redistribution of wealth and assets that aids the majority instead of just those at the top for a change.

In uttering these words I fundamentally believe that Eamon Gilmore, as leader of the Labour Party launching an election campaign, identified the correct question, the correct opponents and the correct moment of opportunity, and that he did so not by some accident. He did so deliberately and strategically.

Lest there be any doubt about how clear, how emphatic, Labour had been on the key choices to be made by the Government after Election 2011 here is another quote. This one was delivered by the current Labour leader, Brendan Howlin, on the national news on 18 February 2011, just seven days before polling day and over two weeks after Gilmore's comments. If Gilmore had got it wrong or strayed off script there was no sign of it in Howlin's contribution. On the contrary, as the election grew closer, Labour was continuing to engage on the key issues in a way that struck a chord with those who opposed austerity taxes that was clear and unambiguous:

> We are not in favour of water charges, we don't believe
> in a flat rate and you couldn't meter everybody in years.
> So our manifesto has clearly set out that we are against
> water charges.

A week later the election took place and the result was a seismic change in the state of the top three parties. The electorate put Fianna Fáil to the sword with the party suffering its worst electoral result ever. They lost a massive 57 seats, winning just 20, while Labour's 19.4 per cent of first preference votes saw them go from 17 seats to 37, its biggest return ever. Fine Gael won 51 seats going from 25 to 76, just eight short of an overall majority.

## Labour's Crossroads

Labour now had a problem. They had 37 seats and were the second largest party elected to the 31st Dáil, well behind Fine Gael but well ahead of the disgraced Fianna Fáil. The nation was in a political and fiscal crisis that would get worse before it got better. These facts were unarguable. Would they stay out of Government or would they enter coalition with Fine Gael and form a Government which, with a 60 seat majority, would be the most stable in the history of the state?

To those who advocated entering coalition the argument was that they could ameliorate the worst excesses of Fine Gael's conservative orthodoxy. They were 'social democrats' and it was their 'duty' to 'act in the national interest'. They could renegotiate the terms of the 'bailout' and ensure that it was those who caused the crisis, and not the weakest in society, who paid.

Those advocating that they should stay out argued that they had made certain commitments, as outlined above, that could not be delivered in coalition with a conservative party. Those commitments were anathema to proponents of neoliberalism and should have been repulsive to anybody advocating neoliberal policies. This was their time to stay out, to hold their ground and build a new progressive movement that they could lead, to reject the tradition of propping up right-wing governments and instead embrace their mandate of opposition. It was the laissez faire policies of the conservative parties that had led to the crisis, and Labour could have ensured that it was those parties who paid the price. At some point citizens were going to fight back, they will have taken enough austerity and would demand real change. When that point came Labour needed to be there to lead the fight.

That last paragraph is about tactics, and there were certainly tactical reasons for Labour not to enter Government in 2011. But politics is about principles, policies, ideology even at some point. If we all stand for the same thing then sooner or later we will discover that we stand for nothing at all.

The prescription of austerity to a nation suffering a fiscal emergency stems from the ideology that is neoliberalism. It takes money out of the pockets of those who spend whatever they get on things they 'need'. And taking money off people for things they 'need' plunges them into poverty – food poverty, fuel poverty, joblessness, homelessness and all manner of deprivations ensue from austerity. Not only that, but it starves the economy of spending, thereby affecting small and medium businesses in particular. Clothes shops, restaurants, bars and hairdressers all suffer when the wages of those on low and medium incomes, or those on social security, are drastically reduced.

The money that is 'saved' or cut by austerity doesn't disappear. It finds its way into busted banks and the pockets of bondholders, both secured and unsecured, and other 'investors' in a real way. And in a less visible way assets which belong to us all are then sold, like Bord Gais Éireann or Aer Lingus, to the rich so they can charge us who used to own them, and push the prices up to boot.

Austerity is nothing but a wealth transfer carried out as part of a 'class strategy'. By this transference of wealth upwards class power is consolidated in the hands of capital. And to those who say 'it doesn't work' you are wrong! It does work. It works perfectly. It works like a dream for those for whom it is meant to work. It makes the already wealthy even wealthier.

Labour knew that this was the game. We are dealing with people of intelligence here. Eamon Gilmore knew what austerity was meant to do when he said it was 'Frankfurt's way or Labour's way'. Brendan Howlin knew that water was one of the key assets that the austerity agenda seeks to push into the ownership of the rich when he said Labour would oppose water charges. Oh yes, they knew alright.

But social democrats do what social democrats always do, and on 9 March 2011 they did what no democratic socialist would ever do. They did what James Connolly or Jim Larkin would never have done. They entered into a pact with neoliberals, manifest in Fine Gael, to ram austerity down the necks of the Irish people. They entered into a pact to make the poor and the working class pay for a crisis caused, in its entirety, by the agents and advocates of unregulated wealth and capital.

That decision, and the apparent relish with which Labour carried it out while the poorest and most vulnerable suffered the most, has meant that Labour are now decimated and currently hold just seven of the 37 seats they won in 2011. We will trace their role in these events throughout this book but, in my view, the pact Labour did with neoliberalism in 2011, at a time when they were needed most, as well as their behaviour since, are actions of treachery from which they will not recover. And they do not deserve to. They no longer deserve the trust of the class they were created to represent and protect.

# 5

# From Horseback to Hope Back

Iwas just a spectator to those events in 2011, though I did feel the wrath of Labour as I tried to ensure that the defined benefit pensions were protected for EBS workers. To me it was distressing that Labour Minister Pat Rabbitte had signed off on the disingenuous accounting outlined earlier, that Labour Minister Joan Burton had failed to enact comprehensive pension reform to put existing workers on a par with retired workers, or that Labour Minister Ruairi Quinn wanted ESB workers to be prohibited by law from striking to defend their rights. To my mind, Labour had been no friend to the workers I had represented while in their austerity bubble with Fine Gael. But that was now in the past and I was at a crossroads myself. I had been in Cuba for the European elections of 2014. Not sure what to do after exiting ESB but happy to come back to Unite, back 'home' in any capacity, I had taken a few weeks to gather my thoughts. I rented an apartment in central Havana for six weeks and went on my own with a bag, a laptop, a bit of Spanish which I was learning at the time and a lot of things to figure out.

It is no exaggeration to say I was struggling with depression at that point. The ESB dispute had taken lumps out of me emotionally. Yes we had won, and if it was football it would have been a thrashing of ESB, which the state and the media had backed. I should have been on a high, right? Wrong. It doesn't work like that, at least not for me. I have always found that when in the public eye and coming under media attack I just keep going as long as necessary. In an industrial dispute situation there is no option but to do the work and try to ignore the highly personalised attacks that come with leading campaigns like the ESB pension dispute. But when it is over, win lose or draw, and the news stories move on, the effect of the attacks hit home and can have adverse effects on my physical and mental health. That the ESB dispute was then followed by the death of my father, who had been reading the newspapers slating me during his illness, brought me to new levels of stress and, ultimately, despair.

And there was more. When I am away from Ireland I often reflect on my country and the good and the bad that goes with it. In April 2014 there was little good. The austerity agenda had been foisted on us for five years by that stage and we had been subjected to lie after lie from politicians and the banks which had left an indelible mark on the national mood. Those who had wrecked Ireland were busy using their political patsies to bail themselves out at the expense of current and future generations of working class people (even if many wouldn't describe themselves as such). Worst of all, however, was that Irish men and women were taken a battering from all directions and there was no fighting back. Not only were the nation's finances broken but the spirit of the fighting Irish seemed broken too. Sold out and led to this shameful state by gombeens for decades, we were suffering from what can only be described as a 'national collective trauma'. The situation seemed hopeless. I was so down at the time that only for my two children back in Ireland I wouldn't have wanted to come home at all.

And so I spent some weeks writing, reading, watching football from Europe and travelling. And yes, perhaps drinking a bit too much for someone in my headspace too while smoking the Cuban cigars I love. Once the expense of getting to Cuba is taken care of one can live there on very little. Rum, cigars and solitude for a few weeks was all that was required. European elections and local elections back home? They seemed utterly irrelevant and pointless to me then. Eventually, my mood began to lift as I got out and about and began to ponder what would come next. Then I heard that my friend and colleague Richie Browne had moved from Education Officer for Unite in Ireland into a more senior position and the Education brief was vacant. And somehow I knew, from 1 June 2014, that that would be where I would find myself. I needed to earn a living and a period away from the cutting edge of industrial relations into trade union education would do me no harm. But would education be enough?

As luck would have it, Richie and my friend from the Energy Services Union, Fran O'Neill, joined me in Cuba for my last 10 days there. By then I was suntanned, rested and a bit more relaxed – more 'positive' as Fran might have described it! Soon after they arrived we headed off for the beautiful Valley of Vinales in Pinar Del Rio province. This is the most famous tobacco growing area of Cuba, a place of staggering natural beauty where fields are farmed on horseback and tobacco growing, drying and even cigar making is all done on remote farms as a family enterprise all year round.

The best way to properly see this place is on horseback as motorised transport is in short supply, quite expensive to hire and, in any event, the network of remote tracks that run between fields can only really be negotiated on foot or by horse. It is no exaggeration to say that it was on the back of a horse, one Saturday afternoon in May 2014, while wearing a panama hat and smoking a cigar that had just been made in front of our eyes, that my involvement in what would become Right2Water was born.

Richie and I had gone on a four-hour trek to visit a family making cigars on their farm when, while smoking some of their produce, conversation turned to my upcoming return to Unite. As an Irish and British union, Unite has 10 'regions' or areas in total and in addition to each having a designated education officer most also have a political officer, though not in Ireland. For reasons linked to the troubles in the North and the historic tensions that remained, Unite in Ireland had never been able to appoint a political officer as such. Where would the appointment come from? From the North or from the Republic? Would the person be a Catholic, a Protestant, or a non-believer like me? Green or Blue? These can become vexed questions when the words 'political officer' are appended so no such post had ever been filled here. This did not mean, of course, that the union was not 'political'!

On the contrary, all trade unions by their very nature are political and Unite in particular (including its forebears ATGWU, Amicus, MSF, AEEU etc.) had always been political in terms of trying to advance the cause of peace and reconciliation for our members on this island and, also, the cause of workers and the working class outside the workplace, as well as inside. It is true to say however that without a dedicated function much of our political campaigning had been somewhat 'ad hoc' and on an issue by issue basis, and responsibility for this had, by default, fallen to the leader of the Union in Ireland, my colleague and friend Jimmy Kelly.

Richie had other ideas though – maybe it was the fact he was smoking his first cigar in 35 degrees heat and it had gone to his head! He was unsure that Education would keep me sufficiently busy and motivated, and believed Jimmy would appreciate some help with the political side of things, at least in the Republic. He thought, almost 20 years after the Good Friday Agreement, that the time might be right for Unite in Ireland to have a dedicated political officer and that I could potentially merge the role with my education role.

As he spoke, and in the following days, this idea seemed to make more and more sense to me. Providing workplace-related education in the areas of shop steward training in organising, collective bargaining, health and safety issues, equalities and pensions is all well and good, but the reality is that whatever gains workers are making in the workplace, even if they are just holding back the tide or stopping the rot in some cases, the advancement of the neoliberal agenda doesn't stop at the workplace gate. The dominant economic model which affects the lives of our members, their families and their communities prevails upon their housing or lack of it, their education and healthcare, their taxation, their pensions and their human and civil rights. I began to think that until we as a trade union movement start to join these dots and develop a way of educating our members and affecting these issues, inside and outside the workplace, that we are only doing part of our job. So marrying trade union education with a political role not only made sense to me, it was an absolute necessity.

Of course, back in Ireland the romanticism of these ideas had to be seen through the realities of what we had to cope with, and when I discussed this with Jimmy Kelly on my return he was certainly open to the idea, but he thought that I should cut my teeth on this new 'political education model' in the Republic in the first instance.

And so I found myself in Dáil Éireann with Jimmy in early June 2014. A meeting had been convened in one of the committee rooms to discuss the fact that later in the year domestic water charges were to be introduced and to see if there was any basis for a campaign against them. Also at this first meeting was a selection of leftist independents and TDs from small parties, including Richard Boyd Barrett of People Before Profit (PBP), who had signed a piece of paper titled 'petition' with Jimmy to be discussed, Ruth Coppinger of the Anti-Austerity Alliance (AAA), Seamus Healy TD, John Halligan TD, Thomas

Pringle TD, Joan Collins TD, Councillor Daithi Doolan and Councillor Brendan Young. Unfortunately, the meeting was a disaster.

On the back of the European elections, Paul Murphy of the AAA had been challenged by Brid Smith of PBP and had lost the seat he had held in the European Parliament. Brid hadn't got elected either, a classic case of the ultra-left in Ireland cutting each other's throats. The atmosphere was both poisonous and depressing as people who all agreed that water charges would be yet another regressive austerity tax and needed to be opposed squabbled about whether a successful campaign could be mounted against the charges, and how. Ruth Coppinger, who I was meeting for the first time, took no time in quipping to Jimmy Kelly that it was great to see the unions standing up for something for once. This was my first involvement with what I became to view as the union-bashing agenda of the AAA and, over two years later, my response now when it happens isn't much less withering than it was then. On the day I pointed out to Ruth that unions such as Unite were always defending workers and that we did not need to answer to her for our role in doing so. It was a sour note to a dreadful and almost hopeless meeting. Oh take me back to that tobacco farm!

The trade union Mandate was represented by Dave Gibney who I had only been introduced to once before. It was clear that Dave was confident something could be developed and so, in order to stop the meeting before we all got completely depressed by the negativity, I suggested that since the European elections had clearly left some discomfort among some of the political groups, perhaps the trade unions should meet alone to see if we could develop a plan to bring back to a future meeting. To be fair, that was readily agreed to and the meeting ended. As Jimmy Kelly, Dave Gibney and I walked back towards Unite's offices in Abbey Street, we chatted about what sort of campaign we could muster.

And so began a working relationship with Dave which has now become a deep friendship as well. It isn't often that you meet someone with whom you can work who just 'gets it' from the off, but Dave and I both agreed about what was needed and little or no time was wasted arguing with each other. Over the next three months, in the background, the strategy and branding for what would become Ireland's biggest single issue campaign ever, and that would ultimately morph into a social movement, was put together.

# 6

# Off Our Knees – Right2Water
# Hits the Streets

The following months saw Dave and I working closely together to try to develop a campaign model that would be different and that would work. It was decided that the campaign would seek to focus attention on the privatisation agenda behind the creation of Irish Water and the resulting introduction of domestic water charges. The unions concerned, Unite and Mandate then, immediately bought the Right2Water.ie domain address and started to put a website in place. So we had the name, the 'brand', if you like.

The next thing we did was to look at how we might organise the campaign. We already had two unions on board and they would soon be joined by the Civil and Public Services Union (CPSU) and the Communications Workers Union (CWU), along with Ireland's plasterers' union, OPATSI. And we already knew that there would be support from parties and independents in the political arena. Of course, we also knew that various Irish citizens were working at community level already. Could a campaign be developed that wasn't trade union, political or community-focussed, but that could bring all three together? The concept of the 'three pillars' of Right2Water was born. When, as promised, we went back to the Dáil to meet the political pillar again the atmosphere was much improved and we began a process of holding open meetings in Unite's offices. These were small at first, with no more than a dozen attending any meeting before Right2Water's inaugural day out on 11 October 2014. We also had a campaign launch and invited a long list of 'civil society' organisations, but from memory only Amnesty International attended and they never came back to us.

But meetings in Unite continued weekly anyway and we put together a plan for the first demonstration. Dave was the key behind this and was keen to build an effective social media platform. I knew little about this but I did know that we were unlikely to get much support from the mainstream media, so when Dave explained the 'reach' and potential of Facebook and Twitter in particular, and how important it was to get the message on these platforms right, there was consensus all round. Two days before 11 October we were asked to attend Store Street Garda Station where it was suggested to us that crowds on Saturday could be up to 20,000. Wow. We were blown away by that. If that happened this would be the biggest demonstration of the 'austerity era' and we were only getting started. We prepared a march route of one mile, for 20,000 protestors, some stewards and a stage truck and sound system that would cover a large semi-circular shape around the GPO.

## Saturday, 11 October, and the Aftermath

What a day! From the moment I left the office I knew something massive was afoot. The streets were packed with people carrying signs and banners for a start, and when I went to the Gresham Hotel to meet some community activists who would be speaking I could hardly get in the hotel. I met Audrey Clancy that day for the first time, a woman from Edenmore in North Dublin who had become a strong and passionate water meter protestor. There were others, too, including a man from Wexford called Brendan (Wacky) Dempsey who was to address the assembly before it departed from the Hugh Lane

Gallery on Parnell Square. Wacky was unwell and on crutches and I remember it took a lot of effort, and the help of the SWP's Brid Smith and her loudhailer, to even get Wacky to that platform so dense were the crowds. Wacky spoke with enormous passion that day about fighting back to reclaim our country in an address that we have promoted several times since, an address that is all the more poignant since Wacky lost his fight with illness just months later.

That day is a blur to me apart from a few memorable incidents, and not all for the right reasons, but history will record that this was the day that Ireland roared. Over 100,000 burst on to the streets of Dublin that day, throwing off the shackles of compliance with austerity to reclaim their pride and reinforce in themselves, and others, that we could fight back, we could rise again, we could rock the establishment and we could win!

After a ropey start when the gardaí in Store Street detected things might turn nasty and asked us by phone if we had 'lost control of the event', I jumped up on the stage, grabbed a microphone and tried to engage the crowd around the GPO with some chants and messages. The demonstration had been lengthened to accommodate the massive crowd extending over several miles, and as a result the event on stage would be very late starting. This caused some restlessness to those already assembled there, so I was basically buying time and trying to build a rapport with the throng. As I ran out of words the wonderful Evelyn Campbell came to the rescue with some songs that created a great atmosphere and, after another bit of music, we were off. I remember looking out from the truck along the full extent of O'Connell Street which was packed as far as the eye could see, right back over to O'Connell Bridge, but it would be overnight as I looked at the videos being loaded on to social media platforms that the full enormity of the first Right2Water day, Saturday, 11 October 2014, would dawn on us.

Sunday, 12 October, was an interesting day. On the one hand I was on a high. The events of the previous day, the colour, the noise and the numbers had blown me away. We were surprised but the media were stunned. Nobody had seen this coming. Videos were emerging on social media sites such as YouTube and others showing the amazing footage of the march. There was one which showed an elderly gentlemen leaning over the balcony of his Dublin 2 'corpo' apartment, looking down at the masses passing and apparently crying and waving. There is spectacular footage available of the beginning of the demonstration as it reached Trinity College on its way back from the extended 5.4 mile route, meeting up with the end of the demonstration as it just left to begin its route. Remarkable stuff. It all looked so amazing and inspiring.

Behind it, however, I knew that something had happened. I knew a steward had been struck and that Jimmy Kelly of Unite had been roundly, and consistently, heckled by a small number of loud protestors near the stage. Jimmy was livid. We just couldn't understand how, having put so much work into such a massive event, anybody would attack Jimmy or Unite. Jimmy was doing an interview with RTÉ TV News that evening and we stayed silent on the incident, but I was under no illusion that we were going to have to get to the bottom of it. We discussed it the following day and decided we had three options. We could ignore the incident and pretend it didn't happen, we could attack the hecklers and condemn them, or we could try to find out who they were and why it had happened to face the issue head on. We decided on the third approach.

And so it was that, a few days later, I was again talking to Audrey Clancy on the phone. I remember the call well. I was in Gatwick Airport coming back from a meeting and I was asking Audrey if she could arrange a meeting with the 'leaders' of the Edenmore group who had been closest to the stage. Audrey corrected me on my use of language, pointing out that the community activists in her area had no 'leaders', but was an amalgam of a number of informal groups. I was happy to be so corrected and Audrey arranged a meeting the following Tuesday night in the Edenmore House bar where I would meet ten or so of those involved. It was agreed that I would go with Dave Gibney and, indeed, we had a meeting later that night in Navan too. This would set a pattern of us, together or separately, attending meetings all over Ireland as part of the campaign but for now Edenmore was the priority. We arrived on time and it was clear from the outset that there would be a lot more than ten or so people present. It was also clear that Audrey was correct that there were no 'leaders' as what was about to happen was completely unstructured.

'Structure' is something I will return to later in depth, but for now all I mean is that as a trade unionist I have always attended meetings with a pen and paper to take notes, and usually an agenda and minutes from any previous meetings. This can be useful in keeping meetings business-like and focussed, but it can also create hierarchy and control. It would soon become apparent that hierarchy and control were feared and distrusted totally by many of these new activists in the water movement, especially those who were becoming active on an issue for the first time.

A strong leader immediately identified herself to me however. Bernie Hughes introduced herself with a smile and a firm handshake. As the lounge filled up (it was ultimately packed to capacity), it was clear that word of our visit had gotten around. The next speaker had a familiar face and introduced himself by name as the person who had struck the steward at the demonstration. He apologised and asked that I pass the apology on to the person concerned. John Lyons, the local People Before Profit (PBP) Dublin City Councillor, then welcomed us and a discussion began with him and Bernie Hughes. Bernie explained quite forthrightly that she would be 'chairing' the meeting and that 'politicians were welcome to observe but would not be taking over or speaking'. John seemed to want to argue his case but relented. It was clear to me that even without a formalised structure here was an example of how a hierarchy naturally emerges.

Dave and I agreed that I would address the meeting and when the room was full Bernie introduced me, thanked me for coming and asked me to say whatever I wanted to say. That was it, basically. There was no easy way to do this. I outlined that I, and Unite, were shocked at some of the events from the previous Saturday, especially at Jimmy Kelly being heckled so strongly. I explained about who I was and where I was from, what I had been involved in and that Jimmy had been talking about defending construction workers against an extremely difficult employer, JJ Rhattigan, when he was abused. I explained that these workers were just like the people in the pub. In fact, some of them could have been in the pub. They wore the same Dublin GAA shirts, they drank the same beer, lived in the same estates and suffered from the same types of social and economic exclusion as all the people there. I explained that in my view Unite was the only union willing to take on such a dispute in that sector. I also told them that Unite and Mandate trade unions wanted to have more great days like last Saturday and that we wanted to work with people in the communities to deliver them.

Then they responded. They stated that they didn't trust trade unions. They explained that, in their community and to them, trade unions were something they associated with the establishment, with Government, and that they had betrayed the working class. They had a right go at the behaviour of the Irish trade union movement in the preceding decades. And they looked to me to defend it.

I couldn't and still can't. They were right. I agreed with everything they said. As a movement, trade unions abandoned working class areas in 1987 when they entered social partnership agreements with Charlie Haughey's Fianna Fáil and, later, with Bertie Ahern's band of gombeen men who wrecked the state. I outlined in words, year by year and agreement by agreement, the betrayal of their communities and their futures. They were right. The trade union movement had let them down in the partnership era and they had felt this betrayal in their homes, in their streets and in their lives. I understood standing there in the Edenmore House that night the social neglect and alienation that a community within a few miles of Dublin City centre had had inflicted upon them by those disgraceful days of social partnership sell out.

I did of course explain that while the trade union movement had done that as a whole, there had always been unions and trade unionists who had fought the social partnership agenda from within the movement. I explained how Unite, and its constituent union forebears, had opposed every single partnership agreement in every single ballot. I described some of the disputes we had been involved in. I explained that Mandate, as an exclusively private sector union of low paid bar and retail workers, was not associated with social partnership either. I said that I fully agreed that the seeds of our economic collapse were sewn by the sell-out of social partnership and, finally, I explained that despite all that, unless the working class can find a way to work 'in union' with like-minded people we had no chance of mounting a successful fightback.

It was a great night. I learned so much that night in the Edenmore House about the inherent decency of the people protesting and the hurt they felt, and about the mistrust that that hurt had engendered. Thankfully, a man emerged from the back of the lounge who I knew. His name was Gerry Kennerk and he had been a senior member of the Building and Allied Trades' Union (BATU), which had decided some years ago to target its officials and staff (Unite members) with appalling discriminatory behaviour in relation to redundancy. Unite, through my personal prompting, had gone on official strike in defence of our members against BATU then, a strike that lasted from 1 May 2009 to 17 February 2010, almost 10 full months! It was the first time that a union in Ireland had taken an all out official strike action against another union as employer since independence, and we had done it for one reason: our belief that a bad employer doesn't become a good employer simply because it is a trade union.

Gerry Kennerk knew this, had been involved at the time, and was able to reassure those present of our bona fides. Whether because of this or the earlier discussion, by the time Dave and I got in the van to go to our meeting in Navan we felt that we could plan the next demonstration together with the people we had met. The air, at least with that group, had been cleared and some new respectful contacts had been made.

Did we know that we were on the cusp of something really massive at this point? Well, we knew that something was afoot but there were many dispersed elements that had not, as yet, fully emerged.

I have outlined earlier the background to the trade union's involvement in this movement and, well, politics and its changing face are littered throughout these pages. But there are other elements that are central to the story. The reaction by the trade union movement and left-wing politicians to the financial crash, the loss of economic sovereignty and the austerity agenda that followed had been abysmal. There had been no calls for protest, for civil disobedience or community uprising, but the people, not for the first time and definitely not for the last, were ahead of the politicians and the official trade union leadership. The first water meter installation protest began in Togher and Ballyphehane South Parish in Cork, and from there citizens in their own communities all over Ireland decided that this was it. They had had enough.

Other protests and movements were also taking place as communities led the fightback. In the small North Cork Village of Ballyhea there began, in 2011, what would be a full five years of weekly community protest against our €67.8 billion socialisation of private banking debt. The protest began when local hurling correspondent Diarmuid O'Flynn decided enough was enough, made a small sign and took to the streets. He, like many, had voted for what became the Fine Gael/Labour coalition of 2011, the one that was going to be opposing water charges, the 'Labour's way or Frankfurt's way' one, the one that would not give another cent to unsecured bondholders or busted banks like Anglo Irish Bank.

But within days it was clear that his vote had been stolen by lies and O'Flynn wasn't just sitting back and taking it. So he inspired a community dubbing itself 'Ballyhea Says No' and not only protested every single Sunday for five years (the demonstrations only ended on 6 March 2016) but inspired many other community groups to follow suit.

Initially, Pat Maloney got involved in the neighbouring 'Charleville Says No' group and then we had the emergence of others, biggest of all of course being the 'Dublin Says No' group. By the time Right2Water as a campaign name, structure and strategy was being developed in the summer of 2014, 'Dublin Says No' had already been marching to highlight how working class communities in the capital were suffering from austerity and bailout. From Spring 2013, in fact, very large crowds of Dublin citizens were on the streets protesting every Sunday, and across YouTube a series of videos sprang up which were 'alternative' in terms of how political debate traditionally had taken place in Ireland. For example, on 15 October 2013 Enda Kenny was intercepted near the Dáil and questioned by a community activist carrying a video camera about the withdrawal of a medical card from a child with down's syndrome, a Government policy that had been implemented while our taxes went to bust banks and unsecured bond holders. Kenny kept his cool as he was questioned before the video was posted on YouTube. Here was a new type of 'political accountability' where community activists were prepared to use their ingenuity and forthrightness on social media to get answers they felt they wouldn't get by other means.

Brendan Howlin was less successful in keeping his cool on 1 July 2013 in another similar video when he was intercepted outside Foley's Pub and was questioned about the Anglo tapes while he seethed and pushed the camera away. The first such video of note had seen Michael Noonan, Howlin's then hawkish counterpart in the Department of Finance, who was visibly shocked when he was intercepted on 13 October 2013 and questioned about medical card withdrawals, elderly people being forced to choose between heat and food, and how he seemed to prefer soft interviews with RTÉ to answering such questions in the street. Readers can make up their own minds how to interpret Noonan's 'sew up your pockets' comment in response to this direct form of questioning. I was intrigued as to who these people were putting our politicians under such richly deserved pressure. When the subject came up at one of the first Right2Water open meetings of trade unions, politicians and community activists, I was told by a leading figure in People Before Profit that 'Dublin Says No' was massive in number, loud, determined and completely undisciplined. In a strange way I thought I liked the sound of that.

Over time the name of the voice behind many of the interviews online, and the weekly marches, kept coming up. The name was Derek Byrne. I first spoke to Derek by phone in the weeks following Right2Water's first demo. He was full of guff and determination and had a completely new, and overly optimistic, view of how quickly simply protesting could turn the current crisis on water, banks and a broken country around. But he, and as it would turn out in 2014 'Dublin Says No', didn't care what I or anybody else thought about them. And I found that refreshing then.

So we were aware that around Ireland local groups were protesting everywhere. Some were in 'Say No' groups, others were in water meter protest groups or committees but now, after the avalanche of 11 October, Right2Water groups began to sprout up all over the country. In every county, and sometimes in every town in every county, Right2Water had caught on. But to what extent and how deeply, how usefully? We just weren't sure. We would have to test it.

The truth was that even before the 11 October event we had already decided that, if there was to be a follow up, it was to be localised for exactly that reason. We wanted to do two things. Firstly, we wanted to find out just how big was the potential for a truly national campaign. Secondly, however big it was now, we wanted to embed it into the communities around Ireland and try to increase it. There had been big single marches in Dublin before. On 15 February 2003, Dublin was one of 600 cities involved in the international anti-war movement where massive protests had taken place in opposition to the invasion of Iraq, and anywhere between 80,000 (garda figure) and 150,000 (Socialist Workers Party figure) had marched from Parnell Square to an event that was addressed by current Irish President Michael D. Higgins. Even further back, on 20 March 1979, the late Derek Davis of RTÉ reported from his helicopter that 150,000 had marched through Dublin looking for tax justice to alleviate the burden faced by the disproportionate tax burden forced upon 'Pay As You Earn (PAYE) workers. It was clear that the numbers, the outpouring, had caught the establishment, and organisers, by surprise then too. But had they worked or been maintained? Not really, at least not over time. Almost forty years later a contracted PAYE sector still carries a ridiculous proportion of the overall tax burden, and the money spinning war machine hasn't slowed down much since 2003. We wanted to know whether the Right2Water protest of 11 October was just another massive but fleeting outpouring, or were we watching something longer lasting and more embedded?

So 1 November 2014 was announced as Right2Water's second day of protest and, on this occasion, the protests would be local. This posed logistical problems because we still had the same 'three pillars' organising model, with all its raw imperfections, to work with. In some places political parties or independents were strong, but in many rural areas neither they, nor the trade unions, had offices or staff. How would we know who these local groups were to be? Could Fianna Fáil infiltrate them for example? There had often been decisions by that party in Government to close hospitals or by-pass towns that were quickly followed by a local demonstration which was headed, brass neck-like, by the local Fianna Fáil Cumann! How could we prevent this form of gombeen 'parish pumpery' infecting Right2Water and driving genuine people away?

In the end the people themselves were the answer and they rose to the challenge spectacularly. We initially started out with 34 planned Right2Water protests on 1 November 2014, a massive undertaking. Local protest groups helped of course. 'Dublin Says No' took control of the Dublin City Centre demonstration and Right2Water encouraged protestors to go there. Throughout the country it was similar. I took a call from another amazing activist who I spoke to for the first time. Her name is Noreen Murphy from Cork and, in the following weeks, we worked to make sure that the group that Noreen was with had resources to plan an event in Cork. We might have helped with news releases, leaflets, messaging, branding, interviews and perhaps a truck and sound system, but the work was put in by the community activists themselves. And all over the nation it was the same. People were getting off their knees at last and fighting back!

And so the numbers of towns holding demonstrations grew and grew and in the days leading up to 1 November we knew the campaign was growing exponentially. All we could do was pray for good weather. What a waste of time that was! It is no exaggeration to say that Ireland was a rain-sodden puddle on 1 November 2014. From lunchtime that day it lashed incessantly. As I looked out my window ready for a busy day this worried me. We had a lot on that day. Just that morning we had the final total for the number of local demonstrations – 106!

Yes, incredibly, the water protestors of just 26 counties of the Republic had put together 106 local protests on Right2Water day number two. All I worried about as I left home to speak at four of them in a single afternoon (Kells, Navan, Drogheda and Dublin) was whether the inclement weather would keep people away. Who was it who said that water doesn't just fall from the sky you now?

As I drove to Kells for the event put together by Seamus McDonagh and his team I was listening to Marian Finucane on RTÉ Radio 1. It was like listening to the coverage of a St. Patrick's Day in Ireland. Throughout the show and on the news it was 'water, water everywhere' as reports 'flooded' in of just how extensive the national programme of Right2Water demonstrations were. The media had missed a trick with the 11 October event and, having failed to anticipate it beforehand, there was now much more interest in what was going on.

I often think the Irish media is so consensus-driven that it can't accurately assess developments in our country at all. It usually adapts a tone set through some of the major outlets and then the entire media engages in a spell of following that message until the news cycle moves on, usually after a period of interminable boredom with the lack of real quality debate. As I said in *Off the Rails* in 2003, the last thing we like in Ireland as a nation, and the media is a key purveyor of this mind set, is for anybody or anything to be challenging the consensus.

Since the crash, the entire tone had been about how Ireland had seen no protests against austerity, no fightback, no public displays of mass anger. This may well have been (mostly) true on a large scale, but it also missed or deliberately ignored a great deal of low level anger and protest.

On 11 October, however, the explosion of Right2Water on to our streets had changed all that and provided the opportunity for the message, the tone, to be changed at last, a change to the national conversation. Now the questions were not, 'Why are the Irish not protesting?', or 'Why are they not fighting back?' Now the questions were, 'Are we seeing some sort of revolt? What is it about? Where is it going?' For the short few weeks between the seismic event of 11 October and 1 November 2014, the media were actually doing their job and asking these questions and facilitating this discussion in an open and balanced manner.

It lashed in Kells as I stood on a truck in the Fair Green and spoke about the need to embed the fight against water privatisation on a local level. I remember looking down and there, looking up at me, was Fianna Fáil's Thomas Byrne. Fianna Fáil, I thought, knew where this was heading even then. Cast on to the opposition benches for their national betrayal, they would try to use this to reconnect with the Irish people.

Without too much time to ponder that it was Fianna Fáil who had been the party (along with the Greens) to put water charges on to our political agenda with their memorandum of understanding with the 'Troika', it was back to my car and off to Navan for a massive protest that packed the town centre in the streets around the Town Hall. Then it was another rush to Drogheda at the invitation of Anthony Connor and the Boyneside Right2Water group. All of this was in constant lashing rain and when I got to Drogheda there was a problem. So large was the crowd that I couldn't park anywhere near the town centre. I had to park out on the hill near the hospital and literally run to the protest before it wrapped up. And I still had O'Connell Street in Dublin to get do.

When I got to the GPO I was startled to be put up on a truck where it was clear that Gerry Beades, until recently a long standing member of the Fianna Fáil National Executive and a close ally of Bertie Ahern, was the MC for the event and he had also, apparently, supplied the truck. I wondered what he was doing there and thought again about how Fianna Fáil's type of politics had led to our problems, not the solutions to them. Gerry himself was polite to me but then he handed the microphone to a man who I now know to be Andy Whelan. Andy was from the 'Dublin Says No' group in the south side and didn't know who I was then. I explained that I was from Unite trade union at which point Andy said into the microphone 'we have a union here, do you think they should be allowed speak?' Other people in the crowd close to the stage knew me and starting shouting for me to speak and I gently eased the mic from Andy and gave a short address, basically announcing that the number of nationwide protests had topped 100 and that the numbers, despite the rain, were massive. The rain-sodden crowd was delighted by this news.

By this point I was drenched to the skin but had to do an interview with RTÉ's John Kilraine in their outside broadcast unit for the 6.00 o'clock TV news. I had to pop into a shop and buy some dry clothes and a towel, go back to Unite's office and shower, and put on the clean dry clothes before rushing off back up to Parnell Square to meet John. Throughout the day Dave and Alex Klemm of Unite had been in communication with me about public relations, the number of protests and the numbers attending them. It was incredible. In 106 locations nationwide with lashing November rain this little nation had seen 200,000 protest on Right2Water day number two. Historic!

We were on a roll now. We had had the big Saturday protest, and now we had had the nationwide protests, also on a

Saturday. But we still needed to test this thing further. And so it was that Right2Water immediately announced that the next protest would be in the middle of the week, Wednesday, 10 December, and that it would not be at the GPO on this occasion. Right2Water were going to the Dáil! We wanted to take our protest against the increasingly bizarre Government policy on water right to the parliament itself, and on a sitting day too.

Now, for the third time, the organising strategy swung in to operation. Again the 500,000 leaflets were distributed, Facebook pages were updated, new 'event pages' were set up with the new date and call to action, and we decided that this was now the time to try to internationalise the campaign.

The phrase 'from Dublin to Detroit, water is a human right' had been a clarion cry since the beginning, a reference to the shutting off of water to thousands of homes in the city of Detroit by a city administration determined to milk dry the poorest citizens, or to make them suffer in the most inhumane way as a penalty if they were unable to pay. We decided that the Detroit Water Brigade (DWB) should be in Dublin to attend our protest on 10 December to explain, first hand, where this ideological journey of the commodification of water and the water meter toll booths would end up. Dave and I had a number of telephone conference calls with the DWB, a group dedicated to not only trying to prevent the shut-offs, but to providing bottled water and other humane relief to those homes for whom the city had literally decided that the taps would run dry. This was the journey we were embarking on, the journey whose consequences Phil Hogan had seemingly taken pleasure in, and the Irish water movement and media needed to be told about it.

And we were not stopping there either. Thessaloniki, Greece's second largest city, had held a citizen's referendum organised by a union-led campaign that fought off privatisation in May 2014. We wanted a representative of that campaign there too.

In addition we decided that, given the expected numbers, the stage, sound, stewarding and content of Right2Water Day 3 would have to be of a better standard. It had to be more professional and have more impact, and so a lot more planning would go in to the actual day itself than heretofore. So there was a lot of work to do. Adding to these elements were two events that also took place between the 1 November nationwide protests and the 10 December event that would have a massive impact on everything else we would do. Those two events were 'Jobstown' and a radical revision to the water charges regime that was implemented by the Government in November 2014.

## From Hogan's Failed Plan to Kelly's

It was clear that even with a massive majority the Fine Gael/ Labour Government was incredibly spooked by the water protests, and that what had begun as a 'campaign' about water charges was potentially developing into a citizens' movement. Right2Water, and the issue itself, had seen people protesting that were not just geographically spread throughout the state, but seemed to cross all social strata as well. This austerity tax was a tax too far not only in the poorest areas but among people who would describe themselves as 'middle class' and upwards. Business people, particularly hard-pressed owners of small and medium-sized businesses, were also in revolt and the Government was struggling to take the political sting out of the issue.

So the Minister who had been responsible for Irish Water more than any other, Phil Hogan, was despatched to the European Union as our unelected Commissioner. At the time I was concerned about this. In terms of motivating protestors, in terms of a Minister engendering anger and getting people worked up, Hogan was the gift that just kept on giving. The man had a way of getting under people's skins that was extremely useful in terms of building opposition to Irish Water.

The Government seemed to be aware of that, so they acted and removed Hogan from the equation.

And then my worrying ended when the Government replaced him with Alan Kelly of Labour!

We'll return to Kelly's particular 'style' later as we assess his period with responsibility for Irish Water through to 2016, but at the time I knew little about him. I knew he was from Tipperary and that he was what some commentators referred to as a 'young turk' (these things are relative in a party that looked increasingly grey and infirm) with a bright future, but his appointment troubled me for a number of reasons. First of all, Labour was already clearly struggling as the smaller party in the coalition Government. The austerity agenda they had agreed to was savage and, even in better times, the Irish electorate had always punished the smaller coalition party come election time. Labour was heading for a similar beating and needed a recovery strategy, not the most poisoned political chalice of our time. Why then did Labour, and leader Joan Burton in particular, allow themselves to be bounced into taking over Irish Water by Fine Gael? Did they volunteer for it? And if they did, had they completely lost their senses? With hundreds of thousands of people protesting and marching, with water meter installations a point of daily conflict, and with the crisis showing no sign of abating, what sort of Labour strategist would take on that hot potato?

Secondly, there was the issue of Kelly himself. A young man expected to have a bright political future he was already the Deputy Leader of the Labour Party and seemingly the heir apparent to Joan Burton. Surely he didn't want this poisoned chalice? Who would? And there was another problem. Alan Kelly has a brother, Declan, who founded and leads a multi-billion dollar corporation on New York's Lexington Avenue called 'Teneo Holdings'. A close ally of the Clintons, Declan

Kelly is the top man at Teneo, a company which advertises it's objectives across the world as follows:

> Working exclusively with the CEOs and leaders of the world's largest and most complex companies and organizations. Leveraging the deep global and intellectual capabilities across all 12 of our operating divisions, we sit at the centre of information and networks, offering unparalleled execution to capture opportunities and solve complex problems.

Before you ask, yes, Ireland is one of the 14 countries whose CEOs and leaders Teneo Holdings 'works exclusively with' and, as they say themselves, it is always 'senior-led and highly specialised'. That's 'behind closed doors', in layman's terms. The Irish connection is not just Declan Kelly either. Senior advisors to the company include the highly regarded George Mitchell, the Clinton-appointed star of the Northern Ireland peace process, and Tory grandee William (now Lord) Hague has also managed to find a place on 'Team Teneo'.

This is very impressive stuff and good luck to them all. There is big money in business and Teneo Holdings are in the business of big money. But in the Autumn of 2014 one had to wonder how a politician, a Labour politician in particular, thought it was wise to take over Ministerial responsibility for a state-owned water company facing historic levels of opposition around the concern – always denied – that the entire project was about privatisation. I would have thought the escape hatch of 'a possible perceived conflict of interest there, Joan' might have been Alan Kelly's response, just as I would have thought that the Labour Party should have told Fine Gael to 'sort out Hogan's mess yourselves, lads' when the poisoned chalice was offered in the first place.

Surprisingly, I have never seen these questions addressed politically or by our media. Surely there are legitimate issues here of public interest?

## Labour Blows Its Last Chance

Earlier I showed how the Labour Party had moved from its democratic socialist origins to the quite different social democracy model, and I suggested that this was as an abandonment of their supporters in a failed compromise with neoliberalism. I outlined my view that in 2011 the Labour Party had a chance to lead in a new progressive direction that could have garnered strong support, but that the lure of being in Government had taken them in the wrong direction. I said then that Labour had one more chance to save itself which I would return to. Well here it is, Labour's last chance.

In November 2014 Labour had an opportunity to completely re-position itself, not as the butt of legitimate citizen anger with its vicious austerity programme, but at the head of a massive social protest movement that could clear Fine Gael out of office and possibly change the political direction of the nation.

Of course from 2011 to the end of 2013, Fine Gael and Labour could argue that they had no choice but to impose the austerity agenda as prescribed by the Troika. They could claim that it was previous Fianna Fáil administrations, with their various coalition partners, that had crashed the economy and that, once in office, Fine Gael and Labour had found themselves in a bailout programme that the European Central Bank was imposing on Ireland. They could claim, notwithstanding their pre-2011 election promises to defend Ireland against this attack, to be victims of circumstance. But that argument effectively ended on 15 December 2013 when, after four long years, the Troika completed their twelfth review of the programme and Ireland became the first EU country to exit the bailout process.

If exiting the programme could have been described as a 'success' in any way, it was one that was paid for by Irish citizens who had been afflicted with the massive socialisation of private banking debt, increases in direct and indirect taxation, savage cuts to public services like health, education, transport and social welfare and many lives wrecked through personal debt, negative equity, unemployment and a resultant upsurge in mental health problems and, ultimately, a suicide epidemic. Some success!

I take the view that those four years are among the darkest and most humiliating in our nation's history, but on the appointed day the Government was more than satisfied with what an Ipsos/MRBI described as a combined 7 per cent rise in their combined support. This of course was in the days when opinion polls were still taken seriously, in the days before they miscalled votes on Scottish Independence, a British General Election, an Irish General Election, our Equality Referendum and the Brexit campaign in the UK. In this context, it seems likely that these poll figures obscured the extent of the anger many people felt about what the bailout had done to them for four years. If that was the case, this misreading of public sentiment was about to go very badly for the Labour Party because they were about to blow their last big chance. With Phil Hogan packed off to Europe and massive protests now underway, the new Labour Minister for the Environment Alan Kelly came to office telling us over and over again that he was a man of conviction and that he would respond to the challenges facing him in his new portfolio.

Imagine what could have happened if Kelly and Company had done the following. Imagine if they had told their coalition partners that water charges had not yet been implemented, that the Troika had departed and that Irish citizens had paid, and suffered, enough. Imagine if Labour had said that Fine Gael's Minister Hogan had made a mess of the Irish Water project

# Water charge - Scrap it ?

blic meeting

# Brendan Ogle
Right 2 Water

# Brendan Young
Community Solidarity

## Tue, 30th Sept, 8.00pm
### Kildrought Lounge
Ibridge

Hosted by Community Solidarity www.facebook.com/CommunitySolidarityNorthKildare

*A notice for Brendan's first
public water meeting*

## RIGHT2 WATER
# A NEW TYPE OF POVERTY

We have food poverty - one-in-ten are at risk of going without food. We have fuel poverty - 13 percent are forced to go without heating. Now the Government is introducing a new poverty - water poverty. Water poverty is defined as spending in excess of 3 percent of income on water bills. The ESRI estimates that up to 6 percent could face water poverty. With over one million people officially described as living in deprivation conditions, this new 'poverty' will pile on new miseries.

## NATIONAL DEMONSTRATION
11.10.14
2:00 - GARDEN OF REMEMBRANCE - DUBLIN

## FACT 2
www.right2water.ie

*Fact sheet for first national demonstration*

*GPO, 11 October 2014*

*Banner drop in Cork with a t-shirted Noreen Murphy in centre*

*Sligo, 1 November 2014*

*Swords, 1 November 2014*

*Right2Water Cabra*

*Jobstown won't pay twice*

*Detroit Water Brigade in the Gresham Hotel*

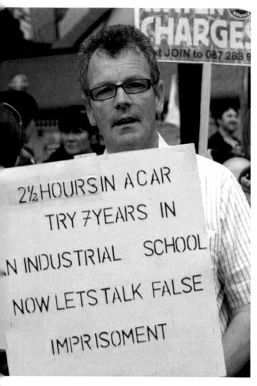

*Protestor with a reality check for Joan Burton*

*The sign says it all*

*Detroit Water Brigade visits Jobstown*

*Ghosts of Christmas future – Detroit Water Brigade collect water for families shut off*

*Brendan addressing the crowd on 10 December 2014*

*Tap Man No. 1*

*Tap Man No. 2*

*Tap Man No. 3*

*Tap Woman No. 1*

with his bullying style, and that Labour was not prepared to continue to punish the people with yet another austerity tax, imposed now *after* the bailout had ended and the Troika had left. Imagine if Labour had decided that this was now a time for the Government, having battered the people for four years at the behest of the Troika, to at last put the Irish people first. And imagine, in that vein, if Alan Kelly then put it to the Government that they should abandon the failed Irish Water project and revert to the long standing and accepted practice of paying for water through general progressive taxation. Labour could have followed up by telling Fine Gael that if they failed to agree with this position that Labour would have no option but to withdraw from Government. They could also have told them that Labour was not going to be a Fine Gael mudguard by simply taking over Phil Hogan's mess and following his agenda, thereby avoiding the inevitable savaging from the electorate when Fine Gael and Labour were ultimately forced to go to the polls.

Just imagine if Labour had changed course when opportunity called and what might have been. Imagine how transformative that would have been for Labour. Labour could have claimed to have steered the country through a bailout crisis caused by Fianna Fáil, the Greens and the long dead Progressive Democrats but, at the first opportunity, to have taken a decision to put the people first. The potential upside of such a course of action appears to me to be so obvious that it is mystifying why they didn't do so. Did they not consider it? Did they discard it because they simply wanted to cling to office for a while longer? By the time Alan Kelly was looking at Phil Hogan's mess Joan Burton had only been Labour leader since July 4, having ousted Eamon Gilmore in a move that looked very much like changing the Captain on the *Titanic*. But just imagine the possibilities. Labour could have connected immediately with a giant protest movement which was on the streets in every county and under a new leader could have then faced the electorate with the wind at its back.

It didn't happen. Instead, Alan Kelly unveiled an altogether different plan. The plan that would sink Labour.

## A Revised Water Plan

When Kelly rose to his feet in Dáil Éireann on 19 November 2014 to announce his revised water plan, he explained how he wanted his 'legacy to be one of achievement, not destruction'. Then he destroyed his own position as Minister for the Environment, and that of his party too.

The key components of what Kelly announced were a capping of bills at €160 for a single occupancy household and €260 for others until 2018. He followed this by announcing a 'water conservation grant' of €100 which could be claimed by anybody just for registering with Irish Water, whether they conserved water or not. He continued by declaring 'there are now only three numbers that are relevant, the two charging structures and the conservation grant'. before announcing that citizens now had a 'fresh opportunity to register' by 2 February 2015 and that those who did not register would be billed at €260 per annum and would not get the 'conservation right'. Furthermore, he outlined how this grant scheme would not be administered by his own Department but would be moved to the Department of Social Protection (another Department with a Labour Minister, leader Joan Burton). Kelly concluded by announcing that the controversial issue of Irish Water collecting personal PPS numbers would be discontinued and that Irish Water would delete any numbers already collected.

So there we had it.

Irish Water had originally been built on a model of collecting revenues of between €800–€900 per annum from households, other than single occupancy ones, meter installation and the 'add on' of PPS numbers which Irish Water would compile into a database that would be an 'asset' that could be sold down the line. As a result of this amended plan, these bills would be reduced by about 80 per cent, but only as a short-term measure. Kelly had considered the hue and cry that Irish Water had caused and had certainly acted, but not in a way that fundamentally addressed any of the issues that had led to such protest, apart perhaps from the PPS number debacle. But in terms of structuring Irish Water as a business, if that was his intention, what he had actually done was close to the worst of all worlds. Firstly, he had failed to reassure the public that the entire enterprise was not part of a privatisation agenda which was, fundamentally, at the heart of much of the protests. And well over €1 billion would ultimately still be spent on a meter-ing project which Engineers Ireland had described in 2011 as spending money we didn't have on something we don't need.

Bills were significantly dropped all right, but only in the short term as a measure borne of political expediency. Cap-ping them to 2018 was seen as a stop gap measure simply to take the heat out of protests. Indeed, it was interpreted by many protestors as nothing more than a cynical political ploy to get Labour and the Government beyond the next general election.

The most outrageous thing about this revised plan, how-ever, was the so called 'conservation grant'. The more Kelly and the Government trumpeted this element the more ridicu-lous the revised plan seemed, and the more the intensity and anger behind the protests grew. The stunt was so transparent that Kelly's plan was busted almost as soon as he announced it. Most thought that he was basically offering a 'bribe' of €100 as a 'conservation grant' to get as many people as possible on the hook into an Irish Water contract, and that he would then allow the bills to spiral again in 2018 after the next election. Conservation of water is an important issue. But the problem was that based on Irish Water's own figures an adult here used

54,000 litres per year in a state-owned, unmetered system. Across the Irish Sea UK customers had, in the main, metered and privatised water for decades. How much water did these meters save? Well a British adult, with a metered utility, uses an average of 68,000 litres per annum, about 20 per cent more.

Everybody agrees that waste should be minimised, but with a water network that leaked over 40 per cent of the treated water into the soil before it got to the taps, and with no evidence that those Irish water users were wasteful at all with the rest of it, Kelly cynically tried to use 'conservation' as a hook to trap people into contracts. It was a ruse and the protest movement, and I suspect many others too, knew it. Consider this. How could conservation be the motive in a flat rate charging regime with a €100 'conservation grant' that everybody gets regardless of whether they conserve water or not? To put it bluntly, a person registered with Irish Water could put all of their taps on full blast for a month yet still get the €100 'conservation grant'. Meanwhile, their neighbour next door might refuse or be unable to register with Irish Water, actually leave the country and not use any water at all, yet would fail to get any 'conservation' grant! Why? Simply because they didn't register with Irish Water.

As if that wasn't enough, there was another sleight of hand that was immediately transparent in the revised plan. By sending the 'grant' to the Department of Social Welfare, Kelly planned that the income would all go to Irish Water while the cost of the €100 'conservation grant' would be borne by a separate Department giving Irish Water a much healthier financial sheen than it actually had. Would the European Union, who was quite open in wanting Ireland to privatise its water system, fall for it? Would the bean counters in Eurostat be assuaged by such trickery? And, critically, would the Irish public fall for Kelly's stunt? Not a hope in either case!

By introducing such a plan to try to split, bribe and trick a protest movement into compliance, Alan Kelly, and Labour, had just blown their last big chance to move beyond this crisis and save their party from disaster. If they thought water had been bad for them under Hogan's tenure, the downhill slide for Labour by failing to grasp the opportunity to reconnect with citizens – ones who should have been their natural constituency – was about to become fatal. Far from taking the sting out of the protest movement, Kelly's revised plan only added to it.

But by the time Kelly had made his announcement he was possibly emboldened by the fact that the water movement was facing its own issues. The movement was now under full frontal media attack, being routinely described as a threat to law and order and even to the state itself. These attacks would reach such a pitch where protestors were said to be creating an 'ISIS situation' by Kelly's constituency colleague, Fine Gael TD Noel Coonan, in what must be one of the most ridiculous utterances ever made in the Dáil. This upping of the tone of attack on the water protest movement began just four days before Kelly's revised plan for Irish Water was announced, and it had its genesis in the reaction to a protest that had taken place in one of Dublin's most disadvantaged areas which involved Kelly's boss, Labour leader Joan Burton.

## Jobstown and Allegations of Political Policing

It was Saturday, 15 November 2014, exactly two weeks after the biggest day of nationwide protest ever, when things turned really sinister. The facts are that Labour leader Joan Burton was invited to an area of Dublin that has been deprived of jobs and proper funding for decades. It is an area where thousands of families struggle to bring up their children amid levels of unemployment, disadvantage and deprivation that are shockingly high. It is an area in need of considerable investment and support, but one where most politicians only show an interest at election time.

Joan Burton's visit came on the back of a quite scandalous statement she had made in the Dáil just a month earlier. Joan Collins TD (Independent) had raised the issue of the worrying behaviour of some gardaí at water meter protests, but Burton's response did little to suggest that she took such concerns seriously. Rather, her response, provided in full below, contained sweeping statements about the nature and behaviour of all of the protestors, and the protests themselves. This is what she said on the Dáil record:

> … well, all of the protestors I have seen before seem to have extremely expensive phones, tablets, video cameras…' [while the Labour leader was saying this some of the opposition started voicing alarm at where all this was going, but she continued] '… sorry, I say this seriously, sorry, a core part of the campaign is to video every single second. There has been the most extensive filming in relation to any of these actions that I have ever seen anywhere, Hollywood would be in the Ha'penny place compared to what's done here. Now just let me say this, you are making allegations here against gardaí, all I can say is all the material, as you would know, from the protests, particularly anything which looks controversial is immediately posted up on Facebook, YouTube and everything else. I certainly have a look at that from time to time and all I can say is if you can show, with all of the filming that's going on, if you can actually say as you are suggesting here that the gardaí are behaving improperly I don't think all the extensive filming which has been going on shows that. Now there is absolutely certainly, on all the films, quite a lot of confrontation.

Here was an elected parliamentarian, the leader of a party which should have been joined at the hip with the working class communities fighting the water double tax issue, on a massive salary paid for from the taxes of those protesting, and not only failing to deal with legitimate questions about the policing of protests, but making snide remarks about protestors and their personal possessions. I do not know who Joan Burton had in mind when she made that remark, so I don't know who pays for their 'phones, tablets and video cameras'. But I do know who pays for hers, and who pays her salary while she looks down her nose at us – the taxpayers of Ireland.

These statements, and the anger that they engendered, were the background to Joan Burton's visit to Jobstown on 15 November 2014. The Tanaiste was invited to visit An Cosan College for a graduation ceremony and arrived shortly after midday with a political advisor. Later on, as the Tanaiste tried to move to St. Thomas's Church, a protest began. RTÉ TV News reported that evening that people initially surrounded the car in a 'sit down' protest with Burton and her advisor inside. The protest grew but the gardaí were on hand and close to the car. As the protest continued chants such as 'Burton in your ivory tower, this is called people power' began from a number of protestors, which at this point included AAA TD for the area Paul Murphy. Murphy later told RTÉ News that an agreement was reached with the Garda Public Order Unit that Burton's car would be slowly walked out of the area but, while doing so, the gardaí decided to move Burton from one car two another sparking what looked like chaotic scenes while a garda helicopter hovered overhead. No injuries were sustained by anybody and two protestors were arrested, one for alleged criminal damage and one for an alleged public order offence, while Joan Burton issued a statement saying that she was 'fine but disappointed the education event was overshadowed'.

The whole event is reported to have lasted approximately two and a half hours. Those are the facts. Now for the fallout.

While Paul Murphy was in the spotlight throughout the day declaring that the event had been a peaceful protest, Labour's Alex White was quick out of the blocks calling the event 'anti-democratic' and accusing Murphy of not acting in accordance with the principles of democracy or socialism. And so it began. What has followed since, and continues to this day, has been one of the most worrying aspects of the entire water protest movement and the nature of the state's reaction to it. Serious issues have arisen, not only about the nature of peaceful protest, but about police behaviour, the courts and the judicial processes at work. The question arises whether the state knows how to respond in an appropriate way to such incidents. Paul Murphy and the AAA have described the reaction to Jobstown as 'political policing', while many of the establishment feel that what happened there crossed a line in terms of peaceful protest. To me, it has seemed like a collective media assault on an entire community that has been over-hyped from the outset.

I must also say, however, that the protest was clearly un-organised, spontaneous and that it grew very quickly. It was also so counter-productive and damaging to the water move-ment that nobody in their right mind would have set out to do such damage intentionally. Despite the fact that nobody was injured, and that only two arrests took place for alleged minor offences, the reaction to Jobstown by the gardaí, the judicial system, the Government and the media was, in my view, out of proportion with what occurred, and deliberately so. I believe the reaction was driven by a desire to use the Jobstown incident to attack and damage the water movement, to present it as sin-ister, malign and even a threat to the state itself. I commented earlier that the Right2Water campaign not only covered the entire country but all social strata, but Jobstown was seized upon by the establishment and the media to try to drive a wedge through that unity and to demonise a community.

How can I say that? Look at what has happened since. In February of 2015, gardaí swung into action and carried out a number of arrests, mostly early in the morning, of over 20 persons to interview in relation to the Jobstown protest. The manner of these arrests must cause concern. I have spoken to senior gardaí who have pointed out that the seniority of the some of the officers present, particularly for the arrest of Paul Murphy, would usually only occur for the arrest of somebody suspected of serious crime or a threat to the public. Because Murphy has a public profile he at least got the chance to explain what most of those arrested had gone through. After his release he admitted to being shocked at 'waking up at 6 o'clock in the morning, six gardaí at his door, taken to a Garda Station and spent eight and a half hours in the station....' Murphy went on to express his surprise at being arrested 'a number of months out from Jobstown' in what he described as 'political policing', 'an incredible waste of garda resources' and 'the use of the gardaí as a political tool of the establishment to damage a campaign that threatens the rule of that establishment'. As I write this, Paul Murphy and 18 others are evidently going to stand trial for 'false imprisonment' over this incident.

Paul Murphy and I do not see eye to eye. While we share a view of the evil nature of neoliberalism, while we share the idea that we need an alternative that delivers a more equal Ireland, we fundamentally disagree on the type of politics necessary to create that reality. As I will outline later, I believe that an alternative needs to be broad, progressive and inclusive, and there have been serious disagreements between Paul and myself, and between the Right2Water campaign and AAA in particular, since the beginning. But I agree with him absolutely that on the water charges issue the gardaí have allowed themselves to be used in a manner unbecoming a fair, objective and impartial police force. I also agree that this use of gardaí is a shocking waste of resources in a force whose numbers were decimated by the austerity cuts agenda adding to a sense of crisis in a city struggling with horrific levels of deprivation, social and economic inequality and drug and gun crime. Jobstown, and the reaction to it, is but one example of this behaviour and Paul Murphy is but one victim. In fact, as a result of Paul's privileged position as an elected TD with a political party machine behind him, he has much more support available to him than the other protestors who find themselves before the courts and the six of whom have found themselves in jail without a single offence being proven against them. The over-reaction to Jobstown by gardaí and the DPP is, in my view, aimed at undermining the water movement and therefore aiding the establishment in their water privatisation agenda.

Six individuals that I am aware of (July 2016) have been jailed for meter protests. Nobody was jailed for hurting anyone, or for committing damage, or even for any proven or alleged offence. Quite the reverse. But on 19 February 2015, Damien O'Neill, Bernie Hughes, Derek Byrne and Paul Moore were locked away for weeks simply for refusing to give a court undertaking not to protest any more. And then in recent months, when we had hoped that the madness of state overreaction had at last subsided, in May 2016 Sean Doyle, a 66-year-old Wicklow resident with Parkinson's disease, and his friend Eamon McGrath were jailed for refusing to give similar undertakings. They spent three weeks in jail before being released on a technicality.

But I am proud and honoured to stand with what is today the largest (per capita) and most peaceful protest movement anywhere in the world. I am proud to stand with Sean, Eamon and all the others who have been traduced for standing up for their right to protest. I am proud to stand with those who refuse to give undertakings not to peacefully protest. They are defending the right to justice and they are acting on principle and in good conscience. More than that, I am proud to stand with the young woman protestor who was flung into a street post by a garda outside the Mansion House, to stand with Gina Ward who had a glass door pulled down on top of her by gardaí showering her and her friends with glass fragments and causing serious injury while they protested, sitting down, outside a Council meeting in North County Dublin. I am proud to stand with the community of Jobstown which has been so unfairly maligned in relation to the events of 15 November 2014.

I have great respect for law and order. But I have no respect for the very small number of out of control thugs in uniform who abuse their oath and their office to attack the ordinary people of Ireland while they are engaged in peaceful protest and, in doing so, cause serious damage to the rule of law that they are paid to uphold. We deserve a police force that is trained, resourced and capable of reacting proportionately to incidents that will inevitably arise. We do not deserve a police force which can put hundreds of officers on streets protecting private companies installing water meters where they are not wanted, but that cannot find the resources or numbers to prevent Dublin being the most violent city for gun crime in Europe. Or, for that matter, a force that is soft on white collar crime and the type of real corruption that beggared our nation. We deserve better than that.

# 7

# Right2Water Day 3: Added Tensions and Meeting Russell Brand

What a week. It began disappointingly on Sunday 7 December when, having arrived to the warmest of welcomes from water warriors in Dublin Airport, the Detroit Water Brigade spoke to an almost empty news conference in the Gresham Hotel. 'Shu', 'AtPeace', Justin and Demeeko (Meeko) had crossed the Atlantic to tell the story of how the City of Detroit was turning off the water of distressed families unable to pay water bills that, in the austerity era, where spiraling out of control. They knew that there was a massive movement of protest and resistance in Ireland as we had been forced to start out on that same journey of installing toll booths on our human Right2Water. They came to tell all who would listen that as 'our ghosts of Christmas future' they had horrific and personal experience of where this ideological journey would eventually end up. But there were very few media present to welcome them and hear their stories the day they arrived. So we held the news conference, answered the questions of the few who did turn up, and took them off to drink Guinness in Temple Bar.

It would be just three days until Right2Water would be back on the streets of Dublin in a single national protest for the first time since its debut less than two months earlier. So much had happened since and we had now declared our core belief that united us all – 'water is a human right' – and one objective that united us all too – 'abolition of domestic water charges and Irish Water'. Many other things divided those of us who shared those two core messages, but by uniting around that simple single belief and objective we had a massive movement on our hands. The movement had rocked the political establishment and forced a massive rethink and concessions from the Government, but unfortunately for them we were not in the business of concessions. We were in the business of changing Ireland for the better. And so December 10 was going to be bigger, but it also needed to be better.

The unions had decided that for safety, communication and professional reasons we were going to have to up the ante in relation to what a protest looked and sounded like. So we had met Shay Hannon and the people at EQ Audio and Events to ensure that Right2Water Day 3 would be the best yet. The location was, initially, simple enough to decide. It would be outside Parliament on a Wednesday. We would be inviting the visitors from Detroit and also from Thessaloniki in Greece, and the event would be in the middle of the day.

There would be star power on the stage that day too in what we intended to be a three hour extravaganza of politics and poetry, music and craic, revolution and revelry, fun and frolics. This was a people's movement and it had gotten attention far and wide, despite efforts at home to make sure it didn't.

I knew it was getting attention a week before when I was in London at a regular Unite Education meeting. As I was getting ready to go out one evening I received a text message from a number I didn't know, an English mobile phone number, which simply asked if I could meet Russell Brand the following morning to record some video about Right2Water. Why not? Text messages were exchanged and by 8.00 am the next morning I was in a black London cab on the way to Russell Brand's home in a chic part of the East End. When I got there I was met by a burly security man in a Mercedes with blacked out windows. He got out of the car and led me in to the townhouse. While we chatted and drank espresso I noticed that the room in which I sat was part sitting room, part office and part television studio. A few minutes later Gareth, the man who had texted me the night before, arrived on a bike. He was young and engaging and talked to me about the campaign and the fact that Russell wanted to record a 'TREWS' (a daily online piece he did for a number of years about, as he put it, the TRuth in the nEWS) about Right2Water and the Irish battle that was going on. Russell would 'be here soon' and it wouldn't take long. Then a woman arrived with an Irish accent and explained that she was Russell's housekeeper and hailed from just down the road from me in County Monaghan. But where was he?

In bed! Yep, as she went upstairs I heard her shouting at him to get up and him shouting back in a jocular way and a minute later, with a bounce and a very sleepy head Russell Brand came down the stairs and we shook hands warmly. We talked about what was going on in the campaign and very quickly we had a filmed conversation that we agreed would be broadcast at a time picked to generate the maximum amount of support for the 10 December demonstration. The piece lasts just under seven minutes and was aired on Monday 8 December. In it a video that was prepared earlier is interspersed with our conversation about the corporate theft of water and how, having already paid for our water through taxation, we were being charged again and again. As a lighthearted piece with a very serious message it worked quite well. After addressing the 'bailout' and our shambolic tax system, Russell finished with an appeal to citizens to attend our demonstration, including for children to stay off school to attend, and hinted that he might even attend himself. The video can be found on YouTube.

But if that was the fun part there was much about the planning around this particular demonstration and, more so than any other demonstration we have had, that had unpleasant undertones that continued up to and including the day itself. The fact that the demonstration would take place on a sitting day of our parliament, outside that parliament, clearly gave rise to increased tensions among the gardaí. Both previous events had been on Dublin's Northside and came under the control of Store Street gardaí, but this one was on the Southside and came under the control of Pearse Street Station. Jobstown, and the media-generated furore around it, certainly hadn't helped and it seemed to us that some people in high authority were more interested in trying to manipulate the event to create a sense of crisis than they were in worrying about any real threat to law and order.

We met the gardaí in Pearse Street on three occasions in preparation for December 10 and, as the numbers were expected to be massive, the event would take place on the Merrion Square side of the parliament. This is actually the front of Government buildings but is generally considered the rear. That however was not the factor that we needed to consider most. We were told by the gardaí that the Kildare and Molesworth Street side 'only' provided for about 30,000 and that, because the streets met in a 'T' shape, there was also an issue about where best to erect the stage and sound system. On the other hand, the Merrion Square West and South streets met in an 'L' shape, and by erecting the stage at the joinder of the 'L' both streets could accommodate well over 50,000 combined with further overflow areas further down and around Merrion Square North and East if needed. We weren't sure about numbers for a midweek protest, but we felt (there were many in the media telling us otherwise) that we would exceed 30,000 quite easily. And so, for safety and logistical reasons relating to a stage, screens and sound, we decided that the assembly point would be at the Merrion Square side of Government buildings.

Some protestors were not happy with this location and communicated it to us which is fair enough. But for every event there has been disagreement on dates, locations, routes, speakers as well as the mix of political and 'entertainment' in terms of stage content. Every single event has seen social media come alive with complaints from protestors themselves about 'Right2Water this' or 'Right2Water that', and given the efforts that go into arranging these events I'll confess I was perplexed with this criticism at times. But it as an inevitable part of making something happen, something we just have to accept and get on with the job. I have come to know that what makes Right2Water so unusual in Ireland is that there are always nay-sayers and discontent with some facet of the campaign, but Right2Water finds a way to move on from that, and at the end of each protest there has been something close to unanimity among water protestors that the event was a success. I have, in a nutshell, come to embrace the differences and realise that most complaints (there will always be a few who will never agree with anything, some with an agenda and others just looking for attention) are sincere and well-intentioned.

However, there was one garda in Pearse Street in the lead up to 10 December who seemed particularly negative and certainly didn't appreciate, or seem to care, that we were trying to marshal this mass movement of protest in a constructive and peaceful way. As we discussed routes and stewarding in a meeting with senior officers, he opined that he had concerns that the 10 December event could be infiltrated by 'anarchists' and a 'sinister fringe'. This was, to put it plainly, nonsense. Because we were in communication with community groups all over Ireland we knew that the feeling was positive and focused on a peaceful, family-friendly day. The establishment and their media mouthpieces may have been foaming at the mouth over Jobstown, but we knew that it was blown out of all proportion and that protestors simply wanted peaceful but effective protest. There were, to be fair, others on the garda team that were having no truck with such drivel and made it clear in the end that a sensible plan was to be put in place. The plan involved each of the following elements:

- The streets concerned (Merrion Square West and South) would be closed from the previous night to allow the stage, screens and sound system to be erected

- The event would run for approximately three hours

- There would be a secure area at the front for the media and performers along with anybody with disabilities or mobility issues

- The access point for this area would be the back of the stage and a laneway on to Fitzwilliam Square

- We would issue passes to those allowed access to this area, or those with proof of infirmity could show them to gardaí and stewards to gain access

- We would publicise all of these arrangements, together with march routes to the assembly point, the previous evening and release them to the media.

The night before the event Dave and I were out late getting some photographs that we would use across social media and beyond. Using a small high-tech lens, the back of a truck and a high powered projector, the Right2Water logo in blue was shone on to some of Dublin's most iconic buildings including the Central Bank, the ESB Head Office (I enjoyed that one), the Department of Energy and Communications and, finally, the General Post Office (GPO) itself. We even shone it on Irish Water's 'anonymous' headquarters on Talbot Street. (I say anonymous because this building stands on a street corner without any signage in order to deter daily protests). But it was outside the GPO that the fun ended and we got tragic evidence of just how sick Ireland had become. As the truck pulled up at O'Connell Street facing Dublin's most famous building we were immediately struck by the luminous jackets being worn by people under the pillars at the building's front entrance. As we looked closer it became apparent that we had come across one of Dublin's homeless charities helping citizens caught up in the capital's then emerging homelessness crisis. That night temperatures in O'Connell Street were in minus figures yet there were over a dozen people in sleeping bags being given hot drinks by volunteers. We felt it was inappropriate to start up the projector but, seeing the van, some of the volunteers and homeless citizens approached us. In a heart-rending conversation they pointed out that down the side of the GPO, in Princes Street, there was a tent with a mother, father and two children asleep. Ireland in 2014!

In the end those present were enthused about the following day's protest but as I went to bed that night Enda Kenny's words, 'It's not about water is it?', were going around in my head. Kenny, you see, was half right when he had said that weeks earlier in the Mansion House. On the one hand, it is absolutely about water. But it is also very much about the deprivation, the inequality and the divisive policies enacted by the likes of him, his party and the other parties that have been in Government in the last numbers of decades. It is that division and those policies that had that family sleeping in a tent on a Dublin street that freezing cold night. As mentioned earlier, homelessness is not some accident that just happened on Fine Gael or Labour's watch. The homelessness crisis in Ireland is the inevitable outcome from decades of Government policy following a Thatcherite model of taking the state out of public housing provision and leaving the field clear for the soulless private sector.

The first task of the next morning was a radio debate on RTÉ Radio 1 with Pat Rabbitte on *The Sean O'Rourke Show*, an interview that I felt went very well. By then we already knew that buses were on the way from all over Ireland and the trains were packed too. This was going to be big! So I was confident, ebullient even, in the studio as Pat Rabbitte tried to hold to the Labour Party line. It was the first time I had encountered Pat since my time in ESB when he had been the Minister for Energy at the centre of the pension crisis. If my life had moved on so too had his as the new Labour leader Joan Burton had removed him from cabinet telling him that he had had his time. Chatting beforehand, Pat was relaxed about this and he told me if the Government went to full term he probably would not run for re-election. He even told me that he was not sure he would advise a young person to do so now as the game had changed a lot since he first got involved. Anytime I have met Pat Rabbitte I have always found him personable and intelligent, but I couldn't help reflect that it may have changed partly because the party that Pat was now in, and a former leader of, had sold its soul in a social democratic pact with neoliberalism, a pact that was never going to deliver for those most in need. As usual, once on air, Sean O'Rourke asked me to predict numbers for that day's rally but this was a near impossible task to do accurately. I confidently predicted tens of thousands before heading into Unite's Middle Abbey Street office.

Once back at base, as on all Right2Water days, the office was packed. On days such as this Unite members and friends arrive at our office where tea and coffee, sandwiches, flags, ponchos, whistles and even vuvuzelas are available, and they usually march together from there. Unfortunately, I am usually involved in arrangements in or around the stage so I tend to miss out on the marching bit. On 10 December in particular I left the office with some 'pop ups' for the stage flung over my shoulder and walked across the city to Merrion Square. The city was packed. Remember, this was the middle of the week, the middle of the winter, and it was absolutely freezing. But the town was choc a bloc with people milling around and heading towards the Parnell Square start point for one of the four march routes to Merrion Square. Everybody seemed in good form with many flags and signs, funny hats and posters that have provided the colour and fun attached to a Right2Water day already on view. To me it felt a bit like an All-Ireland Final day with the numbers, noise and good nature about the place.

As I walked across town I met several people who went out of their way to thank Right2Water and asked us to make sure we kept the campaign going and not give up as so many had before. The mood however gradually started to change as I neared the stage in Merrion Square and it was clear that there was an air of irritability, maybe it was nervousness, from some of the gardaí on duty. I was initially unable to get access to the stage myself as some obstructions were erected by the gardaí that made it difficult to do so. It appeared that there was no plan, despite what we had agreed and published on their request, for those required to get access to the stage and enclosure from the rear, and that was just the able-bodied. There was certainly no room allowed for a person struggling with mobility issues or in a wheelchair. What was going on?

On noticing this I asked gardaí present could they contact the named officer who we agreed we would be communicating with on the day with any issues. Two of them separately told me that they didn't know who I was talking about and when I rang him myself his phone went unanswered. Eventually, I got on the stage but I did feel that if I had encountered such difficulty, which to be honest bordered on hostility, from the gardaí that we had tried to work closely with, what was likely to happen to anybody not known to gardaí if things got any more tense away from the cameras? I was worried.

The event actually began shortly after one o'clock and what a view I had when I got up on that stage. Merrion Square West was thronged with people and they still seemed to be arriving down at the Davenport Hotel end while, to my right, Merrion Square South was jam-packed as well. Everywhere there were flags, colour and noise. On Merrion Square Park itself people were standing precariously on top of fences and even watching from up in the trees. Six weeks after Michael Noonan had declared that Right2Water was having its last day out on 1 November, here we were outside the Dáil in the middle of the day, in the middle of the week, and in the middle of winter. Tens and tens of thousands of us. Magical and massive!

There is a point in any Right2Water event when the optimum amount of people are present, that is, when you will get the best assessment of how many have turned out on the day. As I have said before, some people come for the march, some come for the demonstration and some come for both. I have found that the most people are always present about 15 minutes after the stage event has begun. This means that marchers, including stragglers, will have arrived at the rallying point and even those who aren't particularly interested in the stage event will generally stay to hear the first few speakers. By 1:45 on 10 December 2014, however, massive numbers were still coming. In fact, there were so many people that we had a problem. As the speakers and music got underway on stage, crowds continued to flood in from the rear around Nassau Street. There was nowhere for them to go other than Merrion Square North where there was no real view of the stage and so pushing began and escalated along Merrion Square West. Up towards the stage there were children who were becoming increasingly uncomfortable with crowds still arriving from the rear, and on five occasions I was asked in my earpiece to give crowd crush warnings and asked people to move back. Dave Gibney, who was also in communication with the gardaí, and Des Fagan, who was head of stewarding, passed similar messages to me. I was very relieved to see that by about 2:15 the tension had eased somewhat and people could enjoy the event in some comfort, but all of this made absolutely laughable reports later in the day that 30,000 had attended this event (it is amazing how this figure repeatedly crops up in media reports event after event – maybe their calculator is stuck). That estimate caused a lot of anger around the movement afterwards.

Three hours is a long time to be on stage but I had in my hand a full list of politicians, community speakers, trade unionists, poets, musicians and guests to get through. I was busy and happy. To some of those waiting for a three minute slot, or to those watching, it was a long day as temperatures continued to fall. We had broken the running order into three one hour segments and asked those appearing to come in their slots, but many were enjoying the day and stayed in the vicinity of the stage throughout. Due to the work of Shay and the guys at EQ Audio and Events this was as much a 'concert', certainly an 'event', as a demonstration. Everything was professional and high-tech, from the stage that had replaced the truck to the sound which boomed off the buildings of Georgian Dublin, and the screens and speakers which carried the feed down through the throng. There was a wonderful rendition in duet of 'The Auld Triangle' by Damien Dempsey and Glen Hansard mid-afternoon, and all speakers were welcomed by everyone irrespective of their political affiliation. Gerry Adams got a massive reception from a large Sinn Féin gathering near the stage, and Clare Daly spoke brilliantly, declaring that 'Irish Water is already dead, we're just here to bury it!' There were funny moments too. In co-ordinating Right2Water we hadn't seen sight nor sound of John Halligan TD since the very first fractious meeting in the Dáil the previous June, but there is nothing like a crowd to attract the vote hungry politician so John was at the back of the stage demanding to speak. Dave and I explained to him that he wasn't on the list and that he hadn't been involved, but John is a cute fox and eventually got on stage to 'introduce' a fellow Waterford man, trade union speaker and Unite boss Jimmy Kelly. They say politics is the art of the possible! Then I looked down at the side of the stage and who was also there behind John looking to speak? Rural, conservative former Fianna Fáil Independent Mattie McGrath! Not a chance Mattie!

By the end it was nearer a four hour event than three, and many had to leave before it ended. But to those who persevered the best was kept to last. We had picked up from YouTube a group of traditional musicians who had written a song specifically for the campaign called 'No Privatisation, Irish Water, Irish Nation' and it was brilliant. The video is recorded in the kitchen of a Connemara house where eight musicians used traditional instruments to deliver a rollicking good natured and funny tune which begins with 'Enda Kenny not a penny we won't pay at all, cause corruption up your policies is worse than Fianna Fáil', and also has lines like 'they're charging us for water, that we can't use at all... it has chloride, fluoride and cryptosporidium, flush them out 'cause it's time to get rid of em' and then continues:

> No backing down,
> No concessions will do
> The people have spoken, you know what to do
> The time has come to stand and fight
> And not put up with the same old shite
> We will strike, we will fight
> Water is a human right
> We will stand, we will fight
> Water is a human right
> No privatisation, Irish water, Irish nation, no privatisation, Irish water, Irish nation....

The piece then finishes with a great instrumental segment. There is a video online of the 10 December crowd singing and dancing, four hours after the event began, while this song is belted out on the stage with a selection of guests including the

Detroit Water Brigade trying to learn Irish dancing and jigs. Meeko in particular nearly had a heart attack at the side of the stage afterwards following his hilarious exertions. Brilliant and funny at once. I was on a high as I wrapped up the event on stage and sought out the heat of McGrattan's bar afterwards.

So what had just happened? Well to my eyes we had just had the longest, most professional, ground breaking and peaceful demonstration ever in the state and it had been attended by upwards of 80,000 freezing souls at its peak (1:45 to 2.00 pm or so). The media, and indeed the Government itself, had promulgated the idea that this demonstration would be an effective indicator that Alan Kelly's revised water plan had sucked the energy out of the water protest movement. Well, clearly it hadn't. Throughout the day the message was loud and clear: we do not want concessions, we want abolition. Of course with such vested interests at stake and such profits to be made any hope we might have had that the establishment would acknowledge the success of the event and the campaign was futile. Within the hour I was live in a gale on RTÉ's '6 O'Clock News' and instead of Sharon Ni Bheolain acknowledging the success of the event and asking 'what next', it was 'Brendan Ogle, how dare you bring people on to the streets costing Irish business millions in the run up to Christmas', a line that I still find amusing. RTÉ couldn't acknowledge Right2Water's success; instead we were to be portrayed as the Grinch that stole Christmas.

But that wasn't all. It was only later that I saw the photographic evidence of the garda presence around Kildare Street that looked more like South Africa in the 1980s than an appropriate policing response to a peaceful protest. I had a sharp phone conversation with our garda liaison officer, who only found his phone again after the event, who told me that one of his officers had been injured by a flying missile, while elsewhere there were tales of sit down protests on O'Connell

Bridge and of Fianna Fáil's Gerry Beades having a truck at the GPO in an effort to mount a counter-demonstration while gardaí allegedly directed protestors to that.

Does this sound like a sour note on which to end this section? Well I am setting out accurately from my perspective events that actually happened on the day, and how I felt about them. We have had another five events since and none have had any of this negativity or tension. The protest on December 10 stands out for a number of reasons which, when taken together, explain this tension. It is clear that the Government was surprised by the emerging movement following years of the silent acceptance by the citizenry of one austerity measure after another. They did not know what this was about, or where it was going, and Jobstown in particular was being used to add to a growing sense of concern. The wrong-headed deployment of gardaí in communities on metering projects just exacerbated the sense of disconnection for people who felt that the state no longer cared about them and was only interested in protecting corporate power and that the state, in reality, saw them as the enemy. Alan Kelly and Labour had just gambled what little political capital they had left on a preposterous set of concessions that only added fuel to the anger people felt at Labour in particular. So it suited the establishment to portray a massive peaceful citizens' movement as something sinister and threatening. It was now time to assess over the holiday season where we had arrived and what would happen next. But before we did so we had occasion to write, on this one time only, a letter of complaint to the gardaí about their handling of the 10 December event. I set it out in full below. By the time 2015 arrived the addressee had retired and, thankfully and coincidentally, no such incidents have arisen since.

Mr. Jeremiah O'Sullivan
Chief Superintendant
Pearse Garda Station, Dublin 2

Dear Mr. O'Sullivan,

We write to record our serious concern at the breach of good faith exhibited by An Garda Siochana under your control in relation to the RIGHT2WATER assembly in Dublin City on 10 December 2014.

This breach of good faith has not alone caused great damage to what had, until that point, been a very good and productive exchange between R2W and An Garda Siochana, but put those in the stage area (corner of Merrion Square West and Merrion Square South) in danger at the event.

On 8th December we brought our Head of Stewarding Mr. Des Fagan to a meeting in Pearse Street with senior officers who I do not need to name. This was the 3rd meeting we had attended in relation to this specific event, one of which you attended yourself. We had previously agreed to your request to move the event from Molesworth/Kildare Streets to Merrion Square to accommodate your safety concerns. You also told us that Merrion Square West and South could accommodate crowds of over 50,000 and that in the event of the crowds exceeding that that additional arrangements would be put in place on Merrion Square East and North. Most importantly it was agreed that an enclosure would be put in front of the stage to accommodate media, performers/speakers and those with disabilities and/or mobility issues. These were initially to number 500 but last Monday we proposed to reduce their number to 200 which was agreed. Access to this enclosure was to be through Merrion Street at the back of the stage and passes would be given to those in this area to wear around their necks.

At the meeting last Monday these plans were objected to by one of your Officers, citing worries about 'anarchists' and 'dissidents'. Before we could intervene this Officer was told by a more senior Officer that this access was essential, that Garda should not be over stating these 'anarchic' concerns and that as R2W were the only group co-operating with An Garda in relation to such protests it was crucial that An Garda Siochana accommodate our plans as much as possible. This more Senior Officer also advised his colleague that emergency access was necessary at the back of the stage for an emergency situation that could arise. We were told in relation to Merrion Street that 'you have won the argument' and that stage access would be provided for 200 designated persons through a laneway off Fitzwilliam Place (opposite ESB). An Garda Siochana asked that we publicise these events to the media and on our website no sooner than 7 pm on 9th December and, as requested, we did so.

It therefore came as a great shock to arrive on the day and to find no access to the stage from the rear other than squeezing through the erected fencing and the Georgian fence at the corner of Merrion Square South and West. Efforts to correct this situation to that which we had agreed, and which we publicised at your request, came to nought. Moreover the enclosure in front of the stage was cordoned off by a 'soft' temporary barrier and not the 'MOJO' as agreed on 8th December. Efforts to resolve this situation by telephone or with Officers present were met with rudeness, ignorance of the plans or a complete deaf ear.

There followed over 1 hour within which :

- Gardai repeatedly warned us as organisers of potential crushing at the front and danger to those attending

- There was no provision for emergency access for vehicles in the event of serious injury occurring to any person.

- People with disabilities were not being allowed access to the enclosure as advertised and agreed (at least one wheelchair confined girl and a number of children being very distressed also – on the Government Building's side of the stage)

- Demonstrators in excess of the numbers provided for (50,000) were turned away from the venue back towards a counter demonstration on O'Connell Street (something we had mutually agreed would not happen under any circumstances)

- Gates to Merrion Park were kept locked instead of the park being used to relieve the crowd pressure.

Luckily nobody close to the stage was injured. In our respectful opinion this should not be allowed to obscure the very serious breaches to our agreed arrangements which were implemented by An Garda Siochana without notification to us. In fact they were in flagrant contravention of what we had agreed with you, mostly at your own request.

In fact what was put in place was what had been proposed by the more junior officer at our meeting on Monday 8th and had been rejected by his more senior counterpart. Whatever the motivation for these changes, which concerns us greatly, they were neither notified to us nor consistent with what was agreed as safe and publicised as such. Clearly there will be future, we believe even larger, demonstrations. Right2Water will always be concerned for public safety and order. It appears however that we can no longer accept the word of An Garda Siochana in relation to such arrangements. We will therefore have to review fundamentally how we go about arranging such events and communicating those arrangements to all concerned.

# 8

# Damaged Media = Damaged Democracy

## The State of our Democracy

Do you live in a democracy? Are you a democrat? Here in Ireland we are forever being told that 'we live in a democracy', or 'that's democracy', or 'we have a democratic mandate' or even 'we have listened to the democratic will of the people'.

What is the nature of this thing they call 'democracy' and do we have one? The *Oxford English Dictionary* defines democracy as:

> ... a system of government by the whole population or all the eligible members of a state, typically through elected representatives.

That seems simple enough. Democracy is about 'government' and it involves all the members of the state effectively choosing representatives. So we have one. Right? Well, maybe. Here are a few questions. To what extent does the government of the Irish Republic involve all of the members of the state? In 2011, just 70 per cent of the eligible members of the state entitled to vote did so. And in 2016 it was even worse, just 65 per cent of the eligible members of the state voted.

You may well be of the view that that is the loss of those who didn't vote. But if those who don't vote are predominantly from a certain social, racial, economic or even age-related demographic, can we really say we have a system of government *by* the whole population? Not convinced? Okay, let's try another one. What do we vote on? Every time we have an election we have an array of candidates trying to attract our votes. They make us offers, give us inducements and bandy promises about like confetti at a wedding while they try to convince us that the things they offer or promise us are (1) good for us, and (2) that they will at least try to deliver them to us if elected. What if they lie? What if they have absolutely no intention of delivering to us, or even trying to deliver to us, that which they promised us and the reason we gave them our votes? They are now in Government! Is that a system of Government by the whole population? We do not live in a single party state. We have not elected a single party Government in the Irish Republic since Jack Lynch led Fianna Fáil to office in 1977 on a pledge to abolish rates. Fianna Fáil did something unusual and delivered on that promise and there are those who will tell you that the country has never properly recovered from the damage done to the public finances. And how do we know what we are voting on and what is good for us anyway? How do we know what is a lie and what is not? If, while in Government, we are told by an environment Minister that Europe will not let us change our water policy, how do we know if he is telling the truth? Who is going to tell us the truth, and if you answer 'the media', then the question becomes, Can you trust the media to tell you the truth? Do you believe the media is impartial, agenda-free and honest?

I went to listen to a nun once. If all nuns were like her I might listen to them more often. Her name is Sister Teresa Forcades and she is a Catalan physician and a Benedictine nun. But this nun wasn't talking about religion or God. She was talking about the nature of democracy. I am going to put to you what she said and it is this: there are three phases to any functioning democracy, not one. And I am going to tell you that in Ireland we only have one of them.

## The Three Phases of Democracy

### (1) An Impartial and Informed Media

It should be obvious that in order for a democracy to be fully formed that the people who will choose a Government need to be engaged in an ongoing discussion about the issues affecting their lives, their welfare and how society is best structured to deliver for them. The media, the so-called fourth estate, is the mechanism that is supposed to enable this informed and on-going debate. This debate is challenging to the consensus and establishment 'group think' and it leads to an informed elec-torate capable of selecting candidates that will reflect the real issues facing that society, facing their lives. I do not believe we have an impartial and informed media facilitating such a debate.

### (2) A Free and Fair Vote

A democratic society will have a system of voting for its gov-ernment and for deciding issues in local and national elections and referenda that is based on a free vote and universal suf-frage. I believe that we have this.

### (3) A System of Direct Democracy and Recall for Broken Mandates and Promises

It is one thing to have a debate, and to select your represen-tatives based on commitments, manifestos and promises ac-cepted in good faith. But to then have these promises and com-mitments routinely broken, even ridiculed by those who made them, is not part of any functioning democracy according to Sister Forcades. I agree with her. A functioning democracy will have systems of accountability for broken commitments and promises, mandates repudiated, that go beyond another election five years later. These can involve the right of 'recall' and possibly 'impeachment' or other manifestations of direct democracy such as citizens-initiated referenda. We do not have this.

In summary, I believe that we have a system of 'representative democracy' which provides us with just one of the three necessary elements of a functioning democracy with citizen participation, the right to recall and initiate citizens' referenda, and the ability to be engaged in a perpetual debate on key issues by an impartial and agenda-free media absent. That last point is, in my view, central to the poor quality of our democracy currently.

## The Irish Media

I remember my first real involvement with the Irish media. It was around 1997, almost two decades ago, and I was completely unprepared for it. I wrote about this in my first book, *Off the Rails: The Story of ILDA*, which was published in 2003. I was then a husband, father and train driver who literally found himself pushed forward as a spokesman for my colleagues in a major national industrial transport dispute.

At the time I had done very little study on how the media operated and was still one of those who believed most of what I read in newspapers (I read *The Irish Times* then as I already had a sneaky suspicion all was not well in the Independent Group) and, if I got broadcast news it was generally from RTÉ radio or TV. At that time I would have taken whatever was broadcast as akin to having been carved in tablets of stone.

However, by the time a three-month lock-out by Iarnrod Éireann ended in the August of 2000, my naivety had been illuminated by several years of banging my head against a wall trying to get our message across in what I felt was a fair and impartial manner. The instances of poor behaviour by the print media in particular at that time are catalogued in *Off the Rails*, but suffice it to say it was a sense of deep injustice at the hands of not only my employer and some of the institutions of the state, but from the media itself that resulted in my decision to write that book.

Thirteen years later and things have changed radically. And not for the better. A media that then at least tried to maintain a veneer of impartiality and independence has more or less ceased to bother now. If the problem then was mostly confined to the privately owned print media, the failure of the fourth estate to accurately reflect the society we live in and report on events that are shaping it now runs through print and broadcast media alike. Worst of all, the national broadcaster RTÉ has, in my opinion, at times plumbed the depths in relation to carrying out its statutory function with impartiality, balance and accuracy. So much so that I do not believe we have a properly functioning impartial media at all now, and this is immensely damaging to our 'democracy'.

You think that's too harsh? Throughout the timeline of events set out in this book the behaviour of the media will be referred to as we go, but I think it is appropriate to set out some general examples here. First of all, in my opinion, the ownership of our media is far too centralised around one person, Denis O'Brien. Too much of a media that regularly espouses freedom of speech as a key tenet of a functioning democracy is now substantially owned by a man who can have his lawyers pore over these words in case some honestly held view reflects badly on him or his outlets.

Since the ILDA dispute of 2000 the law has changed in this regard with the enactment of the Defamation Act, 2010. But this act is not a gag in relation to fair comment. It provides defences of 'truth', 'fair comment', 'honestly held belief' and 'in the public interest', but the problem of defamation is a 'tort' or civil matter and is therefore used by those with the deepest pockets who can access the court system more easily and with less risk of losing everything they have.

I first experienced this in that summer of 2000. Eamon Dunphy was then the Presenter of *The Last Word* on Today FM and in the heat of a studio debate about a trade dispute Eamon got a bit carried away and started calling me 'a conman' live on air. This comment was clearly out of scale with the matter under debate, which was a ruse put about by the Department of Transport to damage the dispute by claiming that the ILDA lock-out was putting workers in Irish Fertilisers out of work permanently and the plant was closing. What was actually happening, and what I had been told by then Junior Minister Dick Roche, was that the chemical company was simply closing temporarily for a short scheduled summer break, cleaning and a safety and maintenance check. But accusing me personally of putting people out of work and of being 'a conman' for denying it was the sensationalist type of 'journalism' Eamon engaged in from time to time. That the victim of this tirade was a train driver on a low income, locked out of work for two months and struggling to keep his family and home together made little difference. In reality, he could nearly say anything he liked as I posed no financial threat to him or the station.

This I found out some weeks later when, having returned to work after the dispute ended, I sought legal advice from a senior counsel. Firstly, I was advised that in order to prove that I had had my 'good name and reputation' traduced in the first place a judge would assess my argument against the dark light of the viciously negative and personalised nature of the wider media coverage I had been subjected to throughout the dispute. I was further advised that the then owners of Today FM would be likely to fight the case anyway and revel in the publicity for the station and the host. All in all, I was advised that I was, on balance, likely to win but that it was a considerable risk and that if I lost, selling my house (my only asset) would likely not even be enough to pay my legal bills. In other words, Today FM had deep pockets and, as I didn't, all the risk lay with me if I wanted to defend myself.

Since the law has changed with the enactment of the Defamation Act 2010 many believe that this is more likely to have tilted the balance towards the media and its owners than 'the man in the street'. Not only that, but the ownership of the media, and therefore the scope of debate, has contracted too narrowly. This isn't just my view. This was the view of the then Minister for Communications, Pat Rabbitte, when I spoke to him in RTÉ on the morning of 10 December 2014. We were about to go on Radio 1 with Sean O'Rourke and as Pat and I waited outside I had time to have a bit of a moan about the media. In doing so I expressed the view that the Irish media was too narrowly owned and controlled, and Pat just flatly answered, 'of course it is, but it's a very difficult issue to do anything with'. This from the Minister responsible!

Our Irish media is mostly made up of the state-owned broadcaster RTÉ in terms of television and radio. The other major contributors in terms of news and current affairs are the two national radio stations Today FM and Newstalk, a range of local radio stations and then the print media. We have three daily national broadsheets and a range of tabloids such as *The Star*, *The Mirror*, *The Sun*, *The Herald* and *The Daily Mail*. Of these, Today FM, Newstalk, the *Irish Independent*, *The Sunday Independent*, *The Herald* and a large selection of local and online outlets are owned in whole or in part by Denis O'Brien. In terms of print media, the *Irish Independent* is by far the largest selling daily newspaper we have and *The Sunday Independent* is by far the largest selling paper in the country overall. Not only that, but the *Independent* has been described as a loss-making market leader. In other words, the biggest newspaper in the country is losing money but continues to operate anyway. It would seem that getting the message out is more important to the owner than making money off the outlet itself. Have you got the picture?

The Irish media is so contracted that the reality is this. If you have a message, or you want to challenge the 'consensus' or make a call to action on a national basis you aren't going to get your message out through using mainstream media unless you do it through RTÉ or a Denis O'Brien-owned outlet.

But here is a startling revelation that I have made on social media several times and I now repeat. In my experience with Right2Water and Right2Change, the O'Brien-owned broadcast media of Newstalk and Today FM have shown me as spokesperson more courtesy, objectivity and balance, in addition to access, than our state-owned RTÉ. Before outlining why I think this has occurred, let me give you a particularly bad example of the behaviour of RTÉ in this regard.

It was 16 February 2015 and I was enjoying a Sunday afternoon watching football in front of the fire when my phone lit up and it was showing a prefix that I knew was RTÉ. I knew what this was before I answered. The unions involved in Right2Water had just announced that they were convening a conference to broaden the campaign beyond water. We would be inviting trade unionists, community activists and political parties and independents to engage in a public consultation to see if we could develop policy principles including, but going beyond, Right2Water. These were what would ultimately become the Right2Change policy principles and it was clear even at that early stage that this was a significant political policy initiative. RTÉ wanted me on *Morning Ireland* the following morning, a Monday, to do an interview at 7:15. I explained that this wasn't possible as I had to be at the airport around 9.00 am and wouldn't be able to make it. RTÉ rang back and explained that they really wanted to do this piece as they felt this political initiative was very interesting. Would I, they asked, be prepared to come in early to do a pre-recorded interview which they would air on the show later?

At this point I was concerned. Not only would I have to be out in RTÉ for close to 5:30 am, but I do not like pre-recorded interviews. I have at times experienced such pre-records being used selectively and in a way with which I was far from happy. It's always risky being live on air – mistakes can be made in the spur of the moment – but I have long held the view that a mistake that I made was at least my mistake and something for which I could accept responsibility. A poor, or even worse a malign, piece of editing was a different proposition entirely. Am I coming across as suspicious? If I am it is a suspicion borne of, as you are about to find out, hard and bitter experience.

Back to 16 February 2015. On that occasion I was anxious to publicise the upcoming conference. *Morning Ireland* is the most listened to radio show in Ireland and the researcher was so keen to do the piece that I thought, on balance, we should do it. I therefore agreed to pre-record the interview with Gavin Jennings and to be out in Montrose at 5:30 am. We also agreed that I would do a pre-interview call with a researcher into what we were planning that evening. This is normal practice.

And I did the pre-interview call. It was late when the researcher rang and we had a lengthy conversation where I not only explained our position on Right2Water but how we were looking at nine other policy areas, that we were receiving public submissions, that there would be a vote among the 'three pillars' to finalise any principles and I also outlined all the details of the submission process, the venue, time, format and all relevant details. RTÉ said they were looking forward to the piece and I was satisfied that, very early start notwithstanding, it was a good opportunity to add to the national debate on these key policy areas, as well as to publicise our event.

And so it was that I was met at the door at RTÉ in the Monday morning darkness and gloom by Cathal McCoille to pre-record the interview. Inside I was given coffee and then entered the studio to be met by Gavin. The cursory nods out of the way the interview began. Gavin asked me to confirm the details of the event, which I did, and then he threw a curve ball at me. 'Would the Labour Party be invited?' I emphatically answered no but Gavin had prepared for this response and hit me with a new piece of information, something that had not been mentioned in the long conversation with the researcher the night before. Unite was affiliated to the Labour Party, Gavin claimed. How could we be affiliated to the party and be so critical of them?

If I was surprised by Gavin's question he was visibly shocked by my response. Unite was not affiliated to the Labour Party and had formally disaffiliated following a previous policy conference decision of our Irish membership, and that we could not have been involved in the campaign only for this decision. Gavin didn't seem that interested in anything else about the conference after that and asked me something irrelevant about Gerry Adams. I wasn't biting on that one either and the interview ended. I was happy with it.

As I was leaving the studio Gavin came out with me to the back room where the producers and other staff were. A concerned looking member of staff approached us and asked me was I sure we weren't affiliated to the Labour Party. I answered 'yes' emphatically and they both then confirmed the source of their misinformation. Apparently Unite still appeared on the Labour Party website as a party affiliate. I laughed and told them they would need to take that up with the Labour Party before returning to my car in the morning darkness. I headed for the airport and sat and waited for the interview to be aired at the agreed time, 7:15. It didn't air and wasn't flagged. I waited for the rest of the show. Not a mention of the interview. Nothing. I did formally complain later and was told the interview was dropped to make way for a cricket story that had broken overnight (I kid you not), but I do not believe that now and I didn't believe it then. I fundamentally believe that this was a case where Ireland's most listened to radio station thought they had information that would make me, the campaign and Unite seem like hypocrites on national radio. So they laid a trap. That is the only explanation why this misinformation was not put to me in the very long pre-interview the night before. Editorially, that might even seem fair enough to some. Sean O'Rourke had, in 2013, laid a similar trap for me at the time of the ESB pension dispute turning a planned eight minute interview on pensions into a 25 minute interview, most of which was about a rather unwise speech I had made a couple of years earlier which had subsequently been presented as a national scandal. But while Sean had rightly given me a very tough interview, he had gotten tough answers back and at least it was live, it was on air and in the end it helped garner some much needed support for the ESB dispute at that time. And it certainly made great radio. No arguments from me.

But the decision this time was not to air the interview. To do so would not have shown me or Unite up at all, as seems to have been the intention, but it would have shown up the Labour Party, their policies, Unite's reason for disaffiliating and the reason why we needed this campaign. And because the interview was damaging to Labour and the government, and not the campaign, despite all the assurances I had gotten before agreeing to do a pre-record, RTÉ just dropped it in what I contend was an agenda-laden decision.

There are other examples, too, like the night *Claire Byrne Live* decided to debate whether we should have water charges or not on national television with two panellists only, Eddie Hobbs of Renua who favoured water charges and Fine Gael's Alan Farrell who also favoured water charges. Some 'debate'!

It's not as if the anti-water charges campaign do not have spokespersons, there are thousands of them.

Right2Water and Right2Change are not alone in being effectively cut out of the Election 2016 coverage until the day after voting. I was once promised that if I went on radio one Sunday morning I would be given three minutes uninterrupted to explain the Right2Change platform. That morning even Fine Gael supporter and strategist Frank Flannery described Right2Change as a very important and worthy initiative, but when I started talking I was just over 30 seconds in when I was interrupted by the presenter and shouted down by the rest of the panel.

And throughout the election coverage I listened to how, on show after show, once a spokesperson for any party or Independent even mentioned the word 'water' they were immediately interrupted to such an extent that it seemed as if there was a policy to attempt to shut down the water debate as part of that election. A strategy that, it must be said, failed utterly.

It continues now. We recently had the publication of the Low Pay Commission report which recommended a pathetic 10 cent increase in the national minimum wage. We are a country with the second highest prevalence of low pay in the entire OECD, but on the evening the report was published RTÉ's online coverage gave space to not one, but three, business groups on the issues. While trade unions and the ICTU (the only groups who actually represent the workers involved) had their news releases ignored, Chambers Ireland, employers' representative IBEC and the Small Firms Association were given fulsome coverage as was the Fine Gael Minister concerned. I have checked and can confirm that Unite, Mandate, SIPTU and ICTU all issued news releases and all were ignored.

Readers know that the first Right2Water demonstration took place on 11 October 2014 and that over 100,000 people attended. It was planned months in advance and news releases, press conferences and photo opportunities were all held for the press. But in the month beforehand Pat Kenny had 104 guests on his morning radio show. Only one guest (less than 1 per cent) came from a trade union, however there were 20 journalists (this habit of journalists talking to journalists is a key way of enforcing the consensus in modern media), 16 business people or public relations professionals, eight politicians, eight cultural spokespersons, seven writers, six campaigners, five doctors, two sportspeople and one priest. Twelve were classified as 'miscellaneous'.

The ways in which trade unions are treated have a clear pattern of establishing sub-texts to coverage. Here are some tips. Listen carefully the next time you hear or read about workers winning an increase. I will be surprised if the union that won that increase is acknowledged, and the story will most likely be written with an assurance that the employer has confirmed that the pay rise will not affect jobs. Get the subtext there? Pay rises cost jobs! Over the years we just start to absorb this nonsense in our subconscious as fact. The further context of course is that if we all agree to work for nothing there will be plenty of jobs.

I contend that because the events set out in this book challenge the consensus, and because few countries have a media that protects the consensus as Ireland does (even long after that consensus is seen to be wrong), they need to be seen through a particular lens. That lens is that legitimate debate about the nature of our society, now and in the future, is mostly shut down or presented in a malign way by the fourth estate. If you feel that such a scenario raises questions about the quality of our democracy then I would have to agree.

I believe a free and independent media acting in a fair and impartial manner in debating matters of national importance is crucial to any democracy. And I believe insofar as that media model is damaged in Ireland today that our democracy suffers corresponding damage.

## 9

# Now Let's Build – Early 2015 ...

In just a few months we had gone from being a nation that had taken more austerity than any other like lambs to one with the largest protest movement anywhere, proportionate to our population. So what now? Following the 10 December event the Right2Water unions made a number of conscious decisions in the weeks over Christmas 2014 and as the New Year dawned. We reaffirmed our commitment to staying with this at least until the next general election, which could still be a year and a half away, if the Government went to full term. We committed to building more links internationally to understand the dynamics at play in relation to the global commodification of our water. But we also considered how to build this protest movement into something more permanent, and into something that went beyond protest. Could we build this movement into something that not only attacked these regressive water charges, but delivered much needed real and lasting progressive change in Ireland?

### Citizens Awakened

One of the things that encouraged us were the wonderful people that we had met all over Ireland, people who were determined to make a difference. An excellent example is Karen Doyle from 'Cobh Says No'. Karen manages to be both exceptional in what she does but also somehow typical of the people who have built this movement and who will change Ireland to make it a better place. When I put something on Facebook a while ago about writing this book, Karen told me to get off Facebook and 'write our story'. Well I didn't quite manage the former but in pursuit of the latter I think a few words about Karen exemplifies that kind of hope that had emerged by Christmas 2014.

Karen is a housewife and mother who also works part-time outside the home. She got involved at the outset of the water charges movement in Cobh when she recognised that the austerity agenda was putting Irish citizens like her well down the agenda behind EU diktats and unsecured bond holders. Angered and disappointed at what her country had become, Karen became active in 2010 in opposition to the household charge (another austerity tax presented as a progressive tax on property but targeting those struggling to hold on to their homes, often in negative equity). Karen was active in setting up a local community group called 'Cobh Says No to Austerity' and believed Irish Water was a step too far for many in her town. The citizens of Cobh, like many all over Ireland, formed a 'meter watch' group to obstruct water meters being installed. Every weekday morning someone would rise about 4.00 to 5.00 am and find where the meter contractor vans were heading. Texts alerts would be sent so that by the time the vans arrived people like Karen were at estate entrances to protest. A caravan and a trailer were procured and soup, tea and coffee produced every day for sustenance. Margaret Thatcher would have hated it. Society! People came from their homes, their individual isolated bolt holes, to start sharing their stories about where it had all gone wrong, how their lives had been impacted by the breaking of a nation, which gave them the strength, the determination, to do something about it.

Of course, these groups did not operate in a vacuum and some on the ultra-left saw them as a vehicle for advancing their own agenda (something I will return to later), viewing people like Karen as potential recruits. In this environment, and through the medium of social media, the rhetoric and undertone of the 'debates' that can arise in this scenario can be hurtful to people who got involved in a campaign out of genuine concern for their community and their country, yet find themselves the focal point of bitter and personalised attacks. In the past many have walked away from the campaigns, surrendering them to the dogmatic ultra-left and the inevitable failure to deliver on their promise. But not this time. And not Karen Doyle and many others like her.

Karen Doyle has survived (I don't think that word is too strong for what people went through) that process and become a person determined, talented and confident enough to stand on stages in front of tens of thousands of her fellow citizens and deliver speeches like this one at Right2Water 7 on 20 February 2016:

### Know Your Place

Men and Women – know your place, it is to the forefront of this revolution.

Children – know your place, it is to be cherished equally because you are the centre of our world and this movement is for you.

Students – know your place, use the tools of knowledge to challenge and resist the narrative that there is no alternative to this rotten system (there is).

Politicians – know your place, it is to work for us, to work with us and to break the system which has broken us.

Unions – know your place, it is to support our endeavours as we organise to take back what is rightfully ours. Our water, our health, our education, our homes and dare I say it, our Republic.

Community activists – know your place, it is to hold this revolutionary space to nurture its growth and gift it to the world.

Refugees and migrants – know your place, it is to be free to live and work among us because no human being is illegal.

Homeless people – know your place, it is not on the cold streets of our towns and cities that you should be. But safe in your homes, living your life, and we will not rest until you can.

My friends we have a yearning for a better way.

When our government brings in bad laws that take away our human rights, we will break those bad laws.

We will fill our courts with noble law breakers and supporters of our collective resistance.

Friends, when some insist there is no other way, we will show them how it's done, because my friends, revolutions can be beautiful.

And when the heavy boot of tyranny comes down upon us and they attempt to put us in our place, just remember where your place is.

We will stand united and they will know we cannot be crushed.

Because my friends, my dearest friends, if they won't let us dream, we won't let them sleep.

## Greece, a Water Referendum and the Rise of Syriza

In January 2016, while we considered this, change was happening elsewhere as well. Massive change manifested itself in Greece with the election of Syriza. We had been aware of the process taking place in Greece, a process that had begun around the fight for water, the story of a citizens' referendum by the people of that nation's second largest city, Thessaloniki, on retaining ownership of their water was inspiration for us and the European Water Movement (EWM). Here is a bit of background on what had occurred there.

Greece had been in a bailout before Ireland but, unlike us, they had water companies already established and ready to sell by diktat. Just what the IMF and ECB like so much! Thessaloniki's water company (EYATH) was 74 per cent state-owned with the remaining 26 per cent having been privately held since 2001. But in the memorandum of understanding set out by the Troika, all state assets, including Greek islands and beaches, were to be taken over by HRADF (Hellenic Republic Asset Development Fund) and sold to pay the Greek national debt. I believe this is what will happen with Irish Water eventually if we allow it to continue and our government doesn't sell it first.

In February 2013, HRADF called for an international bidding contest to sell EYATH. However a trade union named SEEYATH reacted to this and promptly called an open public assembly at Thessaloniki City Hall to argue against water privatisation. Everybody was invited, including other unions, civil society groups, the Mayor's office, political parties as well as individual citizens. From this meeting a coalition was established named SOSte NERO (SOS Water). The Greek people were not taking this commodification of their water for private profit lying down! After that SOSte NERO used social media and other means to build a massive citizen-led movement against privatisation. The campaign also reached out to a network of European allies including the European Public Services Union (EPSU), the European Water Movement (EWM), the Italian Forum and the group that was just about to secure the remunicipilisaton of Berlin's water system by getting it out of the hands of Veolia, the 'Berlin Wassertisch' or 'Berlin Water Table'. Then SOSte NERO went further. Rallies were arranged outside City Hall in Thessaloniki that were attended by international personalities renowned for campaigning for the Right2Water from Bolivia, Germany, France, Italy and Turkey, all of whom had had great victories against water privatisation, to talk about their struggles.

The unions considered the water privatisation agenda as an ideological war and therefore felt that they should use every avenue at their disposal. And so, in addition to their other activities, they went to the Supreme Court arguing against EYATH's transfer to HRADF and, although the same movement did not exist in Athens, some individual citizens initiated legal actions in Athens too in opposition to the attempt to sell their local water company (EYDAP). Greek workers and unions also found themselves fighting the privatisation of their energy and electricity sector, their ports, their airports and transport system – practically everything that the state owned. The state of Greece itself was put up for sale in a shameful post-democratic feeding frenzy encapsulated when articles appeared in the *Wall Street Journal* explaining how to buy a Greek island! Everything the Greek people owned was to be taken and pushed up to the 1 per cent.

And so SOSte NERO sought some means of turning meetings, film shows and protests, as well as international support, into something that would be a game changer in their country, at least in terms of water privatisation. In April 2013, in another open assembly, they suggested a people's referendum against water privatisation. The proposal was formally put to the statutory local authority, the Central Municipal Council, and was unexpectedly accepted! Yiorgos Archontopoulos of SEEYATH union, who was central to these events, has told me that they felt very strongly at the time that nobody really believed that a referendum could happen, including them, but that they were going to push it all the way anyway. But by building a massive campaign there was such a grassroots demand for this referendum that the city of Thessaloniki became afraid to say no. People power was forcing politicians, if not to act, then at least to be pulled along in the direction the people demanded. Thessaloniki is composed of twelve municipalities and, one by one, SOSte NERO managed to get agreement from all of them for the referendum.

In February 2014, a date was picked for the referendum, the same date as the local and European elections, 18 May 2014. This decision put local politicians under massive pressure: they would be seeking electoral support in other elections happening on the same day as the referendum! It was a master stroke from SOSte NERO. Unions were central to all of this and it was the EPSU that agreed to send a delegation of 36 trade unionists to play the role of international observers for the referendum, while volunteers were plenty among the local community to make the ballot happen. The EPSU also gathered crucial funds from unions across Europe to help.

A worried administration in Athens, by then completely led by the Troika, reacted late in the day and tried to block the referendum from taking place. On Saturday, 17 May, just a day before the referendum, the Minister of the Interior decreed that the use of election lists by volunteers in the referendum was forbidden. The media, both private and state, fell over themselves to trumpet this announcement far and wide hoping to try to suck the energy out of the following day's event. But by doing so the establishment was scoring a massive own goal. This was just what SOSte NERO needed. Until that day only the local media in Thessaloniki and social media had been speaking about the water referendum, but now the entire country got to hear about it. That day, thanks to the Ministerial intervention, all of Greece finally learned that there was a way to fight back and that people needed to get off their knees.

As the hours ticked down to referendum day, SOSte NERO held another press conference, the second in the same day, where they said that they were going to use the streets outside the schools, the entrances effectively, to conduct the poll as the Government had said they could not use the schools themselves. A high level game of cat and mouse was taking place with the forces of neoliberalism, manifest in the then Greek Government and their Troika masters. But this inept Greek Government, the same one who had presided over the nation's descent to disaster, would soon be run out of office for their treachery by the coalition that became Syriza.

The next day, Sunday, 18 May 2014, more than 2,000 volunteers were out in Thessaloniki with ballot boxes, overseen by an international delegation, carrying out their referendum. On the day more than 218,000 citizens voted and 213,000 of them (98.2 per cent) voted *No* to water privatisation! It still brings tears to Yiorgo's eyes when he recalls seeing the elderly people of his home city waiting patiently in a line to vote, and how encouraged he was that many of them said they had come to vote because of the prohibition the previous day, that they had stayed silent for too long and that here in Thessaloniki the fightback of the Greek people must begin. And, of course, the subject matter was water privatisation. Yiorgos describes the result as a reaction against the neoliberal agenda manifest in water privatisation, as the reaction of the ordinary people to the theft of their country by the 1 per cent. It was a reaction that said a big *No* to Troika-dictated Memoranda of Understanding, that said a big *No* to the policies which were destroying the lives of the Greek people. It was a big *No* to the European institutions working hand in hand with the IMF to take ownership of a member state for the 1 per cent! History will record Thessaloniki's water referendum as the biggest mobilization that had happened in decades in Greece. This was a new type of struggle and in it there were many valuable lessons for the Greek people, and indeed other citizens, to learn. One lesson is that people are out there and waiting to participate – you just have to find ways to connect with them and get them off their sofas.

A week later, in the face of such popular demands the Supreme Court of Greece reached a decision, thanks also to Athens' citizens, that the private sector – driven as it is solely by the profit motive – cannot be relied upon to provide clean water and sanitation to the population so water companies must always be at least 51 per cent under state control.

At the end of June 2014, EYATH held their Annual General Meeting and HRADF made an official announcement which stated:

> Because of the Supreme Court's decision and because
> of social reactions, we are freezing the procedure of wa-
> ter privatisation.

The 'social reactions' reference is a clear allusion to the Thessaloniki referendum, the citizens' court actions and, ultimately, the transformative effect that this anti-water privatisation effort had, not just on a city, but on a nation.

Yiorgos joined us on stage on December 10 to share this tale, and in our discussions beforehand he was amazed at the size and energy of the Irish anti-water charges movement. He marveled at the number of citizens as he looked out from the stage, and could not have predicted that discontent with the Troika was about to see Syriza elected back home. But that is exactly what happened within a short number of weeks.

Today the current Greek government (most of whose parts supported the referendum from what was the opposition at the time) continues to be under Troika diktat and is trying to sell 23 per cent of EYATH so that just 51 per cent will remain in state ownership. However in the near future there are plans to transfer that 51 per cent to the new Superfund (under the guidance and insistence of the Troika) so that the profits of the water company will be used to pay down the Greek debt. The efforts to privatize Greece's water have not gone away. Should this transfer happen, through fair means or foul, the role of the company will thereby change from being there solely to provide clean water and sanitation to one of making profits which, while initially used to pay off state debt, will inevitably become just another means of turning state assets into profit enrichment. Yiorgos describes this proposal as a type of Public Private Partnership (PPP) and assures me that the people are again organising against it. His union SEEYATH remains the cornerstone of the fight against water privatisation.

These events are relevant because while we were considering how to build on the massive start Right2Water had made, Greece had exploded across the news wires with the election of a bizarre coalition calling itself Syriza. This coalition ousted an incompetent right wing administration from office, and the fight against water privatisation played a key role in these events. The similarities with Ireland were striking. Two relatively small nations of proud peoples on the opposite fringes of Europe were beggared by corrupt and incapable Governments over decades. Two peoples were initially in shock but were brought to the streets in opposition to the water privatisation agenda.

But the differences are equally striking. For one thing, Greece remains in what seems like a perpetual 'bailout'. It is not governed by, or for, the Greek people. It is governed by the Troika at the insistence and diktats of the rich. And no matter how well-intentioned those elected by the Greek people may be, they have a gun pointed at their heads in every single decision they make. They are governing under duress to the will of their masters, not their citizenry. Ireland, on the other hand, exited the so-called bailout three years ago and the decision to embrace water commodification was done voluntarily by a sovereign Government acting on its own ideology.

But another difference is key. By the time of the events set out in this chapter occurred, Ireland had had a gargantuan 41 per cent of European banking debt foisted upon it and our then Fine Gael/Labour coalition Government had been elected on the promise that they would secure debt relief for Ireland when the opportunity arose. That they failed utterly to do so, failed to even ask for a debt restructuring package, is the most damning of that administration's many failures. And it was this particular failure to ask for debt relief that led our Government through Michael Noonan, Brendan Howlin and Enda Kenny to behave in a reprehensible manner towards the Greek nation and its impoverished people.

By June 2015 Syriza had made a catastrophic mistake in failing to use a potential exit (Grexit) from the EU as an option in their negotiations with the Troika for a debt write-down. By then Greek citizens had seen wages plummet by 37 per cent and pensions cut by 50 per cent as a fire sale of their country's assets took place. But instead of showing solidarity and using the Greek crisis to make the case for a debt write-down for Ireland, Noonan took the exact opposite approach. By adopting the position that because Ireland hadn't got a debt write-down Greece couldn't either, Noonan lined Ireland up with the forces of financial imperialism over the needs of the Greek citizenry. Instead of lining up with a country in even worse circumstances than us and leveraging that to the benefit of both, our Government lined up with Germany and the ECB and cheerled the kicking of the Greek people. This combination of failure and arrogance was best encapsulated by the then Minister for Public Expenditure, Brendan Howlin, as he delivered his part of the Budget later in 2015, where the failed coalition of Fine Gael/Labour tried to buy the upcoming election with just one budget after years of overseeing austerity. In explaining his case in the Dáil, Howlin let the mask slip as he jibed, 'who speaks of Syriza now?'

Within months it would be clearly demonstrated that Howlin's fancy words had fooled next to nobody as his Labour Party got slaughtered in the polls. Syriza, on the other hand, despite making key mistakes while also facing horrendous threats from the EU, got re-elected with an increased mandate! The Greek people, it seemed, knew that the people they elected were at least trying to act in their interests against almost impossible odds. And the Irish electorate knew that the opposite was the case with their Government as they ran it out of office. If the Greek people found no friends among our Government, they found many in our country among the water movement.

So after Election 2016 in Ireland it might be appropriate to ask, 'who speaks of Labour in Government now?'

## Brussels, Marseille and the Catholics Who Think Water is Free

Early 2015 saw a couple of firsts. Right2Water was invited to Brussels by Sinn Féin MEP Lynn Boylan who had been appointed the Parliament's Special Rapporteur on water following an EU-wide citizens' initiative. Provision for these initiatives had been included in the text of the Lisbon Treaty and presented to the people of Europe as the first truly transnational instrument of modern direct democracy in the EU. That was what people were promised anyway. The idea behind the initiative is that if at least one million citizens, coming from at least seven of the twenty-eight member states, verifiably sign up to it this will act as 'an invitation' to the unelected European Commission to propose legislation in line with the initiative.

Get that? If one million 'electors' want something they can 'invite' 28 unelected mandarins to think about providing for it. Isn't European democracy wonderful?

Anyway, the first (and to date the only) such initiative is on, that's right, the principle that water is a human right. Water was actually decreed to be a human right by the United Nations on 28 July 2010 when the UN passed Resolution 64/272. In doing so, the UN explicitly recognised that clean drinking water and sanitation are essential rights for all citizens. Including the right to life itself! Yet the European Union ignored this move from the UN and remained steadfastly silent on the issue. What is interesting about the EU position, however, is that while it was the Chicago School of Economics that was the birthplace of the modern manifestation of the neoliberal project, Europe is now a major theatre for the latest phase of post-democratic neoliberalism, and it is also home to some of the world's greatest water privatisation corporations, including France's Veolia. But all across Europe concern at the failure of the EU to act on these matters is so acute that this right to water was the subject of the inaugural European Citizens Initiative (ECI). Aided by the European Water Movement and the European Public Services Union (there's unions at the centre of progressive politics again), in 2013 a massive 1.8 million verified signatures (it is now almost 2 million, far beyond the threshold of 1 million) of EU citizens were presented to the Commission.

Now remember that the ECI mechanism was enacted to try to bring some degree of democratic citizen-led participation into a European project suffering from a real and growing democratic deficit. Indeed, in voting for the Lisbon Treaty that is exactly what EU citizens were promised. Yet by January 2015 the Commission had still not acted. In fact, as I write these words in July 2016, it has still not acted. So in February 2015 Right2Water Ireland was invited to Brussels to meet the European Water Movement and address these issues with a representative of the Commission, a representative with whom we had a very interesting exchange later in the day. Not only did this exchange deal with the ECI, but it explored the water campaign then underway in Ireland and our way of paying for water and sanitation through general taxation. During our time there we discussed issues with our counterparts from France, where 'Eau de Paris' had just been taken back into public ownership following spiraling bills and citizen protests; in Berlin, where Veolia had been forced out too; in Italy, where a referendum like the one in Thessaloniki had happened and been ignored; and in Spain, including meeting water campaigners from the regions of Catalunya and Galicia among others.

All over Europe the story was the same. Privatised water was pushing bills inexorably upward and leading to shut-offs in Paris and Rome (you don't need to look to the USA to find water shuts-off, they happen here on our own doorstep) and this was undermining not only the right to water and sanitation but ultimately the right to life itself. And every time we explained our system of paying for water through progressive general taxation the advice to us from our counterparts was the always same – keep it that way and do not let them install the meters for they are the hardware of the privatisation agenda. In fact, once we started communicating with groups from other countries who were further down the privatisation path than we were, I was struck by the fact that we habitually look elsewhere (I think it's a post-colonial national inferiority complex) for ideas about how to do things, how to run our country even. On water, however, by some accident of history, we had managed to find ourselves in a better position in relation to protecting the human right to water. For once, we were the example to be envied and, if possible, to be followed by progressives elsewhere.

I was asked to speak on behalf of Right2Water Ireland when European Commission Representative Jorge Rodriguez Romer of the Water Status Unit met us, looking like he wanted to be somewhere else altogether. But these unelected mandarins need a touch of reality and plain speaking, such as when I told him: 'Water should not be subject to the market capitalist profit system that is being applied across Europe.'

In response to the view that because the EU acknowledged the right to life there was therein an implied acknowledgement of the right to water, I argued that far from rebutting our point, that response confirmed it. If the EU would not vindicate the right to water – as there is no life without water – they could not be said to truly be committed to defending the right to life.

On the Commission effectively ignoring its own citizens in relation to the ECI, and thereby damaging its own democratic mandate, I finished by stating:

> The Commission's attitude to the European Citizens Initiative on the Right2Water was giving citizens the impression that their worries are of no concern to them. I think that is a very dangerous message for the EU to be giving because that has the potential to create all sorts of problems in terms of disenfranchising people and we know in Europe what can happen in terms of political extremism where people feel they are disenfranchised from the political system.

As I write this a year and a half later the chickens may have come home to roost with the Brexit vote in the UK. 'Disenfranchised' writ large!

Mr. Rodriguez Romer was open, cordial and responsive, and quite prepared to put interesting positions to us too. For example, he volunteered at one point, unprovoked, that he was fully aware of the water protests that were going on in Ireland and that, while he didn't want to interfere in a domestic political matter, he could assure us that the Commission saw sufficient space for Ireland to choose its own model of paying for water within the accepted guidelines of the Water Framework Directive. He further acknowledged that the Commission was aware that general taxation was our accepted practice for doing so and had been for many years. For absolute clarity, this was said to us in a formal meeting of European delegates discussing the Right2Water in February 2015.

We left satisfied with this exchange and the contacts we had made, the network that was developing. And we shook hands with some of our counterparts knowing that we would see them again shortly. In fact, four days later Right2Water Ireland had been invited to address the Conference of the European Water Movement in Marseille.

Dave and I arrived in Marseille looking forward to strengthening links with those in the EWM that we had met in Brussels and meeting new campaigners too. We were all on the one page as far as I was concerned so there was nothing to be apprehensive about as we sat down in the auditorium on day one (we would address the conference on day two) and put on our earphones to listen to the translation of the debates underway. Within minutes something very funny happened which shows how our island nation, stuck out on the fringes of Europe, can be viewed at times. As we listened we almost choked on our sparkling *eau* to hear one person say, 'there are big protests in Ireland about water, they do not want to pay for it there. It seems that Catholics believe water should be free.'

Now we hadn't noticed too many copies of the *Irish Independent* on sale in the streets of Marseilles perpetuating the myth that paying for water through tax meant not paying for it at all. Furthermore, the elderly gentleman who had made this comment was Italian, where they are much more likely to believe in free gifts from God than your average Irish person does these days. So we had to stick our hands in air, wave our crucifixes about and get the attention of the Chairman to point out where we were from, and that actually our means of 'paying for our water' had nothing whatever to do with his clichéd view of our country and more to do with avoiding water privatisation and shut-offs for poor people down the line – something they had failed to do in Italy, even with God's help! Something they had failed to do in Rome, even with the Pope living around the corner!

The rest of the Conference went swimmingly after that (we even got a red-faced apology later) and when I spoke the following day the delegates seemed genuinely blown away by the size and impact of our movement and were full of admiration for what the Irish were fighting for. In Marseille, home of Veolia, our message was clear – come to our protests as our guests but keep your water privatisation corporations here in Marseille, thank you very much. And, as with our friends from Detroit, from Thessaloniki, those we met in Brussels and now those we met in Marseilles, the pleading was always the same – do not allow yourselves to be put on the road to water commodification because it ends in extortionate bills, water shut-offs and hardship.

## Right2Water Day 4, 21 March 2015 – Holding It Together

So the plan for Right2Water Day 4 was approached from a position of renewed vigour. It had been three months since the massive 10 December protest and, as usual, the background drumbeat of media-driven negativity was that it had 'gone away', numbers would be down and 'the heat has gone out of the protests'. Well, we'll see about that.

If some in the media were doing their best to make sure Right2Water Day 4 flopped by pretending 'it' didn't exist, we just kept on keeping on, doing the same things behind the scenes while planning openly with the three pillars to make it massive. It was agreed we would go back to a Dublin City event on a Saturday for this one, and there was the usual debate about the mix of politicians and music. In general, it was felt that the 10 December stage event had been very long, stretching out to four hours, and that on this occasion massive Southside and Northside marches should merge and form a parade up to the top of O'Connell Street at the Parnell Street junction. We would use Shay and the lads at EQ Audio and Events for stage and sound again, and we would distribute the usual 500,000 leaflets, hold press conferences and do interviews on national and local media where we could get them (basically Newstalk, Today FM and some local outlets while being completely ignored by the broadsheets and RTÉ Radio and TV). We would once again ramp up the social media machine weeks in advance – all the things synonymous with a Right2Water event.

Of course, these decisions are never unanimous and some madcap suggestions get thrown in along the way, but these are all part of the 'fun' of putting a Right2Water day together. For example, on 10 December, some had felt that four hours in the freezing December cold was not enough for people and we should allow them to use the equipment we had hired out for a later demonstration at Merrion Square or even, for whatever reason, outside the Shelbourne Hotel. Never going to happen! And now, for 21 March, we got a suggestion that instead of having one massive event and rallying point that we should have three stages situated in various parts of the O'Connell Street, Abbey Street and Henry Street areas so that people could 'benefit' from hearing all of the wonderful political speeches in the audio form of triplicate. Oh the joy!

That was not going to happen either, but the facts are that some in the political arena, particularly, but not exclusively, people in the AAA and People Before Profit, see these events as opportunities to collect funds, distribute party newspapers, recruit volunteers and advance their party agenda as much as anything else. To a large extent, although this behavior is criticized by some, it is generally fair enough political activity. If I was a member of a political party I would have possibly done the same. And if part of that party's cause was winning a water war then doing so is not inconsistent with helping the party as well. Party members are quite entitled to see it like that. But it can go too far. Sometimes I worry that supporting the party objective can blind people to the need for unity that, purposely or not, damages the wider movement.

By the 21 March event we were struggling with some of these dynamics. I had worked with people like the Socialist Party and Socialist Workers Party since the ILDA days 15 years earlier, and had always found them supportive. I considered some comrades, maybe even friends. I had in fact voted for Joe Higgins in Dublin 15 in the last three elections in which he ran, and I had made small personal donations and supported my union doing so too at election time. I was never a member of these parties, but I was surely not the enemy either? Yet the unions were pivotal to this campaign for a reason. Remember that first event in the Dáil after the European election when there was such hostility among the political parties present that the atmosphere was poisonous? Remember how it was Dave Gibney and I who went away from that meeting and worked on a union proposal for a campaign to bring back to them? Well, what we were doing there is what unions, by virtue of their 'business' being representing workers, have to do all the time. We were working to come up with solutions that could bring the majority of what are usually members, but in this case water protestors, together. And in this case we were doing it to try to stop them from ripping each other apart on the back of a vicious election campaign that did the 'left' no favours at all.

While some trade unionists may be political, and some politicians may be trade unionists (not as many as should be, or who pretend to be, mind you) they are two entirely separate disciplines. Politics by its very nature is inherently and systematically competitive. In politics, parties do not compete on points of similarity. That would be impossible really, so what they compete on are points of difference, real or invented. At its zenith this 'competition' finds expression in a left/right debate, but when you drill down into social issues such as this the politicians are, by virtue of being in the same campaign, on the same side. So it should be easy, right? Wrong!

That competitive instinct to argue a difference is ever present. You can't be in politics without being competitive, and if you aren't, get the hell out of it before you give yourself a nervous breakdown. But you'll never achieve anything without building consensus either, and sometimes in this campaign that second point has been completely lost on some. If everybody believes that 'water is a human right', and everybody supports 'abolition of water charges', what is there to be competitive about? Unfortunately, some think in terms of what will give their party an 'edge' over the others involved in the same campaign. So issues get 'invented' to cause division.

While I clearly oppose water meters as toll booths on our human right to water, those reading closely will see that water meter protesting, by design, was not a cornerstone of Right2Water's strategy. Similarly, while I am a strong advocate of non-payment and call for it on the airwaves any chance I get, non-payment is not a condition on which support for Right2Water is based. We have stuck with the unifying strategy of having a single belief and a single objective. Why? Because we wanted to build a campaign as broad and strong as possible and this is the best way to achieve that objective.

If we had gone down a different path and built a campaign which, for example, meant you had to be a meter protestor to support it, then I believe it would have been tiny compared to what Right2Water has become. Similarly on non-payment. I may be prepared to go to jail some day for not paying my water bill, but it wouldn't be much of a campaign to insist that everybody be prepared to do so. Many people will absolutely refuse to pay these double taxes. But other people do. Many people who oppose it pay it, not because they want to, but because they feel obliged to or are afraid not to. What sort of strategy would it be to cut to off all those who pay their bills by making it a non-payment campaign? How could we build broad support if we told people like my 84-year-old mother, who has paid every single bill that ever came in her door, that we had no interest in them? How can we look at people who are bullied by their landlord and who have paid out of raw fear that they might end up without a roof over their heads that we were not open to them ? Tell them we have no interest in them? Ridiculous!

Nobody who wanted to build a broad progressive movement open to all with a single belief and objective would countenance such a measure. If, on the other hand, difference is what is needed to advance a political agenda against others in the same campaign, then trying to draw such issues into it, as opposed to leaving them at the door to build unity, is what will happen. And it did happen. For well over a year there was not a single Right2Water meeting where the AAA did not raise the issue of turning Right2Water into a 'non-payment' campaign, long after the logic of not doing so had been explained and accepted by everybody else, including People Before Profit. And if it was bad in the meetings it was worse online. People who were trying to build something broad and inclusive found themselves being told they were 'soft on non-payment' by those more interested in narrow sectarianism. The campaign itself and its broad approach came under constant, and often vicious, attack. And of course those most prominent in defending Right2Water in the public sphere came under the most vicious attacks of all.

When I was involved in the ESB pension dispute a verifiable death threat was posted to my work from a post office in rural Ireland by a gentlemen who was so angered by my defending workers' pensions that he thought threatening myself and my children with death was acceptable. The threat was investigated and dealt with appropriately by the gardaí. They found the person involved, spoke to him, set out the circumstances to me and thereafter neither I nor they had any interest in pursuing the matter further. But however ridiculous the behavior of that person at least he disagreed with me on something fundamental. Something that, had we not won the dispute, would have plunged the country into darkness in December 2013. But it gives me no pleasure to say that the abuse that I, Dave Gibney and others have been subjected to by 'comrades' on the 'left' in pursuance of this campaign has been worse. There have been no 'death threats', but it also hasn't been an isolated instance of a man temporarily losing the run of himself. Instead, what the unions in Right2Water have been subjected to from the ultra-left has been a deliberate plan to try to get the campaign under their control, and then to try to sideline completely the unions supporting it – unions who have supported the left for years. Some solidarity.

Back to Day 4. One stage, and one massive crowd. There was a scaffolding over a building on O'Connell Street to the left of the stage that day which somebody scaled and shot a video from right down along O'Connell Street. It is possibly my favourite piece of film of any Right2Water day, and it captures the scale and the noise of the protests. From early morning convoys of buses had left Donegal, Cork, Kerry and many centres in between and now here they all were. The march from Connolly had passed Tara Street like a never ending snake of people carrying Greek and Irish flags with the usual array of humorous and angry signage. It just went on and on. And marching to meet it from Heuston Station was another group that lengthened along the entire North Quays before joining with their comrades from Connolly at Capel Street bridge.

The hint of menace that was present on 10 December was gone entirely and the gardaí were completely co-operative. A new Chief Superintendent in Pearse Street had reached out helpfully in January after our letter and, in any event, as an O'Connell Street demonstration this was under the control of Store Street Station and all was well. The sun even shone. In

March! It was shirtsleeves all around until an afternoon shower threatened to dampen things down but quickly passed. As usual I only got to see the marches later on the many videos that were posted and they literally blew my mind for scale and good humour. At the stage with Dave waiting for things to start we had taken a phone call from CWU General Secretary Stevie Fitzpatrick who was at Heuston Station, 'stop worrying lads, it's massive'. I am always worried beforehand. I know that our opponents are so entrenched, so bitter and so well resourced that they are just waiting for us, the water warriors, to fall flat on our faces, but Dave is much calmer about these things than me. He spends the days leading up to these events entrenched in our 'social media machine'. Communicating and prompting, and watching and counting. I count 'likes', but Dave focuses on 'reach' to see how it is building. And in the lead up to March 21 he was confident, telling me that we had a social media reach day after day that was deeper than any newspaper could boast and that we would have a massive crowd. And he was right as usual.

We always have to work out who will speak at these events and try to have a mix of political and community speakers. The trade union pillar generally defers a lot of its share of speaking time to the others, the political parties number six or seven (depending on who is talking to whom at a given point) and then there are a plethora of Independents who support the campaign, and those are just the elected ones. So if they all speak, and they are matched by an equal number of community speakers, with a few trade unionists and some music, poetry or performance art thrown in, it is quite a task to pull it all together. Anyway, increasingly it fell to the unions to put the stage together, the running order, the mix and the timings.

John Douglas spoke for Mandate trade union on this occasion. John gave a stirring address and just after him was Sinead Stewart from Donegal Right2Water. Sinead won't

*We just aren't having it*

*Santa hats at 10 December march*

*Dempsey and Hansard on stage*

*Water is a right not a commodity*

*Water charges get the red card*

*Concerns over garda handling of marches*

*Police barriers*

*'Dissidents' or just concerned citizens?*

*Right2Water days are full of fun*

Brendan with t-shirt saying 'We Already Pay'

Lynn Boylan, EU Parliament Rapporteur on Water

*Dave Gibney and Brendan address EU Commission representative*

*Jailed simply for protesting*

*A family affair*

*It's their planet and their future*

*Spectacular blanket knitted by water warriors of Cobh*

*O'Connell Street six days before Election 2016*

mind me describing her as a wee lassie from Buncrana with a big heart. She was very nervous but nobody listening to her would know that. Looking back on video she comes off as natural and solid, but she was weak with nervous tension beforehand and exhausted afterwards. Then came Dundalk's Maeve Curtis. What a woman. Maeve's Dad used to sell me ice cream from his van when I was growing up, 'Charlies Ices'. She is the epitome of the new protestor from 'middle Ireland', but Maeve became so infuriated by the bank 'bailout' that she was central to forming a group in Dundalk. This group is typical of many throughout Ireland and they meet every Wednesday in the Redeemer Hall, my old primary school hall! And what a speaker Maeve is. Here is a bit of what she said on 21 March 2014 to a thronged O'Connell Street:

> We've heard a lot about violence and the violence of protest, but I want to talk today about another violence, the violence of austerity. There are two ways to enslave a nation, one is with the sword, and the other is with 'debt'. And make no mistake, that's what this Government have done, and the previous Government have done. They have enslaved a nation.
>
> We the people have suffered the violence of austerity. I don't have to tell you what these cutbacks have done. We are living with these cutbacks. They have closed hospitals, put 9000 on trolleys in hospitals, they have cut medical cards to the most vulnerable in our society, they have attacked the most vulnerable in our country, they have evicted peoples out of their homes and we have a new work house in our country, it's called 'emergency housing'.
>
> Fifty people caused this debt and cost us €64 billion, €64 billion! It's not our debt. €26 billion of it was down to tycoon builders who got the slush fund, the secret society that is NAMA. They got forgiveness but we got our

mortgages sold, we got evictions, we got the homeless dying on streets in this city and we got a suicide epidemic. Austerity can be directly linked to this suicide.

But there is only one thing worse than corruption, and that is the acceptance of corruption. We have had it for too long but we will not take it anymore.

Phil Hogan you are not getting our water, and Europe is not getting our water, that water is for our future and our children. So when the bills come, and the pressure and the phone calls we will stand strong and not pay this bill and save the water of this nation. All it takes is a 'return to sender' sticker and we will send the bills back to them. We are not ordinary citizens, we are extraordinary citizens and we will win this war. The people of Ireland are off their knees and we will not accept any more political corruption from any political party. No more.

Another massive success, followed up by pints in Mulligans and a decision to up the game. The protest movement was well embedded by this point and its base and continuance were not in doubt in the short term. Concessions had manifestly failed to take the heat out of the protests, in fact so cack-handed were they that they probably helped us become even stronger. But it was the politicians and the political class of Ireland who have let this country down, who have wrecked and then sold it, as captured by Maeve Curtis and others on the day. We were going to have to start joining the dots if we were not only to win on water, but deliver real and lasting change in a broken nation crying out for it.

## Anybody Ever Hear of Political Economy Education?

When I was growing up in Marian Park in Dundalk the men worked in the shoe factories, or one of the town's two breweries, or one of the large engineering plants. Some also worked for the state in CIE, or the Post Office or elsewhere. The odd one was self-employed. I don't remember massive strikes or unrest. I remember that men (and in the 1970s it was mostly men in the workplace) could rear their families, put food on the table and provide a home for them because they earned enough even in unskilled or semi-skilled labour. But I don't remember massive strikes or lock-outs. I don't remember lessons in Connolly or Larkin being given at the tea table, much less Marx or Gramsci. But I knew what a trade union was, what a shop steward was, what a foreman was, what a boss was. I knew the difference between capital and labour, and between rich and poor. We all just 'knew'. And I knew that however the national cake was being cut, houses and streets were packed with children, almost all had food in their bellies and clothes on their backs and there was little, if any, homelessness.

I suppose I knew this because somewhere there was a trade union movement representing those men and making sure they got a fair deal. And there was a boss in whose interests it was to make sure the factory kept producing and a Government somewhere 'up in Dublin' that was more concerned with how its own citizens viewed it than how the leaders of foreign countries or financial capital viewed it. Or Angela Merkel! Then in 1987 the trade union movement entered what would become the disastrous pact of 'social partnership'. I have commented elsewhere on the effect this disastrous course had on the 'wage share' of workers relative to capital, but there was an even worse impact. When the trade union movement chose the comfort of Government Buildings and a 'partnership' alliance with IBEC for 22 years, it abandoned working class areas such as Marian Park in Dundalk. It abandoned its role in providing, by its actions and example, analysis that could serve that working class in understanding the factors that were changing their lives, both inside the factory gate and outside in the world at large.

And so in 2008/2009, when it all came crashing down through the reckless gambling of capital and was socialized on the heads of those people, that class had changed utterly. For a start, few wanted to call themselves working class anymore. People had more education now, more degrees and qualifications, and generally saw themselves as upwardly mobile. Women had entered the workplace, despite being discriminated against in terms of pay in large measure, but households that used to be single income now had two incomes. And yet they were poorer! In the 1970s if a married couple consisted of a garda and a nurse or teacher they would most likely have been on the pig's back. But now the only thing many such couples were on was a spiral of negative equity, personal debt, pay cuts, overtime cuts and being burdened with a massive national debt so that unsecured bondholders could be paid. So if that was what was happening in 2009 to the so-called middle class, or 'squeezed middle', what was happening to those who weren't even that fortunate? Irish Water was waking them up in the morning to put in meters to charge them for their water too, that's what. They were angry, but why, what was it all about?

Trademark Belfast started out on the West Belfast 'peaceline' in the 1980s as the Irish Congress of Trade Union's 'anti-sectarian' unit. What does that mean? It was an attempt to intervene against the usual shower of politicians who were whipping up sectarian and religious hatred leading to young kids in Rangers and Celtic jerseys facing off, causing mayhem, hurting each other or worse, and ruining their own lives in the process. Trademark went about their business, from their own diverse backgrounds, trying to let people see that unemployment was still unemployment whatever tradition you came from, whatever your creed or the colour of your flag. A little red bricked house in a deprived area starved of social services was just that – on both sides of the 'peaceline' – and a budget cut that denied you an education, or cost you your life in an ailing health service, didn't come with a flag on it. The real struggle wasn't between Green and Orange, but between rich and poor. Of course, 1994 heralded a much needed 'peace process' up North, but the promised 'peace dividend' never arrived, unless of course you are some element of the 1 per cent profiting from Stormont's race to the bottom on corporation taxes. But, thankfully, things are more peaceful now. And Trademark now works on anti-sectarian issues only 20 per cent of the time. Still vital work, but much less so.

When I met Trademark in Belfast they were already providing training in political economy to our colleagues in Mandate and the Communications Workers Union, but had not been involved with Unite for some time for reasons beyond the scope of this book. Trademark are Unite members and highly educated and dedicated trainers. And not just in Belfast either. We had a protest movement, remember, full of new activists angry over water and the way their country had gone, but how could it be explained in a wider context? And who could explain it? Trademark Belfast were the very people.

So on Monday, 13 March 2015, Unite embarked on a new initiative. Working with Trademark, we started to run political economy courses for what we called 'non-aligned community activists'. The courses initially took place in Unite's Dublin office and had 17 people on a three-day course. Of those 17, there were activists from Dublin, Cork, Kerry, Limerick, Tipperary and Dundalk. This training was offered free and Unite covered costs while Trademark provided the materials and trainers. We decided that it would be the first of a number of courses with the sole objective of giving activists who were central to the growing water protest movement access to the type of information that would enable them to understand the political and economic agenda behind water privatisation.

When we said that those on the course should be 'non-aligned', what we meant was that they should not be members of political parties. This can sometimes be hard to manage, but in general that provision was adhered to as the courses evolved and it was the right decision to make for two reasons. Firstly, there were so many activists emerging that we were not going to be able to get to everybody, and our first priority was assisting key activists, many of them involved in protest for the first time, to have the information to support their local actions. Secondly, it is not up to a trade union to provide political education out of the pockets of trade union members to political parties. It is for parties who have access to a lot more independent funding than trade unions do to invest some of that funding to provide assistance to their own members. I actually believed that they would as a matter of course. I was wrong about that. They don't. In fact, some of those parties were hostile to the very notion that we would be offering training to activists that were not members of parties. But we were going to do it anyway.

It is all too easy for those impacted by the regressive nature of the domestic water tax to see it and their particular situation in isolation. But through this training we not only helped them connect with each other on a national level, but showed how this tax and the privatisation agenda are global issues. It is part of a global pursuit of shift wealth upwards, and the Irish Government is an unquestioning supplicant to the neoliberal model. Ireland is the best-in-class child of neoliberal servitude, at least within Europe.

Providing this awareness is one of the best things Unite has done, and we clearly owed our working class communities that type of support. By the end of 2015, we had run nine residential political schools throughout the country and over 150 activists had used that knowledge in their activism giving renewed energy as to how to challenge the neoliberal consensus. We have continued it in many ways since, too, making political economy an essential part of all of our meetings, road shows and communications, and we are always trying to provide new ways of adding this analysis to the movement and, ultimately, to the national conversation. To a large extent this training has helped to understand how neoliberalism is communicated to us through the media. The old saying is true: information is power.

So in 2015 we had begun with a period of reflection and analysis, moved on to a focus on building international links and then delivered a much needed education model to help the movement continue to develop. But we had to start looking at what was evolving in the context of an upcoming election too. Would the water movement just ebb away when confronted by the taxpayer-funded party machines in an upcoming election? Or could something else evolve? In fact, it was time to consider whether we should move beyond water and develop a more ambitious platform – a Right2Change.

# 10

# Policies First

Below is the full text of the ten Right2Change policy principles which could be the foundation stone for Ireland's first progressive Government. They naturally begin with the policy on our human Right2Water.

## The Right2Change Policy Platform

## *1. Right2Water*

Water is a human right, essential for life and all human needs. As such, water provision and sanitation should not be subject to the profit motive or the free market, and should be made available to all free at the point of use, and on the basis of need, not means.

Irish Water plc and domestic water charges will be abolished within the first 100 days of a progressive Government being elected.

Irish Water plc will be replaced with a single national water and sanitation board which will be solely responsible for the provision, transmission, sanitation, management and operation of the public water and sanitation supply in the public interest.

This policy will see a full referendum to enshrine a new Article in Bunreacht na h'Éireann. The date of this referendum would coincide with the establishment of the new national water board.

### Article 28 Section 4:2.1

The Government shall be collectively responsible for the protection, management and maintenance of the public water system. The Government shall ensure in the public interest that this resource remains in public ownership and management.

This policy will provide for an end to water meter installation and ensuing costs.

This policy will legislate for conservation measures, including mandatory planning permission requirements, incentivised and subsidised water saving devices, and a public education campaign.

Our water infrastructure is in desperate need of investment in order to upgrade the system and repair leaks. This policy provides for an investment of between €6 and €7 billion to be provided through a progressive taxation model, details of which are available in the accompanying Fiscal Framework Document.

Funding our water services through progressive taxation measures will ensure citizens always have access to water based on their needs without the possibility in the future of water shut-offs due to unpaid bills. It will also ensure our water services will never be privatised and that Ireland remains with zero water poverty.

(The Right2Water Unions acknowledge the support and advice in framing the above referendum position of Seamus O'Tuathail S.C. and Treasa Brannick O'Cillin, candidate Barrister at Law Degree, The Honourable Society of Kings Inns.)

## 2. *Right2Jobs and Decent Work*

After the war people said, 'If you can plan for war, why can't you plan for peace?' When I was 17, I had a letter from the government saying, 'Dear Mr. Benn, will you turn up when you're 17 1/2? We'll give you free food, free clothes, free training, free accommodation, and two shillings, ten pence a day to just kill Germans.' People said, 'Well, if you can have full employment to kill people, why in God's name couldn't you have full employment and good schools, good hospitals, good houses? – Tony Benn, Member of the British Labour Party

Everyone has a right to gainful and decent employment which would provide dignity, respect and a living wage. A full employment economy requires several layers: an expanding public sector including public enterprise; a growing cooperative, non-profit and labour-managed sector; and a growing public enterprise. At the very least, where people cannot find work, the state must act as an *employer of last resort*, directly employing people in socially productive activity.

A progressive government will vindicate people's right to decent work through a revolution in the workplace embodied in a far-reaching *Decent Work Act*. This will eliminate precarious employment, provide under-employed workers with the right to seek additional hours in their workplace when they become available, introduce the right to collective bargaining (by referendum if necessary) – enabling economic and political democracy, end bogus self-employment, and legislate for overtime and unsocial hours pay. Employers who refuse to recognise their workers' right to collectively bargaining should not be able to avail of any tax refunds or benefit from any State assistance.

In order to provide equitable non-discriminatory access to the workplace, a progressive Government will legislate for the right to publicly available, accessible, high quality affordable childcare, part-time, full-time and after-school provision.

This policy will also see the abolition of compulsory or exploitative elements of Government activation schemes such as JobBridge.

The future is wage-led – in particular, the ending of low pay. The medium-term goal should be to make the *Living Wage* the statutory floor.

Exploitation of workers, particularly low-paid workers in vulnerable sectors, is exceptionally high in Ireland while inspections by the National Employment Rights Authority (NERA) and the Health and Safety Authority (HSA) are limited. Legislation providing for inspections from licensed trade union officials in relation to breaches of both employment and health and safety laws – in line with 'right of access' laws in countries like Australia and New Zealand – should be implemented.

The PRSI system should be expanded to include the self-employed in order for them to avail of the same social welfare benefits as all other workers.

## *3. Right2Housing*

Housing is a human right. There can be no fairness or justice in a society in which some live in homelessness, or in the shadow of that risk, while others cannot even imagine it. – Jordan Flaherty

We believe that housing is a basic human right, that this right should be enshrined in Bunreacht na hÉireann and that the obligation on the State to adequately house people should thereby be enforceable by the courts.

As a direct result of the State's failure to deal with this issue our country is now living through a homelessness epidemic.

Having a home is a social and economic right. Without it, a person has no security of person or identity. A progressive policy will develop a range of housing models to vindicate this right, starting with the ending of homelessness and the clearing of social housing waiting lists. The current crisis in rents should be addressed through rent controls and market-based rent supplements in the short term, but in the long term the state needs to intervene in the market to mobilise the investment required to modernise the sector, including the provision of income-related rental accommodation to low and average income earners. The state also needs to commence a national home-building project. People should also be offered the opportunity to own their homes through limited equity ownership or non-speculative housing. Housing policy should be based on need and choice, not speculation.

People will be offered homes through a range of innovative models including limited equity ownership, or non-speculative housing, cooperative housing and community interest tenancies. (These are just some of the alternative models to provision of housing – all based on non-speculative housing. For example, limited equity housing is comprised of a small mortgage/down-payment combined with cost-rental payment which provides ownership; however, when the house is sold the only return is the small mortgage inflation indexed.) A new planning framework will incorporate anti-speculative policies (e.g. the Kenny Report) and socialise unused and derelict sites that will support sustainable housing development. We will provide adequately for Traveller accommodation needs in a culturally appropriate manner. Housing policy should be based on need and choice, not speculation and capital accumulation.

## *4. Right2Health*

> The social conditions in which people live and work can help create or destroy their health. Lack of income, inappropriate housing, unsafe workplaces and lack of access to health care systems are some of the social determinants of health leading to inequalities. – World Health Organization (WHO, 2004)

Healthcare is a human right, from 'the cradle to the grave'. As such this policy encompasses physical health, mental health and emotional well-being, child care and elder care. Access to quality healthcare should not be dependent on income. The long-standing policy whereby successive governments promote and incentivise the private healthcare industry is inefficient and discriminatory against those on low incomes. The role of government should be to create a universal healthcare system free at the point of entry which provides the highest possible level of care for all citizens, irrespective of social or economic factors.

The current healthcare crisis in Ireland, where hundreds lie on hospital trolleys and thousands wait more than 12 months for appointments, must be addressed. Any future government must acknowledge errors in past policies and invest in the mental and physical well-being of the nation, instead of a private industry. A well-funded and efficient public healthcare system would provide economic and social benefits for individuals and wider society in general.

- The right of access to all healthcare services regardless of income will be ensured through free primary health and dental care, heavily subsidised prescription medicine and access to tertiary and outpatient services free at the point of use. In addition, we will substantially increase investment in nursing home care and mental health services.

- This policy provides for the right to accessible, high quality, affordable care, including respite care, for vulnerable adults

The care of vulnerable elderly and children is increasingly commercialised. The complete absence of a public care infrastructure and the commercialisation of personal care coincide with a rise in forms of employment that are forcing people to live in ways that are so time-pressed they have no time to care for those they love. The rise in precarious and insecure work, long costly commutes and emigration make 'caring' unsustainable over time.

Civil society organisations are both the means and expression of more engaged citizens. The fundamental democratic role of these organisations should be acknowledged and actively supported. We will provide community-focused policies and investment which will build on the voluntary activities of people and communities – in particular, in rural areas through strengthening the local infrastructure from re-opening garda stations and post offices, to more developed infrastructures such as transport, telecommunications and housing. As part of this approach, we will place community arts at the heart of cultural policy, thus increasing access to and participation in arts and cultural initiatives. We will reverse the cuts to community development programmes and restore the autonomy of these groups to engage in critical action.

We will validate the importance of unpaid caring in families and communities in a constitutional amendment that removes the gender-biased article 41.2.2 (which assumes that only women are carers) and replaced by a care-recognition article that is gender neutral; a significant investment in caring in the community including supports for carers, and a new child-raising allowance that allows parents to spend more time raising their new-born children.

## *5. Right2Education*

> I speak – not for myself, but for all… I raise up my voice – not so that I can shout, but so that those without a voice can be heard. Those who have fought for their rights: Their right to live in peace. Their right to be treated with dignity. Their right to equality of opportunity. Their right to be educated. – Malala Yousafzai, youngest ever Nobel Prize Laureate

Everyone has the right to education. The provision of education should be truly free – without the necessity for 'voluntary contributions' – up to at least primary degree level. The provision of professional and technical education should be affordable and available to all and should be equally accessible.

Three basic priorities for any new government should be:

1. To reduce the ratio of students to teachers from among the highest levels in the EU to the lowest.

2. The restoration of and increased provision of Special Needs Assistants (SNAs), which should be seen as an investment in the most vulnerable of our children.

3. Investment in early childhood education should be provided in line with a progressive childcare policy which would facilitate the option for parents to enter or leave the workforce.

Education is an investment in the future of the nation whereby we can develop a productive and cohesive society. More funding for the apprenticeship programme and a coordinated jobs policy promoting labour-intensive industries should form part of any future government education programme. A modern dynamic economy is dependent on well-educated citizens, increasing employment opportunities and providing the opportunities to create new services and technologies.

Multinationals benefit from our highly educated workforce and therefore a proportion of corporation tax should be ring-fenced to fund third level education following the elimination of fees by this Government.

## 6. Right2Democratic Reform

> A community is democratic only when the humblest and weakest person can enjoy the highest civil, economic, and social rights that the biggest and most powerful possess. – Asa Philip Randolph, leader in the African-American Civil Rights Movement

We need to undertake a programme of substantial democratic reform of our local and national democratic processes which would put citizens at the heart of decision making. We will ensure the right to greater democracy throughout the economy, society and, most importantly, the political decision-making process: popular initiation of constitutional referenda and parliamentary legislation; the right to recall TDs; citizen nomination of Presidential candidates; direct elections to the Seanad; and parliamentary committee membership and chairpersons overseas voting and mandatory voting for all electorally registered citizens.

Citizens should be strongly encouraged to participate in the electoral process. Elections should be held at a convenient time for the vast majority of the population.

Our parliament is a key function of our democracy to which many of our citizens feel disconnected and disempowered. We will enact parliamentary reform measures that will address the number of sitting days, holiday terms, numbers of members in the chamber, a curbing of the whip system, election for Ceann Comhairle by secret vote and other measures to address parliamentary behaviour.

Government Ministers and TDs to draw down pensions on reaching normal (State) retirement age. In the event of proven corruption by public representatives, including Ministers, the forfeit of pensions should occur.

We will reduce the number of TDs to the minimum allowed in Bunreacht na h'Éireann and conduct a public debate as to whether this number should be further reduced through a Constitutional referendum.

We will reduce the powers of local county managers and transfer those powers and accountability to locally elected representative councillors.

Hosting one general election every five years provides too large a gap for real democratic representation, particularly as there is no accountability for broken political promises subsequent to an election. A reduction in the electoral cycle in general elections from five years to four should be implemented in order to provide more collective democratic accountability.

Corruption in democracy is democracy denied; therefore, we will establish an Anti-Corruption Agency on a par with the Criminal Assets Bureau (CAB) to investigate and recoup to the state any assets and incomes accrued through political corruption. This agency, with similar wide-ranging powers to CAB, will investigate public and corporate financial corruption, fraud and tax evasion.

Any functioning democracy requires a diverse media and media ownership should not be disproportionately in the hands of a small number of wealthy individuals or corporations. We will expand the Irish media landscape, facilitating democratic ownership and participation by community groups, NGOs, civil society groups and trade unions.

# 7. *Right2DebtJustice*

Blessed are the young for they shall inherit the national debt. – Herbert Hoover, 31st President of the United States

The past recklessness of financial speculation is imposing an intolerable burden on people's future. Debt justice requires a European Debt Conference to restructure and write-down sovereign debt throughout the Eurozone; the introduction of a Financial Transaction Tax in order to repay states for the private bank debt they assimilated; the effective repudiation of Anglo-Irish debt through retention of the Anglo-Irish bonds in public, an end to bank-driven mortgage debt resolution through a state-led and democratically accountable programme of restructuring and writing down of mortgage debt with a halt to evictions on the basis of inability-to-pay; and restructuring of money-lending debt which traps people in 100 per cent interest loans.

Two further steps are needed to address the debt crisis in Ireland, Europe and globally:

- Build alliances with progressive citizen-led movements in Europe to develop and promote alternative proposals for realistic and responsible debt reduction strategies for people across Europe.

- Establish a Debt Audit to determine the level of debt attributed to the private financial sector as a first step in recouping that money from those who caused the financial crisis, and fully participate in the UN Committee on Sovereign Debt Restructuring.

## *8. Right2Equality*

> When I was poor and I complained about inequality people said I was bitter, now I'm rich and I complain about inequality they say I'm a hypocrite. I'm beginning to think they just don't want inequality on the agenda because it is a real problem that needs to be addressed. – Russell Brand, actor, entertainer and author of *Revolution*.

The right to equality encompasses social and economic rights which are implied and un-enumerated rights in our Constitution. These rights should be protected in legislation which will address the issues of poverty.

Given the historically emotive nature of the debate on abortion in Ireland, we believe this matter can only be resolved by the people, who are sovereign. Therefore we will provide the Irish citizens with a Constitutional referendum to decide whether to repeal the Eighth Amendment of Bunreacht na h'Éireann in the first year of office.

Many people still face workplace and service-related discrimination based on disability, gender, age, colour, sexual orientation, Traveller status, ethnic origin, family status, marital status and religious/other beliefs. We will run major education and mobilisation campaigns to end discrimination both in the workplace and in services generally, and we will introduce stronger sanctions for breaches of equality legislation; we will repeal Section 37 of the Employment Equality Act; we will democratise the national and secondary school systems.

We will reform the work permit system to make it easier for workers to leave exploitative employment situations without threatening their immigration status.

Improving access to work for migrants, including reforming Ireland's labour migration policy, revising the eligible categories of employment and the right of employees to change employer, and lowering the salary threshold required for new employment permits for sectors where a shortage has been identified.

Over 4,000 people are consigned to Direct Provision centres, including over 1,500 children. Detainment in these Centres represents a form of institutional abuse that denies adults and children basic human rights. We will end the system of Direct Provision and we ensure that the children of asylum seekers suffer no discrimination in relation to health or education due to their parents' asylum status.

Market inequality undermines economic efficiency and social solidarity. Alongside strategies to end low-pay we will establish a High Pay Commission to propose measures to reduce income inequality.

## 9. Right2ASustainable Environment

> Our economic system and our planetary system are now at war. Or, more accurately, our economy is at war with many forms of life on earth, including human life. What the climate needs to avoid collapse is a contraction in humanity's use of resources; what our economic model demands to avoid collapse is unfettered expansion. Only one of these sets of rules can be changed, and it's not the laws of nature. – Naomi Klein, *This Changes Everything: Capitalism vs. the Climate*

The dominant economic model is 'at war' with the natural world. Unfettered capitalism and globalisation continue to place unsustainable burdens on the earth's natural assets including its water, air, fauna and flora and threatens the very continuation of mankind.

Fighting climate change is not a 'cost' – it is a necessary strategy for human survival which simultaneously provides another means to promote a collective and democratic economy. The first steps in this struggle will be the introduction of a Green New Deal – a sustained and substantial drive to bring all buildings in the residential, commercial and industrial sector up to the highest level of conservation necessary, to expand and upgrade the quality of public transport with significant reductions in fares, the increased mobilisation of R&D to urgently progress the development of ocean/sea-based renewable energy to complement other forms of green technology.

We will legislate for ambitious and binding climate change targets, including a ban on fracking, a transposition of the Rio de Janeiro Agreement into domestic law, and we will use Bolivia's Law of the Rights of Mother Earth as a guide.

## 10. Right2National Resources and a Fair Economy

That's the standard technique of privatisation, defund, make sure things don't work, people get angry, you hand it over to private capital. – Noam Chomsky

The assets of our nation were declared in the 1916 Proclamation as belonging to the citizens of Ireland, a Proclamation which also pledged to cherish all the citizens of the state equally.

The Transatlantic Trade and Investment Partnership (TTIP) is one of the biggest threats to people's ability to provide labour, social and environmental protection, and represents a proposed transfer of economic and political sovereignty from the Irish citizens to multinational corporations. A progressive government will oppose TTIP through whatever mechanisms possible. Should TTIP be ratified without the consent of the Irish people, a progressive Government will provide for a referendum on our continued membership of the European Union. Opposition to the Comprehensive Economic and Trade Agreement (CETA) and Trade in Services Agreement (TiSA) should also be a priority for this government and any other trade agreement that contains an Investor State Dispute Settlement mechanism (ISDS).

This government will re-commit to neutrality and a non-militaristic foreign policy starting with the banning of the use of Irish airports for military purposes.

In Northern Ireland, we will work for the full implementation of the Good Friday Agreement and the Saint Andrew's Agreement. Further, we will provide full support to the people of Northern Ireland in their rejection of austerity – to be vindicated through inter-governmental negotiations.

Solidarity with the developing world will be reinforced through meeting official development assistance targets and political, diplomatic and economic assistance with victims of occupation, in particular, the Palestinian people. Trade sanctions should be implemented against countries who breach international laws – up to and including the banning of imports of all goods. The ambassadors of countries who commit war crimes should be expelled.

Further, we will join with other progressive Governments to restrain the undemocratic activities of the International Monetary Fund and the World Bank.

**Indigenous Sector**: We need a prosperous indigenous enterprise sector – to provide decent jobs, social security, and economic growth where money is reinvested in local communities. We need a plurality of enterprise models to maximise the shared benefits of growth throughout the economy.

Rejecting privatisation, we will expand public enterprises into new economic activities and provide for local government enterprises and new business models based on co-determination between public, private and civil society ownership.

We will promote worker-owner co-operative enterprises, whereby workers share in the decision-making process, and in the risks, profits and benefits. In these companies the right to work is prioritised and employment-security is an integral objective of the business model; limited wage differentials promotes sustainability. We will establish institutional supports for this sector to provide access to capital, patient banking and management assistance; provide employees the option of buying out companies that close down and introduce tax incentives for new cooperative ventures.

We will establish a new basis for supporting indigenous enterprise through job creation agencies in a programme of Companies of Excellence, which can lead the modernisation of the indigenous sector; in these companies employees and employers accept co-responsibility as the fundamental principle of managing the company: commitments to R&D, investment, innovation, labour rights and participation. This will form the basis of sectoral planning frameworks to grow Irish businesses in a coordinated and focused way.

**Income Supports:** A major reform of income supports to provide security for people in paid work and out of employment is required: pay-related unemployment and sickness benefit; pay-related state pensions; enhanced family supports (maternity benefits, paid paternity benefit, care and family leave and child-raising allowances). A priority will be the introduction of a 'cost of disability' payment and the ending of child poverty and deprivation which focuses on access to adequate resources and quality services along with enhanced labour market and social protection supports for one-parent families. We will bring all social protection payments up to the minimum essential standard of living over the medium term. These reforms require moving from a welfare system based on poverty-avoidance and means-testing to a system based on social solidarity and mutuality through an enhanced social insurance system and universal payments in which everyone benefits, including the full participation of the self-employed. To this end basic income strategies will be actively explored.

This effective New Social Contract will be funded by a long-term phasing in of an enhanced social wage, or employers' social insurance, to the average paid by employers in other European countries.

**Natural Resources**: The natural resources of Ireland belong to the people of Ireland. The campaigns over our oil and gas reserves, woodlands, clean seas, archaeological and heritage sites, and community life point to the growing issue of 're-source democracy'. We will constitutionally enshrine the ownership of natural resources with the Irish people. Natural resources will be entrusted to public and transparent control providing people the right to benefit from sustainable developments.

A national programme of repatriation, and subsequent nationalisation, of surrendered natural resources will be initiated with those who seek, or who have been allowed to secure, access to our natural resources free or without proper re-imbursement/value to the Irish people. Where this requires negotiations these will have the objective of securing maximum value to the Irish citizens from their resources in a manner applicable in similar sized nations with potentially similar resources such as Norway.

**Public Banking and Insurance**: The fundamental lesson of the crisis is that we cannot rely on private banking based on short-term shareholder interests. We need a national public banking system for both households and enterprises – one with a mission statement that makes the bank partners in people's living standards and business success, and promotes the public interest. We will promote public interest and mutuality in banking and insurance. To this end we will set up Public Banking and Insurance Review to promote public banking and an insurance system based on mutuality and co-operation rather than profit.

That's the lot, at least for now. You have just read ten policy principles that when implemented can change the nation we live in for the better for each and every one of us. It is for the betterment of our children and our grandchildren and all who follow. For our world even. If you are reading them for the first time do you notice anything strange?

Well, it may not have struck you immediately but you are now engaging with political ideas and policy principles, and there isn't a political party, a banner, a flag, a 'personality' or a family dynasty in sight. In short, you are engaging with politics as it should be, but not as it has been in Ireland for a long time, if ever. These policy principles arose in the first six months of 2015 from people wondering if those who were protesting could agree on an alternative, progressive and costed policy for our human Right2Water (and they had), what other policy principles might they agree on? What would those policies be, what areas would they cover, what specifics would be in them, how would they be arrived at, agreed, endorsed, followed and ultimately implemented? Did you notice that the 'implemented' bit is last on the list? Let me explain.

Key to this process from a trade union point of view was a two-day meeting in the Ballymascanlon Hotel, Dundalk in the first week of February 2015 where the General Secretaries and Assistant General Secretaries of the Right2Water unions did something rather unusual for trade unionists. They, along with some others, cancelled all their meetings and took the time together to assess exactly where this was going and what resources they had available to pursue the campaign on water, or anything else.

It was crystal clear at this point that it would be union members who would be footing most of the bill for anything that developed. Once there, we considered the three massive days of protest so far and the hunger, the need we were sensing, for some political re-alignment. The word change kept looming large. But unions are primarily industrial representative organisations who may, or may not, engage in political campaigning and lobbying. Unite, for example, has a rule book that is quite specific on this. We are not only entitled, but obliged under rules, to mount political campaigns and actions that benefit our members and the conditions of their lives. All unions, however, are not the same. Another Right2Water union, the Civil and Public Services Union (CPSU), represents the lower paid of the civil service grades and is prohibited from affiliating to a political party, for example. Their General Secretary, Eoin Ronayne, was emphatic that while the CPSU was well up for a water campaign anything that might look like of a political party was off limits for them. But that was not the mood anyway. A party without policies? There was no appetite from anyone to go down that path, but there was strong and clear consensus that we should look at what kind of process could bring people in to build broad support behind those policies and, insofar as possible, then seek support among the fractured body politic as a further step. It was a bit like the first meeting in the Dáil before Right2Water was formed when it looked like the unions were best placed to set out a process that could enable the community activists and political pillar to continue to develop the movement. Once again, at this point it was felt that union support, resources and perhaps leadership would be crucial. As we left Dundalk after a very productive couple of days it was one of those present who probably summed up the mood best when he asked the rhetorical question, 'If not us, who?'

There is a view that politics in Ireland is party and personality driven and that it is mostly about noise, spin and bluster, and hardly about the policies that the majority of the people want or need at all. I strongly hold that view. I don't think it is controversial to say that for many decades the bulk of people voted for either Fianna Fáil or Fine Gael based on a combination of their notions of the civil war, often handed down through the generations, or on the basis of the cult of local party personalities, or even family dynasties of those party personalities. There has never been much policy difference between our two largest parties, and there is hardly any at all now. I also don't think it is controversial to say that both parties are right of centre parties. They mostly describe themselves like that (except when Bertie Ahern described himself as a Socialist akin to Joe Higgins, but I'll let that go as just one of Bertie's more entertaining and less damaging viewpoints). Where precisely you might put both parties on the right of the political spectrum is a matter of opinion (I personally think that Fine Gael are a pretty far right party by any economic policy measuring stick) but they are both certainly to the right of centre, a political centre that itself has shifted distinctly rightward in the current era. I have set out previously my opinion of where Labour are on that spectrum, and without going into it again I think they behaved in Government much as Fine Gael did. I think they are socially liberal in tone but economically conservative, and even if they don't see themselves that way, the truth is that they were far too compliant with EU diktats to be anything different from the main parties. And then we have Sinn Féin who make no secret of the fact that they are predominantly a nationalist, all-Ireland party. That is fair enough, but it doesn't pin them on the left, or the right, on a permanent basis. There is also a plethora of smaller parties on the left from the Social Democrats to various parties that are often described as the ultra-left. And then there's what's left of the Greens.

Now you may disagree with some or all of this, which is exactly my point. We could argue about this for hours and get very excited about it, yet that argument would be based on a single paragraph that spoke about politics as 'party' and 'spectrum' yet never addressed one substantive policy. It is my contention that such an approach to political discussion sums up

Irish politics. A lot of heat, not too much light and the same policies being implemented over and over again no matter who is in power. It is about getting elected for the sake of getting elected, and all that has been required is some coverage, some recognisable personalities, a lot of money and a bit of spin. Use all that to throw promises about the place while always conducting the debate in a tightly squeezed ideological space, but don't get too bothered about policy development, and certainly not on delivering electoral promises. As Labour's Pat Rabbitte told RTÉ about broken election promises just months after Labour had entered Government in 2011, 'well isn't that what you tend to do during an election?' But there is another striking, more recent example of this rush into politics without any clear policy position that is worth remembering. The role of the cult of personality in Irish politics should never be underestimated. During the events outlined in this book that cult was strong enough to introduce to Irish politics, however briefly, an actual new party – remember Renua?

Renua was launched in a blaze of publicity on 13 March 2015 while at the same time communities all over Ireland were having meetings that ultimately became the Right2Change policy platform. To my mind, Renua was everything that Right2Change is not. For a start, Renua only emerged because a very strong and articulate politician fell out with her party on a matter of conscience. Lucinda Creighton was a hawkish Fine Gael Minister on economic matters when she was Minister of State for European Affairs from March 2011 to July 2013. If she had a problem with austerity, wealth distribution or citizens carrying the can for banks, it's not apparent from anything she said or did in that time. She was regarded by her party and European colleagues as a loyal member and was considered by all to be talented and hard working. She was even tipped as a future Fine Gael leader.

But Lucinda Creighton holds very strong views on the contentious issue of abortion, opposing it even when the mother's life is threatened during pregnancy, and when Fine Gael wouldn't allow a free vote on the Protection of Life During Pregnancy Bill, 2013 Creighton refused to abide by the party whip and voted against the Bill. She was subsequently expelled from Fine Gael's parliamentary party and took up life as an Independent. And so a politician tipped for great things found herself out of Ministerial office. Whatever one feels about the issue – and I fundamentally disagree with Lucinda Creighton on a woman's right to choose – she was a rare thing in Irish politics: someone prepared to lose Ministerial office on a point of principle.

But in less than two years she had teamed up with another larger than life personality, Eddie Hobbs, and Renua was born. It is the nature of that political birth, the dawn of a new party and its entry into our political discussion, that best makes my point. Renua was launched at a press conference in Dublin and was immediately given massive media coverage. In fact, Irish broadcast media was almost taken over by this launch with hourly updates throughout the day. But there wasn't a policy in sight. Not even a policy principle. There was, of course, a name, there was of course a flag, and there was a new image, lots of image. And there was a smattering of some public personalities. But on actual policies Crieghton had none, and she was honest about it. She said the day Renua was launched that she wanted the party to be open-minded and available to all and that they just were working on 16 policies that would be developed later but were not a 'fait accompli'. Renua also declared, however, even before these policy developments, that the party would be positioned on the centre right and that its policies would be 'pro-enterprise, pro-business and geared towards entrepreneurship'. Nothing new there then! It announced that financial commentator Karl Deeter was the party's 'ethics officer', and it soon hired respected political commentator John Drennan to head up its communications functions, long before it had anything to communicate.

If this seems like I am criticising any of the individuals involved I am not. I do not share their views on many things but that is not the point. The point is that a new party was launched on personality and a bit of ideology without policies, and that intelligent and experienced people thought that this would work. And they thought it would work because it had always worked in Irish politics. Names, labels, ideological notions and media bluster are often enough to get people who never had an original political thought in their lives elected in Ireland. And, to be fair, you would think that people like Lucinda Creighton, Eddie Hobbs, Karl Deeter and John Drennan had a lot more going for them than some others who have made careers out of that kind of politics, some of whom have been sitting on back benches for years yet are hardly known outside their own constituencies. So of course there was a view that Renua could work, and the tone of the coverage almost suggested it was inevitable that it would work. But it didn't. In fact, it bombed completely and ended in disaster. Why?

Whether the political establishment like it or not, and whether the media report it or not, Irish politics is changing. More and more people are seeing through the spin, the promises that are so often broken they are almost a laughing stock at this point, the image over substance. Some are disconnecting, just walking away from any interest in politics as if by doing so the forces that affect their lives will no longer do so. If only it were that simple. Increasingly, this is the outlook of the under-25s who are the generation that will pay more than any other in their unemployment, under-employment, education cuts, social welfare cuts, forced emigration and low paid and precarious work, not to mention the near impossibility in the current housing market of ever owning their own home.

This generation is abandoning the politics of the past and just walking away, feigning disinterest. In the February 2016 election just over 65 per cent of those entitled to vote in a country ravaged by economic inequality bothered to do so.

But there is another, much more positive approach with massive potential taking root. Every word that is in the ten Right2Change policy principles came from a submission that was open to the general public. The ideas, thoughts and opinions that form this particular policy platform come, in a unique way, directly from the people themselves. Those submissions then went through an independent panel for collation and were then considered and voted on at two conferences set up specifically for that purpose. These conferences were attended by representatives of the three Right2Water pillars – political parties and Independents, trade unions and, in the case of the majority, new community activists that were in neither union nor party. These people were motivated by the water movement and came to consider wider issues with no agenda other than understanding what was going on in their country and taking steps to change it for the better. While Renua was being launched amid such fanfare that it was almost deafening, the media either missed or deliberately ignored the fact that a conversation was taking place throughout Ireland to develop these 10 policy principles.

In the hall of the Communications Workers Union on 1 May 2015, a day-long conference took place with 200 people in attendance. Thirty-five TDs either attended or sent a representative, six unions were present and there were citizens from all over Ireland making up what we call 'the community pillar', one-third of the total in fact. This conference mostly studied what was happening in social movements throughout Europe, and something was definitely happening. Syriza was in power in Greece and they made a presentation. Eduardo Maura flew in from Madrid to tell us how his anti-austerity party Podemos had emerged from the *Indignados* (the indignant ones) movement of Spanish people gathering in their local communities to try to understand and address the root causes of their nation's rapid economic decline, massive unemployment and growing inequality.

The conference also had Dorothea Haarlin from the Berlin Water Table focussing on how citizens in Germany managed to win back public ownership of their water and force Veolia out as bills went through the roof and water quality and investment dropped. It had the Belfast Trades Council as well explaining how in Northern Ireland activism from the ground up, across both communities there, had beaten water charges at least for now. And of course, as with everything we do now, there were elements of political economy education because if we don't understand what the dominant global economic model is doing we forego the ability to resist, change or even ameliorate it. By design, it was a day when mostly we listened, something some of us find harder to do than others. But it was an important step.

Six weeks later, on 13 June, we were back. This time there was plenty of time for talk. The unions agreed to boost the community pillar significantly by giving them 50 per cent of our seats, meaning that about half of all those who discussed, and later voted on, these policy principles were community activists. Of course, we advised the media that this was going on. We invited them, threw open our doors and issued press releases. But they weren't interested. They only cared about Renua and what Ireland's newest party was going to do. So we just got on with it. This was politics from the ground up. The morning was broken into ten workshops where initial wording from the submissions and the collation process was debated, discussed and amended. Each workshop had representation from the three pillars. Those ten workshops then proposed final wordings which were presented to Dave Gibney and myself (the only two people with no votes on the day) and each final wording was then put to a full plenary session of the conference in the afternoon for voting/endorsement. As the chairperson of each workshop came to make the presentation, there was some lively debate, some things dropped and others added. But the ten policy principles at the beginning of this chapter are what emerged from this process and were endorsed all but unanimously. For transparency, every second of this process was put on the internet and remains available for viewing.

Communications Workers Union General Secretary Stevie Fitzpatrick then wound up the day by saying that we were now going to take these policy principles on the road, and that we would hold meetings in every county possible between now and the general election to try to gain public and electoral support.

So what is Right2Change? Right2Change is a policy platform. It is broad, as opposed to narrow and sectarian, because that is what people wanted. Right2Change is not about people being a big part of something small; it is about us all being a small part of something big. It is progressive as opposed to regressive because we have had enough of inequality and wealth transfers upwards. It is socially liberal and economically progressive, but it would not be considered particularly radical in any time other than the present. It would be positively moderate if the dominant neoliberal model was not so repressive and iniquitous.

Not everyone will agree with all of the above, but then everybody shouldn't. But Right2Change was a sincere attempt to change the way politics is done. A society with problems needs its citizens to engage with and understand those problems and the dynamics that create them. Informed citizens are then able to come up with ideas to address those problems. Those ideas develop into policy principles and then some sort of a political vehicle seeks support, is engaged in and afforded fair and reasonable debate and if elected implements them as the mandated position from the electors.

Sound radical to you? Maybe it is. It used to be called democracy but that was back in the day when democracy was participative throughout the electoral cycle, permanently, and not solely about casting a vote come election day.

## Costing the Change

It is clear to all that whatever changes we want or need in our society will have to be paid for by someone. So I'm going to talk here about tax. When the Right2Change policy platform was launched it was soon followed by a full published Fiscal Framework which set out how, by adopting an alternative view of the tax base, this progressive platform could be paid for. The purpose of the paper was to estimate the fiscal space available to a progressive government to drive economic and social investment and create a modern European social state.

In 2015, RTÉ's *Primetime* aired a segment showing the social services available to French citizens. The programme outlined how well French citizens do in relation to affordable childcare, unemployment benefits, rent supplements and healthcare, and compared them to Ireland, a country where childcare can be like a second mortgage for struggling couples, where we have seen cuts in unemployment benefit which is not, like France, linked to income in previous employment, and where our health system still struggles to cope with what increasingly looks like a deliberate plan to prop up private healthcare. Plus we have rampant and growing homelessness. Back in studio a panel discussion took place and the consensus was that Irish taxpayers would never pay for the type of benefits they have in France. Here's the problem. Irish taxpayers *already pay* as much tax on income and consumption taxes – two of the three tax collecting mechanisms – as they do in France. And not just France either.

So what do you know about tax? You probably think you pay too much of it. I bet you look at your payslip and gasp a wee bit and think of the things you could do with all the money which is whipped out in tax. Your income would mostly double, right?

Or are you unemployed with a very low income from the state? Maybe you are a student and not earning yet, educating yourself and relying on family support, grants or loans to keep you going. Or maybe you are retired having spent some or all of your life in work and you rely on your pension or your savings, maybe if you are lucky some investment income, to survive in the 'golden years'.

I'm not a tax consultant, an accountant or an economist. I don't understand all of the nuances, thresholds, bands or exemptions, but I am going to try to make tax simple. And I am going to try to make a very serious, fundamental and challenging statement stand up. Here is the statement:

> The services that a society needs to function are in decline because those who can most afford to fund them refuse to, and are allowed to so refuse.

So what are those services? What is it we all need to function as a part of a society? As we have seen, we need healthcare from the very start right up until we die. We need shelter so housing is an issue. We need food, water, sanitation and in a modern society we need energy and communications. As we reach the age of four or so we can add the need for education, which will continue for a significant proportion of our lives. We need a transport network and we need to work in order to earn an income, to provide for us and our dependants. We live in a time of rapidly increasing longevity so pension provision becomes an issue. There are, of course, other things a functioning society needs such as a police force to maintain law and order and other emergency services.

Most, if not all, of these essential elements to a functioning society have two things in common in Ireland: they are available either publicly or privately. Those that are available publicly are generally provided on the basis of need and funded through taxation. Those that are available privately are solely funded according to means, not need.

Of course, funding things such as health care on the basis of means, not need, has very obvious consequences. If you need an emergency operation or transplant and this is only available in a private institution you won't get it unless you can afford it. If you need cancer screening or care and there is a two-year waiting list for public patients those two years could cost you your life. But if you can pay – often the same consultant in the same facility – privately you can jump the queue and have a two-year jump on your ailment. Money, or the difference between tax-funded or privately-funded healthcare, can literally be the difference between life and death. It applies to education too. Is your child struggling with honours maths in the run up to the Leaving Cert? Have you money? Get grinds! Money can provide a distinct advantage. As to private schools, don't get me started. Education provided to certain kids and young adults not based on aptitude and hard work, but on the means of their parents or families?

We will return to which services should be funded exclusively from taxation but, for now, let us be clear of where the tax take is collected from, or not, as the case will be. All taxes can be put into one of the three following categories:

1. Income taxes

2. Consumption taxes, such as VAT and excise duties, and

3. Taxes on wealth and capital.

The collation of the taxes that we, or any country, collects from these areas are what we use to run our public services and pay down the national debt including, in Ireland's case, our massive banking debt. When the Right2Change fiscal strategy was launched, it set out how, within current EU guidelines, a new tax base could be structured that would lead to a better and fairer Ireland (see www.right2change.ie).

This framework pointed out that Ireland would have to increase spending on public services, income supports and investment by €11 billion a year to reach the EU average. This lack of investment in our social infrastructure and income supports results in two deficits: First, in an under-performing economy – underinvestment reduces productivity and inefficiency in the economic infrastructure. Second, in high living costs, which includes paying market rates for healthcare, inflated public transport fares, lack of affordable childcare, reduced family supports, and the lack of pay-related benefits for workers in the event of sickness, temporary unemployment, occupational injury or retirement.

But it is also the case that we pay close to the EU average in terms of income taxes and consumption taxes such as VAT and excise duties. So where is the shortfall? How are we not collecting enough taxes to have comparable public services to our peer countries in the EU? Well, in the only other tax category, wealth and capital, we are collecting just one-third of the EU average. In addition to collecting Corporation Tax and Wealth Tax, something Michael Noonan himself trumpeted, Unite's Michael Taft revealed a startling figure in this report. The 'social wage' is the proportion of your wages retained by your employer and paid to the Government for investment in public services. These public services are exactly the ones a functioning society needs to maintain equality in the short term, and social structure in the long term. And by providing these services from the tax base, that leaves money in workers' pockets to spend in the real economy. Money that they might otherwise be spending on childcare, education subsidy and healthcare costs, as well as extortionate housing costs, gets spent in the real economy, in the indigenous business sector thereby stimulating our entire economy.

So what was the startling figure? Our employers pay just about one-third of the EU average in Employer's Social Insurance. In 2012, they paid 7.7 per cent while the EU average was 20.5 per cent. Staggering.

The Fiscal Strategy can be studied in more depth, but it addresses this issue by slowly getting the larger employers, some of the richest corporations in the world, to step up to the mark and meet their obligations, thereby releasing real incomes for real spending in the businesses we all need to survive. A bottom-up spending stimulus that will drive the economy in a sustainable way. The four-year strategy, which is called 'Finding the Resources to Drive Investment, Prosperity and a Shared Recovery', provided for the phasing out of the Fiscal Deficit by 2020 as allowed under EU rules, and not by 2018 as determined by a Government more interested in being 'best in class' than doing the right thing for Ireland.

## We Must Not Be Afraid of a Debate On Tax

By developing the Right2Change policy platform citizens had set out their priorities for a fair and more equal Ireland. And by publishing the Fiscal Strategy the unions had used the knowledge and skill of Michael Taft to set out an alternative, workable way of paying for it. There are many other ways and measures but to conclude this chapter let me say this.

We only have one way to pay for the public services we all need – taxes – and as we have seen the only three pots from which to collect those taxes are income, consumption and wealth/capital. If we are going to give a free pass on tax to employers and corporations, particularly the largest and most profitable, we are forever going to live in a country with a high cost of living because we will to have to pay for the services out of our net incomes. To be blunt, we are paying out of our net incomes for the services large employers fund through tax in other countries. When these costs are added to taxes on our income and consumption that are already at relatively high levels, that means we have less money to spend which is bad for business, particularly small and medium-sized businesses. And when those incomes contract, or disappear due to unemployment, retirement or illness, people will be faced with a personal abyss – something clearly already happening in Ireland today.

Do we want it to stay like this or to get even worse? Let's not be afraid of the debate. I don't believe many employers will leave Ireland just because we raise their taxes to the same or similar levels they pay in other countries in the EU. This is a ruse and scare tactic perpetuated by the agents of big business and corporate greed, a ploy that is often swallowed lock, stock and barrel by the media, the agents of the small and medium businesses it harms, and even by some members of the public who are slipping in to the very poverty or homelessness that it causes.

We set out to change much with Right2Change and one of the most important things we set out to do was to help to change the national conversation on tax. And in Election 2016 that is exactly what happened.

# 11

# ICTU Conference Victory – 'No Way, We Won't Pay'

Whatever would become of these ten policy principles the cornerstone of them, and of the campaign, remained Right2Water throughout the summer of 2015 and beyond. In the months that followed the campaign became more and more 'political' as an election loomed large, but on Wednesday, 8 July 2015, the issue of domestic water charges ignited the Irish Congress of Trade unions (ICTU) biennial conference in Ennis in a way that hadn't happened in years.

The background was fairly routine. With Labour in Government and implementing austerity with zeal, there was always going to be a motion on the abolition of water charges before the conference. This was, after all, the first time that the trade union 'family' would get to debate the issue since charges had been implemented. As it happened, motion 41 came from the Waterford Trades Council and it demanded:

> That the Waterford Council of Trade Unions calls on Conference to reject the imposition of water charges on the Irish people and calls for a Constitutional Amendment that ensures water remains in the ownership of the Irish people.

You will recall that there were five unions affiliated to Right2Water at the time (TEEU technically affiliated later) but there are almost 50 unions affiliated to the ICTU so, clearly, the vast bulk did not seem to be motivated around supporting the abolition of water charges. Not only that, but although Unite is one of the larger unions, about two-thirds of that membership is based in Northern Ireland. Mandate General Secretary John Douglas was then the ICTU President but would step down at the end of this conference having done an excellent job of steering his union through a difficult dispute with Dunnes Stores, while also supporting Right2Water and the evolving Right2Change platform. John's prominence and likeability could not however disguise the fact that his union was not one of the larger ones, nor is the excellent Communications Workers Union led by Stevie Fitzpatrick. Of the two remaining Right2Water Unions, OPATSI is a small craft union with few votes and, potentially worst of all, the CPSU were by then entering merger talks with the much bigger public service union, Irish Municipal Public & Civil Trade union – IMPACT.

So when it was the very same IMPACT that put in an amendment to motion 41 it should have been game up for the Waterford Trades Council motion. The amendment read:

> Conference supports the Congress demand for an increased free allowance to equate to the normal domestic need for each household for treated water and recognises that this can be achieved in a number of ways. Conference also supports the Congress demand for a constitutional referendum that ensures that water remains in the ownership of the Irish people.

SIPTU was very much behind the IMPACT amendment as well. That meant that there was a mountain to climb as SIPTU and IMPACT, ICTU's largest two affiliates, had never lost a vote at a conference when they had voted together. So, as I drove to Ennis to play my part with the Unite delegation, we had no real expectations of victory. It seemed obvious that this IMPACT amendment would carry comfortably. The three teachers' unions and the nurses and midwives, among others, would most likely toe the IMPACT and SIPTU line, and Dave and I discussed tactics on the phone as we drove south separately. Our view was that we were going to have the debate, roll the dice, and attack this amendment as something that was more about saving the Labour Party's blushes than being about workers, water or citizens' rights.

We expected, in the way these things go, that the Waterford Trades Council would be asked not to cause division at Conference since they couldn't win anyway. They would be prevailed upon to do the 'decent thing' and withdraw their motion. But the mover of the motion was Tom Hogan, a Unite member and a good friend to Jimmy Kelly and me, and I was determined that they would not withdraw the motion, that the debate would be had and to hell with the result. I needn't have worried, Tom was equally as determined.

In the hotel the night before Conference, however, there was something in the air. A lot of people were unhappy that the IMPACT amendment didn't look like an amendment at all. It looked like a completely different position to motion 41, and there was some disquiet that it had been accepted as an amendment by Standing Orders. And that wasn't all. The Northern Ireland unions were looking at it closely and noticing that it made no distinction for them. They had defeated water charges in the North, but if this motion was passed it could mean that they would now be part of a Congress that was looking for 'free allowances', and those 'free allowances' by their very nature must clearly be linked to some charging mechanism.

And so it began. Tom Hogan and his colleague Una Dunphy arrived and were immediately prevailed upon by Congress officials to withdraw the Waterford motion. When Tom said no, meetings were arranged in rooms upstairs which continued on and off as Conference began the next day. I was to be at some of them with Tom, but I wasn't needed really. Tom was having none of it. Some of the arguments made for withdrawal were preposterous, but as the hours passed and day one went in to day two and beyond it became clear that, behind the scenes, people were talking and there was quite a bit of support for the Waterford position. Or, to be precise, the Right2Water position.

Joan Burton arrived at Conference on the morning of day three. Here was the Labour leader and Tanaiste just months before an election coming to talk to the trade union movement in an era of austerity with a garda escort. I can't tell you what she said because the Unite delegation walked out 'en bloc' as she entered the conference hall. John Douglas was at the top table chairing all this and he was utterly professional through-out, as he would be later in the day when the great water debate hit the Conference floor.

Just before the afternoon session there was a conversation in the hotel foyer between Dave, Jimmy Kelly, Stevie Fitz and myself and we were prevailed upon one last time to talk to Tom about withdrawing the motion. It was suggested that IMPACT might even withdraw their amendment and rumours were flying everywhere about which union might vote which way, about which unions were applying a 'whip' to delegates and who was giving a free vote. Water was the only show in town at Congress 2015, and the IMPACT amendment to motion 41 and how it was put together had backfired spectacularly. The amendment was seen as being fast and loose with the rules by some, and of ignoring the Northern colleagues and their victory on water charges by others, but one way or the other it had shone a light on the Waterford motion and Conference was buzzing. Water, water everywhere. As we prepared to enter the hall for the afternoon session one final person suggested we might be doing the wrong thing here. I responded, 'Are you fucking joking? We might just win this!'

The debate happened late in the afternoon and followed a sweep of the hotel by both sides to make sure as many of their voting delegates as possible were in the hall. IMPACT President Gerry King began by passionately arguing that his members in water services needed to be protected against outsourcing and privatisation. SIPTU's Jack O'Connor later argued this line too, and said that if charges were abolished the Government would have to find €500 or €600 million which was currently being spent on public services. They were passionate and strong. But wrong. Unite have members in water and sanitation too, and we argue that their jobs are threatened, not protected, by establishing Irish Water as a privatisation vehicle. When I got to the podium I also addressed a ridiculous assertion that we didn't want people to pay for water:

> Of course, we pay for water, this is about *how* we pay for water. We currently pay for water through progressive general taxation. While water should be free at the point of use, nobody thinks water is free. Water needed to be paid for through tax.

I was back in my seat when Terry Kelleher of the CPSU tackled the argument that this was about funding our public services and described the charge simply and succinctly as 'a bailout tax'. Then Mandate's Dave Moran gave a strong defence of the Waterford motion in what *The Irish Times* referred to as an acrimonious debate. We also had strong interventions from the Northern Ireland Public Services Union (NIPSA) and others who felt that the IMPACT amendment supported by SIPTU was utterly reckless with regard to our members up north. By the time the debate was over the hall was in ferment. The speeches on both sides had been passionate with some heckling added to the tension, and nobody knew how this was going to go. Could we possibly win a vote against the block votes of SIPTU/IMPACT and their effective defence of the Labour Party who would face an election within a year? Would the entire trade union movement back this motion from little Waterford Trades Council, which effectively was the Right2Water position when Right2Water was a campaign led by just five affiliates? Could we succeed in making the formal ICTU position be about the abolition of water charges?

John Douglas called the vote and hands shot up in the air. Tellers were called into action as hands were held up. The vote was for the amendment first. If the amendment passed the original Waterford motion automatically fell. There was a massive block of SIPTU hands up at the front right, and IMPACT hands behind them. Elsewhere there were others up in the air too. People were straining and standing up counting for themselves. Then the tellers nodded at each other and John called for those opposed to the amendment to put their hands up. Up they went. Different hands. More counting and more straining of necks. Junior Coss behind me whispered, 'we have it, we fucking have it', down in front of me Dave gives me a signal that he doesn't think we have it. Richie Browne is confident. Who knows? The tellers know and they hand something to John, the ICTU President and General Secretary of Right2Water's Mandate. John whispers to Patricia King, the incoming ICTU General Secretary who has just left SIPTU to take up her position, and then he calls the result:

'In favour of the IMPACT amendment – 194

Against the amendment – 203'

The amendment fails by nine bloody votes and the roar nearly lifts the roof off the hall. Nine precious votes. People are hugging and pumping fists and shaking hands and congratulating each other. The Waterford motion has of course now passed by the same margin. What a bloody result! This was a victory for the Right2Water unions on behalf of the thousands of water warriors nationwide. In that room we were David struggling not to be emasculated by Goliath, whereas we knew outside of the room that the working class movement was what most trade union members actually supported. A political arm to the industrial struggle. Later I would tell the press that:

> The decision by delegates to effectively call for the abolition of water charges reflects the views of trade union members throughout the country – tens of thousands of whom have attended national and local Right2Water demonstrations.
>
> Our campaign is delighted that Congress is now in step with the trade union movement, and we look forward to working with other unions, in addition to those already affiliated to Right2Water to ensure that these charges are abolished.

The cheering and congratulations that took over the hall after the vote was a spontaneous manifestation that a people's movement was fighting back within a Congress that many thought had abandoned the working class in the social partnership era. But now we were fighting to claim our movement back. Then, the defiant chant of the water movement, of the water marches broke out, 'no way, we won't pay, no way, we won't pay!'

I knew if I went to enough of these Conferences I'd enjoy one eventually!

# 12

# Right2Water Day 5 – 29 August 2015

By the time Right2Water had its fifth formal protest on 29 August 2015, it had been five full months since the previous one. That's a long time, the longest there had been between any two Right2Water demonstrations since the beginning. But we had promised to be around at least until the general election and to make water charges the number one election issue. To that end more than protest was needed and since the previous demonstration the Right2Change policy platform had been developed, we had held two seminal conferences, built on our international links and won a major battle to change the ICTU policy on water charges. Not bad while 'we were doing nothing', as some would have described it.

Demonstrations however are crucial to the campaign. They motivate, create awareness, optimism and belief and (usually) unity and momentum. So it was time to hit the streets again, this time O'Connell Street, and it was held on Saturday, 29 August. The organising was similar to previous ones with 500,000 leaflets and a massive social media push. A week beforehand, people like Noirin Murphy, Keith O'Brien, Anne Kavanagh, (my sister) Sinead Stewart, Terry Curtis, Vivienne Farrell and Padraig O'Rourke had arranged something they called 'BOB'. They teased and taunted me about what 'BOB' might mean for a week or two, but on the morning of Friday 21 August it was revealed that 'BOB' stood for 'Banners Over

Bridges' as all over Ireland activists draped banners from public bridges publicising Right2Water Day 5. This reflected the initial shock, and then anger and frustration, of activists with what was all but a media blackout of the campaign at that point. Maybe 'blackout' is too strong, but in the context of the size of the campaign the media seemed to be deliberately downplaying everything we did. Those of us experienced in how the media react to anything outside the consensus were only surprised at the scale of the shutdown, but to those who were newly active and had never seen anything as big as this in their lives the lack of a media response was shocking. So in villages and towns all over Ireland, on their own initiative, these activists decided to bring their own publicity to a bridge nearby. Meanwhile, the unions were preparing a banner drop or two of our own!

Banners or not, the attendance was once again marvellous. Even *The Irish Times* reported 'tens of thousands' and, as usual, shortly after the speeches began the attendance was at its height. Five months later, Right2Water had done it again. These mobilisations were not only historic in size but they were now consistently so, and they were being done mostly by people power and social media. A phenomenon had been born.

There were several highlights of the day. Dave Gibney did something uncharacteristic for him: he made a very personal speech when introducing the next speaker. Dave outlined how his grandfather aged 80 had been brought into hospital and put on a trolley for two days with a 'lung infection'. It turned out to be lung cancer and two weeks later he died. A year later his wife, Dave's grandmother, was also brought into hospital and the woman died at 5.00 am with the nurses asking the family not to disturb the eight other people who were in the ward with her as she passed. Dave spoke not because this story is unique, but because it is normal. The ordinary people of this nation are being denied dignity and respect even as they pass away, in many cases having worked every day of their lives until retirement. We all know somebody this has happened to. We all know the truth of Dave's words. Whether it be homeless people dying on streets, or families being evicted and sleeping on park benches, Dave stressed that they all deserved better and that the people have a Right2Change from a country based on:

> ... corruption, cronyism, speculation, profit and greed to one that's based on equality, social justice, democracy and respect. But it won't happen on its own. We're going to have to fight for it. We're going to have to fight hard because the forces against us are very very strong. They will tell us that there is no alternative. That this is the only way. But there's always an alternative and there's always a choice.

While these words were being spoken Billy Wall of OPATSI and my dear friend Padraig O'Rourke, some activists were hanging precariously from the top of a building on O'Connell Street unfurling a massive Right2Water/Right2Change banner that we had made up for the day. This spectacular sight was done with help from a businessperson on O'Connell Street who came in, opened his business for the afternoon and gave the lads access to the roof. When the massive crowd below eventually realised what was being unfurled, a wave of enthusiasm and determination swept through the throng. It may have been five months since our last demonstration, but this was symbolic evidence that our promise to fight right up to the election would be fulfilled. The massive banner would reappear in an iconic photograph on Croke Park's Hill 16 the following day. Dublin were playing Mayo in the All-Ireland semi-final and the lads on the Hill managed to display the banner long enough for SKY TV to capture it while RTÉ turned their camera away. How such a giant banner got on to the Hill is a story that must remain untold, but suffice it to say that while we were celebrating another massive Right2Water success in Mulligans on Saturday, 29 August, the banner was already secreted in Croke Park waiting for its sporting debut.

Some people call things like this 'stunts', but I prefer to see it as all part of the colour, imagination and excitement associated with Right2Water. Since the beginning the campaign has been determined to break new ground. A key part of this is the role played by artists at our events. I have already touched on how our event on 10 December 2015 was as much a rock concert as a demonstration, and again on the 29 August the fantastic Don Baker and his band provided a long stint of musical entertainment from the stage before the actual demonstration took place. Because of the nature of the campaign, all of our artists, musicians and poets give of their talents on a volunteer basis, and I often marvel at how Evelyn Campbell, Don Baker, Damien Dempsey, Glen Hansard, Dean Scurry, Red Empire and the many others acknowledged in this book are such great examples to us all, especially the young, showing how to combine youth and talent with hope and inspiration to help deliver a fairer better place for us all.

Poetry is vital too. The power of the written word in the hands and voices of those with creative talent can put our problems as a nation in a deeper context that can inspire. Andrew Galvin from Donegal left those who heard him speak at our March demonstration awestruck by his talent and passion for change. And on 29 August we were joined for the second time by the amazing Stephen Murphy. Like Andrew, Stephen lives in rural Ireland – Leitrim in his case – and from that lovely county he assesses the tribulations of ordinary people and puts them into words that connect with anyone who hears them. Not only his words, but his passionate delivery has brought tears to my eyes on every single occasion that I have heard him.

Stephen appeared at the very first Right2Water demonstration where he had recited a letter he had written to the Taoiseach called 'Dear Enda'. But now, on the day that Right2Change got formally launched at a demonstration, Stephen produced his masterpiece called, 'This Isn't Just About the Water', which is reproduced in full at the end of the last chapter.

# 13

# Be a Big Part of Something Small, or a Small Part of Something Big?

The success of the 29 August event provided vital momentum for what lay ahead which was going to be even more difficult than we had anticipated. When Steve Fitzpatrick of the CWU had marked the voting on the Right2Change policy principles by announcing a nationwide 'roadshow' to try to build support he wasn't speaking off the cuff. By then it was already clear that the trade unions were fulfilling a particular role. It wasn't a role we were afraid of, but if wasn't one we had sought out either. In actuality, it was a role created by the momentum of the water movement which was now evolving into a wider campaign for change. People were asking, legitimately, how are 'we' going to get the politicians who support the proposals to work together?

That this role fell to the unions was probably natural. We all had contacts, experience and history of working with and supporting the various elements of the 'political pillar'. Whether it was the historical support that Unite gave to Socialist Workers Party (PBP) or Socialist Party (AAA) candidates, along with a plethora of Independents, or the fact that Sinn Féin was working with the unions to try to build an understanding of workplace-related issues, the fact was that the unions had it in our DNA to try to find common ground and get people to work together. Now that the policy platform had been agreed at the 13 June Conference, the next step was to try to build a strong, unified alliance behind these principles. Everybody was aware, however, that the closer the next election came the stronger the natural political impulse to find difference, rather than commonality, would be. Could an alliance be built to rise above that fracturing impulse? In essence the question was:

> Were 'we' interested in being just a big part of something small, or could 'we' all learn to be a small part of something big?

And so the roadshow began. All of the meetings had the same structure. Each had a presentation on the ten policy principles which followed a political economy presentation, and then there would be a question and answer session which generally turned into a debate. The first block of meetings included Tralee, Limerick, Dublin South and North, and Donegal by early October. Ultimately, there would be 24 meetings with over 2,000 attendees. At these meetings the unions were often asked to 'make the politicians work together' by frustrated community activists, and there was a strong feeling that unless we found a way of uniting behind the principles we could be looking at another FineGael/Labour Government. While no opinion poll at the time suggested it, there was an increasing sense of something akin to panic all the same, a sense that lack of unity could deny us the opportunity for real and lasting progressive change. But clearly the task of forging that unity in a historically fractured 'left' meant that we were headed into new and difficult territory for all concerned. Who would be up to the task? It was these questions, which came up over and over, that inspired a union-led attempt to formalise a structure within which, we hoped, people could work together. And on Friday, 16 October 2015, the unions called a meeting of the 'political pillar' in Unite's offices to do so.

There was an early indicator that this process would be fraught with difficulty when the CPSU Executive decided that the Right2Change policy platform was too political for them and they couldn't support it. Readers will recall that CPSU General Secretary Eoin Ronayne had made this point clear at the crucial meeting in Dundalk, and that this had been accepted unquestioningly. Now, however, despite the fact that Right2Change was specifically structured to be about policy and not party, there were evidently those on the CPSU Executive whose party loyalties were still threatened enough for them to unite against it. I believe that this was a deliberate misinterpretation by some for party reasons of what Right2Change was all about and how it sat in light of CPSU rules. Anyway, the Right2Change unions would be Unite, Mandate, the Communications Workers Union and OPATSI.

While this episode was instructive we were pressing ahead anyway and on 16 October 2015 we did just that. The meeting was very well attended given that nobody knew in advance why it was being called. I took a back seat on the day, preferring to take extensive notes, so the top table was made up of Jimmy Kelly (Unite), John Douglas and Dave Gibney (Mandate) and Steve Fitzpatrick (CWU). The following parties attended: AAA, Communist Party, People Before Profit, Sinn Féin, Social Democrats, Workers' Party, RUAG (Unemployed Network Tipperary) along with Independents including Clare Daly, Joan Collins, Mick Wallace and representatives of several others. After a short opening address three questions were put to the meeting. On behalf of the 'trade union pillar' and the 'community pillar', we wanted each element of the 'political pillar' to formally answer these questions. They would be given until 30 October (two weeks) to do so, and we told them that we would reveal their responses publicly to a special meeting of the 'community pillar' on Saturday, 31 October 2015. The three questions were:

1. Do you support the policy principles?

2. Will you agree now to form a progressive Government based on the Right2Change principles if the numbers allow?

3. How will you work together to deliver this objective?

Given that all of those present were in the CWU when the policy principles were unanimously voted on 13 June, we weren't expecting anybody to demur from question 1 (we would be wrong about this in the end), but on that Friday the AAA (Paul Murphy) and People Before Profit (Richard Boyd Barrett) had issues with question 2. Both spoke at length about their wish to replace the word 'form' in the question with the word 'support'. The Workers' Party also spoke in support of this proposition, but Sinn Féin (Mary Lou McDonald), as well as Independents Clare Daly and Joan Collins, told us that they didn't need two weeks and that they were answering questions 1 and 2 in the affirmative there and then. Clare spoke passionately on the day about how it was important that this meeting had been called and that clarity was needed if unity was to be pursued. Some debate took place between the union officials present and those seeking a word change. This required some assessment. What exactly was the difference between 'forming' and 'supporting' a Government? Paul Murphy was the most up front on this topic in explaining that he could see AAA supporting a Government led, for example, by Gerry Adams, but entering it was a different question entirely. Paul was clear, long before the election of the current minority Government set up was even thought of, that this was a possible electoral outcome and that the AAA felt that a commitment to Government formation was not something they could commit to at that remove, while supporting a minority administration was potentially on the table.

It was a positive meeting and afterwards most of the trade union leaders found themselves in a discussion as we left the building. The view that we should change the word 'form' to 'support' was expressed, but there was the alternative majority view that the meeting had confirmed that we had asked the right question, and that the question had exposed a fault line that we were better to understand now than find out about later. While this question was being debated the matter was cut across when John Douglas entered the room. John had been detained in conversation with Paul Murphy who had explained to him that Socialist Party rules prevented his party from forming a Government within the current capitalist system, and that this made question two impossible for the Socialist Party/AAA to answer in the affirmative. While this seemed to cut to the heart of the debate, it was agreed that the unions would offer to discuss such issues with any party or individual before the 30 October deadline for clarity.

In the event two such meetings took place. The first was with the Socialist Party and AAA, and the second with the Workers' Party. On Thursday, 29 October, John Douglas, Steve Fitzpatrick, Dave Gibney, Cormac O'Dalaigh and I met with three executive members of the Socialist Party including Joe Higgins TD. The meeting was almost three hours long and productive at times, but also somewhat fractious. Much of it was spent discussing their concerns about Sinn Féin, both historically and in terms of that party's behaviour in the Northern Ireland administration. From the point of view of a rival party, these concerns were not only legitimate but inevitable. Our view, which I expressed, was that by working together areas of convergence could emerge, while working apart would only illuminate and exaggerate differences. It was, at least to me, the inevitable difference between an approach based on the pursuit of unity for the common good as opposed to one based on difference for a sectional advantage. To our surprise, however, issues were raised about not only question two, but also question one. Specifically, the Socialist Party felt that as the policy principles endorsed the Good Friday and St. Andrew's Agreements that they could not endorse them, and they also felt that the Fiscal Framework underpinning the platform did not go far enough. Unfortunately, Paul Murphy did not attend but the position with regard to the Socialist Party rules was again made clear.

Before the meeting ended the Socialist Party/AAA told us that they would not be answering the questions positively or becoming involved on that basis, and that they would follow this up with a letter, which they did. The letter set out their response in detail. It stated that, in relation to question one, while they 'generally' supported the reforms, 'we believe for the principles to be realised will necessitate going much further than the projected spending increases in the Fiscal Framework Document'. And on question one another problem was set out in relation to the Northern Ireland peace process:

> We don't agree that the Good Friday or St. Andrew's Agreement offer a way forward as the failures of the last 17 years show. They institutionalised sectarian divisions whereas you need unity of working class, Catholic and Protestant, to overcome sectarianism and the sectarian parties which are a barrier to real change in Northern Ireland.

The answer to question two was also negative but this came as no surprise as the letter was consistent with the long meeting we had had. For their own reasons, the AAA were out but, on the same day, we received a letter from PBP which was positive. This came as a slight surprise given that Richard Boyd Barrett had also strongly sought to change the wording of question two, but it was welcome news nevertheless.

The following day we met with the Workers' Party at their request and the meeting was remarkably similar to the previous day's, both in tone and content. In fact, at this meeting we could have spent as much time discussing what had happened in Belfast in 1973 as what was happening in the Republic in 2015. But the outcome was the same. In terms of positive answers to the questions put, the Workers' Party, who unlike Socialist Party/AAA had no parliamentary presence, were out.

The issue of Sinn Féin has been difficult throughout. To many in Ireland they remain a party joined at the hip with the horrific carnage that took place in Northern Ireland throughout the 1970s, 1980s and first half of the 1990s. To others, they are a hope for a new kind of politics that can embrace nationalism and progressive policies which might break the Fianna Fáil/Fine Gael hegemony. Feelings run so high, justifiably so to those affected by 'the troubles' and opportunistically by some others, that sometimes it feels like the best thing is to just give up. It certainly felt like that to me when people in my union in Northern Ireland, my colleagues and friends from a loyalist working class background, started contacting me in 2015 about rumours that I was working behind the scenes to advance the cause of Sinn Féin and using union members' contributions through Right2Change for their benefit. Worse was that I was said to somehow be a secret member of Sinn Féin and that I was going to be running for them in the next election. These utterly baseless and deliberate untruths were in my belief fostered by those fearful of Right2Change in the Republic and prepared to use difference of background (I was, after all, born into a Catholic family in Dundalk) in the North in a disgraceful, even dangerous, manner to undermine me and therefore Unite's role in Right2Change itself. I had several dark days and nights when it seemed I was under a veil of suspicion, and I felt uncomfortable in my own office in Belfast, but in the end the sheer nastiness of such tactics fortified me in my determination to push on.

It wasn't all bad either. The decision by Sinn Féin early on not only to endorse Right2Change but to publicly call for a vote transfer pact with others gave the policy platform much needed exposure, but the benefit of that exposure was offset by the loss of support for Right2Change from a section of protestors who had backed, and still back, Right2Water. I got a number of messages from people with no party affiliation or agenda who espoused the view that they just could not support any platform that had Sinn Féin involvement. To me this struck at a certain toxicity many people feel for that party, one which is also manipulated by the media, and which Sinn Féin needs to overcome if it is ever to be in Government in the Republic. To those people who just cannot conceive of ever supporting Sinn Féin but who want Ireland changed for the better, the extent to which Sinn Féin is a vehicle for progress or an obstacle to it is an open question. But it is not one unique to Sinn Féin. For altogether different reasons it is also a question that can legitimately be put to their sworn enemies in AAA and People Before Profit – vehicles of progress or obstacles to it? For the record, I have never been, and will never be, a member of any of these parties. Only by working together around policies, as opposed to flags or dogma, can fundamental change be achieved in Ireland in the long term.

## Wynn's Hotel – 31 October 2015

We met with the 'community pillar' (on Halloween of all days) to outline the responses we had gotten from the 'political pillar'. The Social Democrats had by then sent us a letter, widely reported in the media, which stated that while they broadly supported the intent of the initiative they would not be supporting Right2Change as they intended going before the electorate as a 'fully independent party'. They also felt that the

Right2Change platform 'amounts to a manifesto', and that they would be developing their own programmes. And so, for whatever reasons, stated or otherwise, the Social Democrats, Socialist Party/AAA and the Workers' Party were out. On arriving at Wynn's I was approached outside by a stalwart AAA member from the Midlands who wanted to shake my hand and express how appalled he was by his party's decision. I had had a lively online exchange or two with this man and the fact that he was of this mind was a portent of a difficulty ahead. But I will return to that at the end of this chapter.

The media were also invited to this meeting and it was attended by both *The Irish Times* and the *Sunday Times*. While explaining the background and the list of the parties that we had approached, I noted that Fianna Fáil, Fine Gael and Labour had not been included as we engaged only with those who had worked with us in the water movement. I also said that those specific parties were 'not part of the solution to our inequality, they are the reason for our inequality'. We (the 'trade union pillar') began by setting out a proposed 'Mission Statement' and to establish agreement on two 'facts':

1.  That no single party, individual or component of the 'movement' can offer the electorate a choice for a progressive Government, and

2.  That to do so we should focus on policies and that they should be broad and progressive.

We then set out the three questions, and to those on social media and elsewhere who suggested that we had asked the 'wrong questions', I said that just because some could not provide the 'right' answers did not mean the questions were wrong. On behalf of the unions, I pointed out that having asked these three questions and collated the answers that we were fully prepared to walk away from this process now if the 'community pillar' felt that our role was no longer needed. I also outlined that we felt that the 'community pillar' was:

- very large
- mostly non-aligned to parties or individuals, and
- not uniform and lacking in structure and discipline.

On behalf of the unions I offered to help the 'community pillar' to develop structure and discipline, explaining that our way was always to try to find compromises and that we had much experience in doing so. We were happy to bring that experience into the political sphere if it could help.

I then, one by one, set out the responses to the three questions. Or at least I thought I had! When I had gotten through them all the summary was quite clear. Socialist Party/AAA, the Social Democrats and the Workers' Party had declined to sign up while the following had: Communist Party of Ireland, Direct Democracy Ireland, National Citizens Movement, People Before Profit, Sinn Féin, Clare Daly TD, Joan Collins TD, Mick Wallace TD, Thomas Pringle TD, Tommy Broughan TD, Seamus Healy TD, Declan Bree, Barbara Smyth, Michael O'Gorman, Cllr. Paul Hand, Cllr. Cieran Perry, Cllr. Francis Timmons, Cllr. Brendan Young, Cllr. Joanne Pender, Cllr. Pat Kavanagh.

The last on this list was a courageous Councillor and animal rights activist in Wicklow. Pat Kavanagh had been a stalwart from the inception of the water campaign and had supported Right2Change from the beginning. She felt it was an essential first step to bringing about necessary change. By the time this meeting took place Pat was fighting illness, a battle that she would lose soon afterwards. Pat knew this at the time but was in touch with us nevertheless to give encouragement. It was important to her that her name was on that list and it was important to us too. Pat is greatly missed within the campaign.

## No Looking Back

I set out the events in this chapter in some detail for a number of important reasons. Firstly, I believe the Right2Change policy principles, or a future incarnation of them, *will* lead to our first progressive Government at some point in the future. I believe they will do so because sufficient numbers of people will see in them broad egalitarian and inclusive principles that will change all of our lives for the better. And so, before measuring how much progress was made in Election 2016, and hopefully will be made in future elections, I think the birth pains of this process need to be recorded for the record from the inside.

By the time November 2015 arrived people had developed, from the ground up, policies that a massive 106 candidates would run under in Election 2016. That all of this was done among a fractured and often sectarian left is, I believe, remarkable and a sign for hope. There are lessons to be learned too. Mistakes were made and opportunities lost which we will explore further in the remaining chapters. Can we learn from those lessons and go further to vindicate our Right2Water, our Right2Change? Only the future will decide.

For now there is one final part of this chapter that needs to be said. In closing it within these pages I am also closing it in my head and heart. It is the way the Socialist Party/AAA reacted to these events by accusing Dave Gibney and me of falsifying their answers to the Right2Change questions and then making formal written complaints to our employers about us. It took until 5 November, almost a week later, for this personalised attack to emerge. The AAA member from the Midlands wasn't the only member perturbed by the party's responses. I wasn't, Dave wasn't and nobody in the unions was. Once we understood their rules a lot of their behaviour throughout the campaign suddenly made sense and, while I don't believe we need a worldwide revolution to improve society, I respect their views to the contrary.

What I don't respect, or accept, is that they launched a scathing public attack on us (mostly me) because their answers to questions one and two were appended with the word 'No'. And they were. When Dave prepared the slides the night before the meeting in Wynn's Hotel he did so on the basis that we would be providing the answers to 'yes' or 'no' questions. But despite the fact that they had said 'no' to both at our lengthy meeting, despite the fact that the text outlined then and now in this book clearly means no, once their members started asking questions, once it looked like their dogma was going to backfire on them for once, Paul Murphy went on record on 5 November and said, 'we did not say no'. In doing so, he did not explain how specifically not agreeing with Right2Change's key Fiscal Strategy component could be a 'yes', he did not explain how not agreeing with the Good Friday and St. Andrew's Agreements, key parts of the platform, could be a 'yes', and he did not explain or refer to his remarks to John Douglas about their rules or his absence from the key meeting at which they clearly said no to us all.

Without any contact with us a flier was produced, appropriately in yellow, and with the word 'Falsification' emblazoned across the top with the sub-heading 'Right2Change falsifies & misrepresents AAA's answers'. The words 'No' were encircled as if a smoking gun had been produced to the crime of the century. As an exercise in tabloid-type presentation and hyperbole it seems the AAA were taking lessons from their enemies in the tabloid press. They then spent days pushing it all over social media and into the hands of journalists who mainly treated it with the appropriate level of disdain. Yet between 31 October and this 'sting' on 5 November not a single call, email, text or other contact had come from the AAA. When Dave saw it on social media Paul Murphy spent days avoiding his phone calls.

Now this is a party I had voted for in the three previous elections. It included people who I considered, if not friends, then comrades. I had even provided small donations to it in the past. And Unite had often been the only union in Ireland where their brand of utopian fundamentalism would even get a hearing, let alone financial and logistical support. For months I had been the subject of damaging rumours perpetuated against me for the sin of doing nothing other than trying to build unity. And now, for asking the hard question and closing down the deliberate ambiguity in their grossly negative answers, a personal onslaught was embarked upon.

That it involved written complaints from a party of the left to the employer of two trade unionists beggars belief. It is only now, on mature and calm reflection, that I believe I understand the tactics used against Right2Water by the Socialist Party, and the origins and intent of those tactics. The Socialist Party in Ireland, founded in 1996, is aligned to the Socialist Party in the United Kingdom, which was formed after that party's predecessor, Militant Tendency, was expelled from the British Labour Party under leader Niel Kinnock. In an excellent book written by Channel 4's Michael Crick, *Militant*, he sets out a grossly exaggerated claim that it is the remnants of 'Militant' manifest in the Trotskyist left that have boosted the British Labour Party membership in support of Jeremy Corbyn. Crick is around long enough to know that there are no more 300,000 Trotskyists in Britain than there are little red communists under his bed, but he is nevertheless doing some service in exposing the modus operandi of these groups and how they sought to wrestle control of Labour before being expelled. Anybody who attended a Right2Water meeting in the last two years at which the Socialist Party/AAA were present will recognise the Militant tactic used to infiltrate Labour meetings, which Crick claims included:

*The Hill have their say*

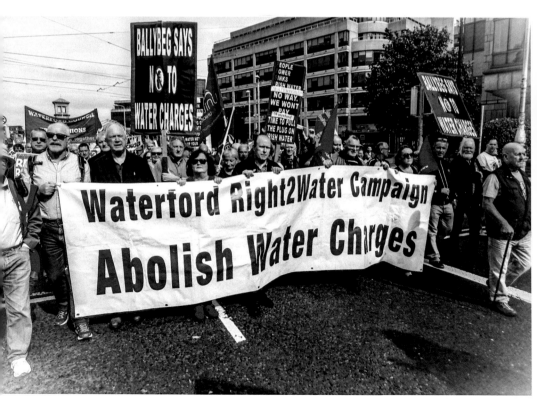

*And so does Waterford*

*An emotional Stephen Murphy
addressing Right2Water*

*Red Empire and support from Right2Water
for water warriors in North Dakota*

*Homeless families on stage, February 2016*

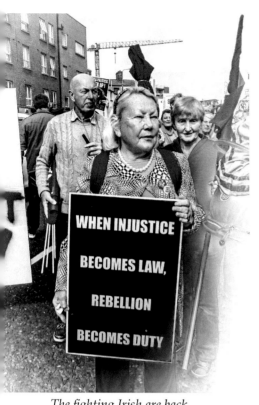

*The fighting Irish are back*

*Maeve Curtis*

*Ministry of Thirst with Rita Fagin*

*Water is a Human Right – Bill Wall, John Douglas, Dave Gibney, Maude Barlow, Brendan*

*Right2Change policy principles vote*

*Russell Brand and Brendan*

*Another massive turnout*

*Fiscal Strategy launched – Dave Gibney, Michael Taft, Mandy La Combre, Brendan, Stevie Fitzpatrick*

*Varoufakis speaks in Mansion House via video link*

*Unite ad*

*Two Irelands leaflet*

*Victory at ICTU Conference*

*Our €13 billion apple heads the 17 September march*

*They came again in massive numbers on 17 September*

> Make the event adversarial. Uncomradely questions to sitting councillors and the MP, challenging the chair's method and motive, defining the politics of the speaker before they have defined their own. This behaviour basically reduces the attendance of the remaining sensible types. Then the meeting (is) ours to control.

Suffice it to say there will be no more votes, contributions or logistical support from me. And it's not because I support another party. I do not. It is because whether from the right or the left, if a party is going to treat one of its friends like that I don't want to be around it when it deals with its enemies. And in twenty years of dealing with intransigent employers, of having fought some of the biggest and most controversial industrial disputes, some of which I believe few others would have taken on, none of my opponents, no matter how vicious the argument, has called my personal integrity into question. Nor have I theirs.

# 14

# Building towards Election 2016

There had been seven public meetings to consider the Right2Change policy principles by the time the politicians had decided whether they were in or out in supporting the policy platform. For the unions there was much to do. We had another 17 such meetings before the February 2016 election which were attended by more than 2,000 people in over 20 counties. Some of the meetings, such as the one arranged by Noirin Murphy and chaired by John Lonergan in Cork, were superb, and at meetings such as the one we held in Wexford came the gratifying news that Independent Mick Wallace's team and People Before Profit were working closely on the ground in exactly the manner we had hoped for. It would be election count day before we could measure how beneficial these informal arrangements would be but, in the end, those who co-operated most got considerable electoral benefits and those who didn't – well they didn't.

As summer passed into autumn, trying to build unity behind the policy principles among those who had signed up to Right2Change took many forms. Parties were considering how many candidates would run and the news that Sinn Féin in Donegal would be running the excellent Gary Doherty alongside Pearse Doherty and Padraig MacLochlainn clearly threatened Thomas Pringle TD's Independent seat. Along with local Right2Change stalwart Sinead Stewart, I came in for considerable attack in the North West when I had the temerity to simply ask if there was room for four Right2Change candidates in Donegal. No matter that there was no criticism of anybody involved in my question, least of all Padraig MacLochlainn who ultimately became the victim of this serious miscalculation when he lost his seat, we were heading into an election and it was becoming clear to the politically inexperienced like me that everybody – and everything about them – was fair game and truth was by no means an essential element in the discussions either. Particularly the online ones.

## To Run or Not to Run

At this point I was considering whether to run for election. I have never seen electoral politics as my natural home, and I have never understood why some see electoral office as the 'be all and end all' to such an extent that they spend years build-ing profiles to try to make it to the empty benches of Leinster House. For me the question about running wasn't so much 'how can I get elected', but 'why the hell would I want to'?

My starting position hadn't changed for many years. For one thing, I believe that my union and I make a difference any-way in what we do. I believe whether it is working to save the defined benefit pensions of ESB workers, to secure the jobs of apprentices and others, to protect insofar as possible the terms and conditions of workers, or anything else that we do that we have as much impact for people as many of those who spend years in the Dáil. There are some great parliamentarians for sure, but there are also far too many who do little or nothing and are only expert in playing the system to get themselves elected and re-elected. So, I suppose you could say, I have always had a negative attitude to the idea of running for, let alone being elected to, Dail Éireann.

But there were new things to consider in the context of Right2Water and Right2Change. The campaign was actively looking for new candidates from communities and from trade unions if they emerged. It is a bit much to be hoping other people might disturb their lives to run for office without at least giving it some consideration yourself. I also fully accept that my cynicism about our politics is open to the criticism that giving out about it isn't going to change anything for the better. So I was asked at the Wynn's Hotel meeting from the floor, and I undertook there in response, to give the matter fresh consideration. So what were those considerations? Well there were essentially three things to think through:

1. Was running for electoral office the role in which I could play the best part at that time?

2. If so, where would I run?

3. Would I get elected?

These questions didn't come in any particular order, and it seemed to me they were all linked anyway. On the one hand, there were people in the campaign, and in the Dáil, who were telling me that if I was elected if would be a great boost to the campaign, but I often countered with the view that if left the campaign to join the election race I was unlikely to be replaced by my union, and that the union role in the campaigns – which I believe is essential – would be damaged and might even cease. Right2Water may have made a massive impact, and I some-times think people believe that the campaign is packed with staff and call centres, but from a union point of view it is essen-tially co-ordinated by a very small number of people who do it almost voluntarily in addition to their existing union roles. So far nobody has been released from their other union activities, in any of the unions involved, to work on the campaign.

In any event, the unions had committed to being involved in the campaigns up to the election only, and any commitment after that would be decided later. So there were clear counter arguments to all points. And even if a positive decision was reached, where would I run? I am from Dundalk in the Louth constituency and I did feel that there was some possibility of a strong Independent winning a seat there. I felt Peter Fitzpatrick of Fine Gael, from the Dundalk end of the constituency, was extremely vulnerable, and that Ged Nash would lose his Labour seat too. So yes, I was thinking about it.

My mother pleaded with me not to. She had just lost her husband and memories of the treatment of me by the media during the ESB dispute while dad was dying were still very fresh for her. She asked me to promise not to run while my sisters asked her to ease up and gently encouraged me to do so. In the end, the decision regarding Louth was made for me. While I was still pondering, Garrett Weldon announced he would be running for People Before Profit, the first time a candidate had run for them in Louth. I knew Garrett and his family since childhood and I went to meet him. Garrett is a gentleman, an activist in his DNA with a very big heart. He was already building his network and was fully behind the Right2Change platform. He believed it was the only way forward. We discussed People Before Profit and their overarching Socialist Workers Party and I knew Garrett was unfamiliar with their particular philosophy and methods, but he had made the decision to run and I thought good luck to him. With Sinn Féin running a second Right2Change candidate in Drogheda there was no space for me and so my considerations about running in Louth, to my mother's great relief, went no further. Garret subsequently did well coming within touching distance of claiming a seat.

I didn't live in Louth anyway, I lived in the Dublin West constituency. This was a crowded constituency where Leo Varadkar was a 'shoe in'. I attended a public meeting held by Fianna Fáil to promote young Jack Chambers in Westmanstown, and felt after that that he would win a set. He was endorsed by the political chameleon Colm Keaveney, but I still felt he could overcome this and was likely to win the seat formerly held for Fianna Fáil by the late Brian Lenihan. That left two seats and it was clear that Tanaiste Joan Burton was under pressure from AAA TD Ruth Coppinger and Sinn Féin candidate Paul Donnelly. Every time I considered running here I had a recurring nightmare that if Coppinger, Donnelly and I ran with other Independents too that we would only succeed in allowing Joan Burton to slip through the gap and retain her seat. I actually had sleepless nights over that scenario as I knew that I would be the one that many would blame if that happened. So, in the end, I ruled it out. I was right to as well. With AAA having walked away from Right2Change they and Sinn Féin would never work together in any way and set about trying to cut each other's throats with venom. It was Coppinger who won this battle of the alternative candidates, and sure enough Joan Burton took full advantage of the division among her opponents and, as Labour poured resources into the constituency to save their leader, she won her seat more comfortably than I think even she expected.

My decision about Dublin West was spot on, at least on that occasion, and that would have been the end of my deliberations if it wasn't for Bernie Hughes in Dublin North West. Bernie had declared her candidacy within days of her release from prison after she had refused to undertake to cease her right to engage in further water meter protests. But there was an impetus among many for me to run and Bernie has a generous nature and a heart like a lion. Bernie offered to stand aside if I would run in my neighbouring constituency and to work might and main to get me elected. To Bernie it was about the bigger picture and her offer did give me pause for thought. I spoke to some people in that constituency who I knew from previous work and I got positive feedback. It was felt that Labour would definitely lose a seat there (they did) and that a possible Independent seat could be won.

In the end, though, I decided not to. I did consider that I could potentially, on a good day, have won a seat but the thought that my role in the unions would end the day I was elected brought me to the view that there was a wider project to be developed, and that if I wasn't in Unite it might not happen. Or at least it might not happen with Unite in it. This potential was, in my considered view, more worthy of exploration than the benefit of one potential back bench Independent seat in the Dáil, even though the Right2Change Independent group is becoming more of a force in redefining political debate along progressive lines. I do not see 'politics' as narrowly defined by who sits in elected office. I see it as a living thing that we all can play a part in, sometimes very different parts, and in working for greater trade union connection with our communities in a strategic way my role seemed just as important as any in the Dáil, in my opinion. In the end, Bernie did run and did the best of all of the community candidates nationwide.

## AAA/People Before Profit Alliance Formed

One other thing of significance happened in October 2015. Many had wondered for years what the policy differences were between the Socialist Party/Socialist Workers' Party or their front parties AAA/People Before Profit, and so when it was announced that they would be running in the election as a single alliance, or on a common platform, it shouldn't have been a surprise. In fact, it should have been a welcome development in clearing up what was often portrayed in the media as a chaotic 'ultra left' that was strong on rhetoric but light on unity and  workable or costed policies.

The problem however was that by the time this otherwise logical alliance was actually formed People Before Profit had signed up to Right2Change and their new partners the AAA had not. Given that the AAA differences with the Right2Change platform and Fiscal Strategy were so fundamental I was unable to explain to anyone, least of all myself, how this could work. Specifically, if two elements agree to form an electoral alliance and one has committed to Government formation with those elected under the Right2Change platform, but the other has ruled it out, what exactly happens if that scenario arises? Sceptics suggested to me that this was a strategic alliance cooked up between the two parties, one of the objectives of which was to diminish Right2Change from the inside and the outside simultaneously. That it happened without People Before Profit informing, let alone strategically discussing, this with anyone in Right2Change seemed to add to this view, and it certainly meant there was no agreed strategy to explain it to voters or the media in the teeth of what would be a heated election.

The same question reverberated again, 'do we want to be a big part of something small, or a small part of something big?' Whatever the answer, the confusion in the heads of voters about this alliance only went to show up one of the shortcomings of Right2Change. It demonstrated that as the platform was simply an alliance around policy principles, it had no mechanism to deal with this apparent contradiction. Right2Change was on the map and making waves, but without formalised structure it was open to such manipulations. I believe that any future incarnations of Right2Change will have to address this flaw from the outset.

## Full Steam Ahead for Election 2016

By now all of our efforts were centred on using a series of events to create momentum in the run up to the General Election 2016. Once we got the date (26 February) we already had the shape of what we wanted to do. There would be three events which would be accompanied by the publication of the first edition of a newspaper, *Change News*, that we were determined would help 'change' the national conversation, at least for those interested in an alternative analysis.

Much has been written about the media treatment in the UK of Jeremy Corbyn, a politician that – whatever your views of him on policy – has the highest personal integrity, is corruption-free and has never gone to war with anyone. But the media ownership is concentrated in the hands of powerful interests that are threatened by his views and plans. Noam Chomsky recently opined that this manifests itself in a sort of 'self-censorship' by journalists that ensures that the views of the owners of media outlets, which not by accident coincide with the needs of the dominant economic model of neoliberalism, are reflected in media reportage to such an extent that any alternative approach gets battered then shut down. I have lost count of the number of times that Corbyn was reported to be 'unelectable' or on the point of losing his leadership of the Labour Party. This stuff gets reported not because it is fact, which it plainly isn't, but because media editors and owners want it to be fact. This type of reporting has also now infected state-owned broadcasters and when Andrew Marr of the BBC challenged Chomsky, his riposte of 'I am sure you believe everything you are saying, but what I'm saying is that if you believed something different, you wouldn't be sitting where you are sitting' was witheringly to the point.

I have already outlined how 'our' media here are no different. And so in addition to intensifying our online communications through the social media platforms we decided to produce a free 36 page ad-free newspaper. *Change News* was paid for by the trade unions and its first two inside pages carried a list of all of the austerity budget cuts, year by year, from 2009 to 2016. Another two pages carried the 10 policy principles. The centre pages listed 97 election candidates (later to rise to 106) running in all 40 constituencies who had endorsed the policy platform. This was by far the biggest cross-party policy platform in Election 2016 and it was stitched together *before* the election on policy principles, not after it on expediency. I would have expected that it was newsworthy.

The rest of *Change News* was packed with articles from quality writers the like of which you would seldom, if ever, have seen in the mainstream media. Whether it was Donal Fallon, tracing the link between the 1916 Proclamation and the current political scenario faced by the electorate; Niall Crowley, writing about the need for a 'Robin Hood Tax' already supported by Germany, France, Italy, Austria, Belgium, Greece, Portugal, Slovakia, Slovenia and Spain but not tax haven Ireland; Eoin O'Murchu, on the exciting opportunity to develop progressive politics; Peter McVerry on homelessness; or Maude Barlow on our Right2Water from a global perspective the paper set out to tell voters what they needed to know about the state of their country. It set out what many voters felt but could not access in terms of information anywhere else. And in order to get the message out we went big – 200,000 copies big! In all, volunteers delivered more than twice as many copies of *Change News* as the *Irish Independent* sell daily, and it was a massive undertaking. But it was a necessary one. In an era where the media work to reinforce the establishment rather than to challenge it, this publication was among the best things we have done to date.

## Three Events Leading to Polling Day

By this point the political parties and independents were in full campaign mode. New community activists were declaring their candidatures, but doing so unilaterally and often without any experience, resources or back-up. There was no time to develop a structure for support and insofar as the unions did try to help, in the autumn and winter of 2015 those efforts fell flat. It was too soon in the process and with an election on the horizon the efforts to build structure were too pressured and agenda-laden to have any chance of working. So we did what we could do with the limited time and resources available.

Fantastic community candidates did come forward and considerable personal risk and expense was taken by people simply interested in working for a better Ireland. Barbara Smyth in Longford/Westmeath, Keith Gilligan in Carlow Kilkenny, Damien O'Neill in Dublin Bay North, the aforementioned Bernie Hughes, and Michael O'Gorman in Kerry were examples of candidates who joined experienced hands like Declan Bree, Clare Daly, Thomas Pringle, Tommy Broughan, Mick Wallace and Joan Collins in supporting the policy principles.

The unions focussed their resources on events and a plan was considered by their executives. Every union has its own rules but in Unite the process of resourcing Right2Change was particularly interesting. As noted earlier, many of the representatives of our members in Northern Ireland were concerned with a perception that our resources were funding Sinn Féin. To those of a Protestant background, and to some who weren't as well, this unease related to the perception of Sinn Féin as a nationalist party with links to the IRA, and also as a perceived party of austerity in the Stormont administration. They didn't want our members' money spent on these candidates and I agreed that that was not what we should be doing anyway. I felt that Right2Change offered us in Unite a chance to break with funding of any candidates or party to which we were not affiliated (we had funded left parties and Independents in the past) and to instead direct our resources into a people's movement behind a progressive policy platform. I believed that if that movement led to a political formation at some point in the future that that could be discussed then, but in February 2016 I was vehemently opposed to a single cent of Unite's political fund going to any candidate or party. And so were our Irish Executive. So Unite endorsed and agreed to co-fund a programme of events, along with the publication of *Change News*, and other initiatives up to a maximum amount.

Dave and I had presented a full programme to the Right2Change unions that was expensive and logistically difficult, but that we believed if implemented it would help ensure the outgoing FineGael/Labour coalition simply could not be re-elected. In the end, even a slimmed down version of that plan helped to deliver a quality debate and surprisingly positive results for a first outing of a new policy platform. The three events that formed the centre piece of that plan were a day of local mobilisations on Saturday, 23 January 2016, a one day conference in the Mansion House assessing alternatives on 13 February, and a major national demonstration in Dublin on Saturday, 20 February, just six days before polling day. To be honest, the first two events could have been better supported, yet they still had a massive impact in terms of building momentum, debate and awareness.

On 23 January, in awful weather, thousands took part in 30 protests across the state in an effort to build constituency-based awareness of the Right2Water demand for abolition of water charges, the Right2Change policy platform and the local candidates supporting it. On that day John Douglas of Mandate reminded people that 'we promised over a year and a half ago that we would make water charges the number one issue' for the upcoming election. Echoing this, I outlined how that day's protest was just the first step in a significant pre-election campaign by Right2Water, adding that:

> ... while today is about water it is also about a number of other issues facing Irish society. It's about inequality, unfairness, cronyism and corruption. It's about soaring poverty levels and mass emigration. It's about deprivation and homelessness. Water has been a catalyst in the fight against austerity, but people are crying out for a change in how our country is run and that will be visible on the streets of Dublin, Cork, Limerick, Galway and Donegal, among other counties today.

I was probably most looking forward to the one-day confer-ence in the Mansion House. I do not believe that there has ever been assembled in Ireland a platform of speakers so informed and impressive on matters that the nation was about to vote on.

Maude Barlow flew at great inconvenience from Canada to be with us on that day. No one in the world knows more about the water 'debate' that we were having in Ireland and how it sits globally than Maude, but despite calls and emails to radio stations and reporters the week before she arrived, not a single outlet wanted to interview her. Not a single journalist had any interest in the planet's foremost 'water warrior', the woman who had spearheaded the United Nations declaration that water and sanitation are a human 'right' and who was the Senior Advisor on water to the 63rd President of the United Nations General Assembly, author of 18 books on the subject and National Chairperson of the Council of Canadians.

John Hilary from 'War on Want' is the foremost campaigner against the Transatlantic Trade and Investment Treaty (TTIP). This proposed trade treaty between the EU and the USA would effectively put the trading and investment rights of corporations beyond the democratic control and accountability of sovereign states. Throughout Europe there is a massive fightback against this threat, and its sister treaty between the EU and Canada (CETA), to such an extent that German courts are faced with their largest class action suit yet from their citizens in history challenging CETA's constitutionality. But the media were not interested in John Hilary either. There was a 'Slab Murphy' story to chase instead.

John Barry joined us from Queen's University Belfast and explained from an environmental point of view how neoliberalism was, as Naomi Klein wrote in *This Changes Everything*, destroying the planet. No media takers there either. And the wonderful and entertaining Ann Pettifor demystified economics, money and financial capital in a way that everybody could understand, and warned us that our failure to learn the lessons of the last financial crash and build proper regulation mechanisms meant we were ill prepared for the next which will soon be on the horizon. No takers for Ann either.

We had poetry (Stephen Murphy) and rapping (Dean Scurry) along with a political debate on the election and the policy platform featuring Clare Daly, Mary Lou McDonald, Richard Boyd Barrett and myself, chaired by Eoin O'Murchu. All in the centre of Dublin, all open to everybody, all well publicised, and all of which the entire media were invited to in the teeth of an election campaign. The coverage amounted to a few seconds on the RTÉ News and a critical piece in the *Examiner* newspaper, but none of the speakers were asked to be interviewed or to elevate our election debate above the banal with their challenging perspectives. But … then there was Yanis!

The week before the Mansion House event, Right2Water had been invited to speak at the launch in Berlin of a political entity called DiEM25 (Democracy in Europe Movement 2025) headed by Yanis Varoufakis, former Greek Minister for Finance. When I spoke at one of the sessions I asked rhetorically whether the European Union had already gone too far beyond democracy for a movement such as Diem25 to succeed, a theme I will return to when we assess the Brexit vote that has occurred since, from an Irish perspective. We had initially been invited by Yanis Varoufakis and agreed to attend only on the basis that he would reciprocate with a visit to our Mansion House event, although this reciprocation never materialised. Varoufakis did, however, make a video especially for that conference which gained quite a bit of media attention. In addressing the conference he appealed to Right2Change to assist the Irish people in contesting the general election 'in the way that the Irish people deserve'. He spoke about his experiences with our Finance Minister Michael Noonan and our outgoing Government when he had been Greece's Minister for Finance. He observed how:

> The Irish general election will either condone and legitimise the Irish people's violation at the hands of an unscrupulous local regime and a brutal European Central Bank. Or the general election will repudiate and condemn those who violated the Irish people. Your government did what all oligarchs wanted them to do – they blamed the victims. (Enda) Kenny said Irish people went mad borrowing. Really? What happened is that a small band of Irish international bankers, developers and politicians built up a gargantuan debt that you have to take on. Now you have a chance to send Mr Noonan packing. Our struggle was also a struggle for the Irish people. If our moderate proposals prevailed, a template would have been created for Irish debt restructuring for the end of debt in Dublin.

Varoufakis' comments about Noonan did get some coverage in the following days, but my overall view of the Mansion House event was that the unions had expended massive resources to not only change, but elevate, the national conversation. We had put together a platform which was of the highest order and went to considerable expense to put it on in a suitable location. Those who heard the presentations from the speakers over the day told us they had learned so much. It was all part of our process of bringing a political economic focus to the maximum number of people, to illuminate and explain the issues that were determining our lives and our challenges. But the opportunity presented to the mainstream media to engage with these speakers, these ideas and their perspectives was rejected and, in my view, quite deliberately so. Nevertheless, Varoufakis had, in his own inimitable fashion, described the challenge voters would be faced in two weeks.

## Right2Water Day 7 – 20 February 2016, Dame Street

There had not been a mass mobilisation of citizens during an election campaign in Ireland since independence, but in fulfilment of our promise to run this campaign right up to the election we were determined that there would be one this time around. Finding a suitable venue for it was more difficult than normal, however, with Dublin's main street in rubble with the Luas extension and so for safety and capacity reasons our favourite O'Connell Street location was out. An alternative venue wasn't obvious either as Dave, Billy Wall, Cormac O'Dalaigh and I went walkabout checking various locations. In the end, we chose a Dame Street venue with a stage to be erected at the Trinity College end looking up towards the Central Bank and Christchurch.

As usual, EQ Audio and Events were engaged to provide sound and large screens, and the gardaí in Pearse Street were helpful in facilitating the event and the march beforehand from Parnell Square. We again produced 500,000 leaflets but for the first time some of these were not picked up by some of the 'political pillar' who were busy dropping their own election literature in doors at that point. To be honest, we were more stretched in relation to the organisation of this event than any of the previous ones. For starters, instead of having the optimum six weeks to organise it we had effectively been organising three events in that timeframe and a lot of our time and energy had gone into the Mansion House event. In addition, there was a sense (even among some in the union fraternity) that we were getting too close to the electoral space and this was causing some discomfort. Could we not just put our campaign away and stop trying to actually shake the country up for a while? Well, no actually. To the vast bulk of the campaign this was what we had been building for and we were on the cusp of having a serious role to play in the election result, and for the better too.

It's funny the things you enjoy. For all the interviews I did, the demonstrations, the meetings and even some travelling that we had to do during the campaign, the days I enjoyed the most were when I was giving out Right2Water leaflets on O'Connell Street on my lunch break or delivering *Change News* around the homes of Castleknock and Carpenterstown. Some people do not like that kind of thing, and I thought I wouldn't either, but I loved it. I could sense by the reaction of people I met during those activities that the movement was making a difference far beyond anything you would have thought if measured through media coverage.

The day of the demonstration, Saturday, 20 February, was great. I left the Unite office where people were assembled as usual (including my two sisters in Unite ponchos) and went over to Dame Street with Padraig O'Rourke (Podge), my friend from Dundalk who travelled to all our events and helped to provide stage security along with other friends and ESB staff representatives. I picked up some t-shirts we had got printed especially for the day and, after checking that all was well with the stage, sound and screen locations, I got to actually see one of the marches for the first time! Podge and I walked back across O'Connell Bridge and took up position on the O'Connell monument. As we waited we were confronted by a sea of people walking down O'Connell Street towards us and already the message from Dave back up at Parnell Square was positive. It was massive!

The marchers made their way chanting and waving banners along the south quays to Winetavern Street and turned left at Christchurch before filling Dame Street like a human tide as they moved down to the stage. As they did so the voice of Labour's Eamon Gilmore boomed from the sound system off the buildings in a video that was prepared which included all the electoral promises that had been broken before the last election. The stage event was the usual combination of speeches, poetry and music, but there were some amazing highlights. It began with the excellent music of Evelyn Campbell who frequently writes and performs musical pieces specifically for events and campaigns such as this. Stephen Murphy then brought all who listened to him to tears again with his talent and passion, just as he had reduced Ann Pettifor to tears in the Mansion House a week previously, while Cobh's Karen Doyle inspired us with 'know your place'. There was a special moment when a large cross section of the 106 election candidates who had endorsed Right2Change climbed up on the stage for a group photograph, but the real reality check was yet to come. Just six days from an election homelessness in Dublin was at crisis levels, yet we were hearing an election campaign conducted on a 'keep the recovery going' message. It was sick!

I know it was sick because I was the one who introduced to the crowd families, including beautiful little children, who were not only in emergency accommodation because of home-lessness, but who were being evicted from that emergency accommodation the day before polling. The plight of these women and children was not even exceptional, it was becoming commonplace as the housing policies of successive Governments putting builders' profits ahead of homes for children came home to roost. As we headed into an election, the choice was clear to all who cared enough to listen – do we really want to vote for more of this?

Whatever the answer that would emerge, one thing was clear: Right2Water had delivered on its promise, made by the unions concerned a year and a half earlier, to make this issue much more than about a protest or two. The people of Ireland had, in massive numbers, disabled Irish Water through protest and boycott, maintained and developed their awareness of the forces impacting negatively on their lives, and built a movement that would shape the election agenda and outcome.

Job half done!

# 15

# Elections Results and the Aftermath – All Is Changed, Changed Utterly

*A century after the 1916 Proclamation do we even live in an independent state, or are we just citizens of a dependent or vassal state?*

One of the essential attributes of a state under International Law is external sovereignty – that is, the right to exercise freely the full range of power a state possesses under international law. Recognition of a state as independent necessarily implies that the recognizing states have no legal authority over the independent state. The status of a fully independent state should be contrasted with that of dependent or vassal states, where a superior state has the legal authority to impose its will over the subject, or inferior, state. – *West's Encyclopedia of American Law*

Let's be clear. A state that must keep voting in European treaties until it gives a result acceptable to the European Union is not independent. A state whose budget must be approved in the German Bundestag before it is presented to its own parliament is, de facto, a state that has surrendered its sovereignty to a foreign power. A country who has external authority imposed upon it is no country at all – it is a dependent, or vassal, state.

On the last Christmas before the centenary of the reading of the Proclamation declaring an egalitarian Republic, 1,571 children and over 5,000 adults were officially homeless in this state. Yet the media loudly boasted how, on St. Stephen's Day, €5 million an hour was being spent in shops. As a state we have utterly failed to deliver the promise of the Proclamation while surrendering our sovereignty in all meaningful ways to a foreign power, the European Union. This would be disgraceful even if the European Union was still the one that we joined, an anti-imperialist, social Europe advocating continent-wide and worldwide peace and equality. But instead it has been supplanted by a vehicle for German imperialism (economic on this occasion) – the very thing it was set up to prevent. The fact that it has also become an aggressive and bullying advocate for neoliberalism makes the betrayal of the promise of the Proclamation shameful.

How did we arrive at this state of affairs? By decades of voting for either tweedledum – the populist and utterly unprincipled Fianna Fáil – or tweedledee – the neoliberal Fine Gael which has its origins in the fascism of Eoin O'Duffy. Also by handing key functions of the state over to a corrupt and abusive church which delivered decades of political dysfunction and generations of abuse victims.

From this mess any real debate or political analysis of alternatives was always absent. This was never a state where challenge was welcomed. It was always beaten down, first with a tommy gun and then with a belt or crozier. As a nation we seem to distrust and batter any dissent to a pulp. The 'consensus', which is always conservative and lacking in vision in Ireland, is protected by the state at all costs. The result? A lost Republic.

How did we allow it to happen? Every state has its birth pains and certainly the bitter civil war meant that a slow start for an independent Irish Republic was understandable. But how does it explain Charles Haughey as Taoiseach in the 1980s? Or electing Bertie Ahern three times with his chimney full of cash that he claimed to have won in the bookies, telling doubting economists to commit suicide, and even now blaming innocent citizens for the collapse of the state? How do 'birth pains' explain the citizenry choosing to vote for politicians of the 'calibre' of Ray Burke, Michael Lowry and Liam Lawlor, not to mention hundreds of parish pumpers, most of whom have never had a single original thought that didn't involve self-interest? 'Birth Pains' 100 years on? No. It's a betrayal. The state has been betrayed by those we elected to run it, and by continuing to elect them we betray ourselves.

The last decade has been the most preventable of the 10 decades to date. First came the greed, the vulgarity, and the over borrowing by state and citizen. Of course, for every irresponsible borrower there is an equally culpable lender, but no lender ever paid a price for what they did to Ireland. Anyone with sense knew it would end. And it did. But all we had was a very ill Minister for Finance being bullied by an arrogant Frenchman speaking for a European Union that is now in democratic, fiscal and political crises all of its own making.

Capitulation, 'bailout', socialism for the rich and reckless, capitalism and inhumanity for the poor have followed. This was the scenario when we reached Election 2011. Fine Gael was there with their usual 20-30 per cent, boosted considerably by the beating a stunned public gave to tweedledum. But they still were far short from what was needed to form a Government to face the horrors Fianna Fáil had left for them.

Labour were asked and, instead of solemnly assessing their position and their responsibility to their supporters, Gilmore and Burton leaped around the stage of the RDS as if they had won the lottery. You would never have guessed they had just knowingly inherited a broken state without sovereignty or independent power. As I watched the ridiculous, stomach-churning celebrations, I knew they didn't get it. And because they didn't get it they wouldn't do the right thing in Government. But these are intelligent, educated people. They know about neoliberalism and the tactics of disaster capitalism. They know that it waits like a vampire for times such as this to take assets from the working class and give them to the 1 per cent. They knew it in 2011 and they know it now.

Since 2011 Fine Gael have done what they were established to do. They have protected and enriched the wealthy at the expense of the rest. Unfortunately, Labour, which was created to do the opposite, has done exactly the same.

It's not just about the homeless children and families at Christmas. It's about the 37 per cent of citizens suffering deprivation. It's about the 300,000 citizens driven abroad. It's about the real unemployment rate of 12.9 per cent pre-Election 2016. It's about the complete supplication to the economic policies Germany needs which are, almost always, the opposite of what we need. And it's about Irish Water.

The Government responsible for all this could not have been re-elected. And it wasn't.

Before the election was called I wrote a blog wondering how a Government could be formed and what, in 2016, will we, the heirs of the Republic once envisaged by great men and wmoen, do to reclaim that vision?

There is no need to provide a full breakdown of the Election 2016 results here but the main points are clear:

- The Fine Gael/Labour coalition government got routed from office

- Labour lost 30 of the 37 seats they had entered that government with, over 80 per cent of their seats lost

- Fine Gael also had an awful election losing 26 of the 76 seats they won in 2011, over one-third of their seats lost

- The key outgoing government initiative of attempting to buy the election by cutting taxation was rejected by the vast majority of voters more concerned with the state of essential public services

- Almost 100 of the 158 seats were filled by candidates who had campaigned on an anti-water charges platform

- Candidates who endorsed the Right2Change platform won 36 seats

- The results meant that, for the first time in modern Irish politics, a majority Government could not be formed

- Almost 35 per cent of those entitled to vote did not.

Some of the casualties of the election were spectacular and Irish politics has since been in a state of disarray. Fine Gael now heads a minority Government that only stays in office by the grace and favour of their sworn enemies in Fianna Fáil, and the fact that the two large parties of the right are being forced together befits parties with no major policy differences. We currently have a Taoiseach whose party cannot command the support of even one-fifth of those entitled to vote.

Labour has been eviscerated for their betrayal of their core supporters. They cannot get the backing of 5 per cent of those entitled to vote, and Alan Kelly's pre-election prediction that they could still win at least 15 seats and return to Government was wildly off the mark. A bitter leadership contest followed where Kelly was kept off the ballot paper by his own parliamentary party and Brendan Howlin was elected to lead those who remain. On 11 August 2016, Labour's public relations guru Pat Montague took to the national airwaves to explain how the party had carried out an assessment of this disaster. When pressed on water charges, he announced his support for them on the basis of 'conservation'. Odd that they never had that view before the 2011 election promise not to introduce domestic charges and that they were emphatically opposed to them. The spin doctors continue to spin their nonsense while the party is over for practically all but those who get a living out of it. They never listened!

In February 2016, Fianna Fáil loudly celebrated the second worst election result in their history. Fine Gael may have suffered savage losses but they were still comfortably ahead of Fianna Fáil both in terms of seats and vote share. That the latter saw this as a success indicates just how far they had fallen. The historic fact of Election 2016, however, is that both parties together could not command a combined majority of those who voted, let alone those who are left cold by the current state of Irish politics and just stayed away. But Fianna Fáil did react to the national mood in the run up to the election. The party that, more than any other, wrecked the nation with its 'dynasties', its brown envelope culture and its embarrassing cronyism went all sympathetic and cuddly in the run up to Election 2016. Suddenly they were concerned about inequality, deprivation and unfairness. They even had the neck to talk about tax reform and making those at the top pay their share – as if they ever did such a thing when in power – and then in their manifesto they gave the following commitment on Irish Water and domestic water charges:

### (ii) Abolish Irish Water and end water charges

Irish Water has been a complete failure on the part of the government. Since it failed the Eurostat test, the very reason it was set up, it is incapable of delivering major investment in our water network. Instead it is imposing a water charges regime where families are paying for a service that does not deliver, operated by a quango that simply is not working. People should not be expected to pay for a service that is not up to standard. We need a 21st century water system that will attract global business investment, allow businesses and agriculture to expand and provide safe water to homes. Irish Water has failed to achieve basic public legitimacy, has diverted resources away from the water infrastructure and does not have the capacity to focus on its most important tasks. We will: – End the failed water charges regime. This will save families €160 per year and allow the better use of state resources. – Abolish Irish Water and create a new slimmed down agency to deliver the national water investment programme. The National Water directorate will develop a nationwide approach while local services will be handed back to democratically elected local authorities with on the ground knowledge.

According to the Department of the Environment the net cost of scrapping water charges would be of the order of €210m annually. This would be replaced by a direct state subvention to the new National Water Directorate, which will be run at an approximate cost of €16.2m per annum. We would also fully provide for the costs of winding down Irish Water, at a cost of €9.1m and abolish the government's botched Water Conservation grant to save the state €110m.

That is clear enough isn't it? If words mean anything those words mean that Fianna Fáil pledged to abolish Irish Water and water charges, and they gave pretty solid reasons for doing so too. But in Irish politics, as Pat Rabbitte pointed out, words in an election campaign or manifesto mean little. They are simply confidence tricks politicians play on voters to ride whatever popular mood exists at the time to get themselves elected.

Since February, Fianna Fáil has done nothing to build support with the other 50+ TDs who share their view on that issue. Instead, they have worked with Minister Simon Coveney to set up an 'independent commission' of people hand-picked by the Minister. The commission is charged with delivering on terms of reference that specifically requires it to retain Irish Water. The terms of reference also exclude the commission from assessing the social impact in relation to how we provide our most precious resource – water. Coveney appointed veteran trade unionist Joe O'Toole, a seemingly safe pair of hands, to head the commission, but O'Toole's hands didn't prove to be that safe as he went on to wax lyrical all over the media, effectively announcing the commission's findings before the commission had even met. Joe and the commission were just there to make sure water charges would, according to O'Toole, 'have enough sugar on it to make the medicine go down easily'.

O'Toole had been retired for a while from his trade union position so could possibly be forgiven for forgetting that in gombeen Ireland things aren't done by being as honest and straightforward as that. So he was replaced as Chairman before ever attending a meeting, but the commission's terms of reference remain and the political gamesmanship continues.

## Brexit, Europe and the Unelected European Commission

In the intervening months since the election the unelected European Commission seems determined to show the Irish just how undemocratic it can be. But before turning to that, it is important to first address the biggest thing to happen in politics in 2016 so far – the decision of Britain to leave the European Union, Brexit.

The question as to whether Britain would vote to 'remain' or 'leave' the European Union was one that many believe should never have been asked. It is certainly one that the establishment does not want to be asked here. I stayed awake until 6.00 am on Friday, 24 June 2016, to get the answer to that question.

What a night it was. The night the British said 'enough' to the European Union. I was going to go to bed early. The markets had predicted a comfortable win for the 'remain' side and the bookmakers were almost completely ruling out a 'Brexit'. There was a YouGov poll just in as the voting closed at 10.00 pm and, although narrow, it confidently predicted a 'remain' outcome. An earlier poll had predicted a 'remain' win by as much as 10 points.

There's that 'consensus' again!

You know the result by now, but you have possibly forgotten how, on that historic night, the turnaround began with a very narrow win for 'remain' in Newcastle where a comfortable win was expected. Minutes later, from the Tyne down to the Weir and Sunderland, a very strong 'leave' resulted. Within minutes the faces had changed. UKIP's Nigel Farage had conceded before a vote was counted (some judgement he has!) and was now withdrawing his concession while the experts in the BBC studio were looking for direction. The markets gave it as sterling lost 6 per cent in just 10 minutes and bookies started to adjust odds rapidly. As we moved into the 3.00 to 4.00 am period the results were rolling in and the pattern was clear. Scotland (hoping this Referendum would give them another shot at independence) was solidly 'remain', Northern Ireland less solidly so, and Wales was edging towards a 'leave'. And so to England. It couldn't have been clearer. The old industrial heartlands in the North and Midlands were voting solidly to leave the European Union, while London City and Centre, basically wherever there was wealth, were voting 'remain'.

But by now it was too late. As I took my final hot whiskey to bed at about 4.00 am to continue to watch the TV from there, the bookmakers had stopped taking bets on a 'leave' result, the market for sterling was in freefall and would soon be joined there by the euro as well. By 5.00 am both BBC and Sky had called it as a 'leave' result. I put the TV on mute and went to sleep for a couple of hours but was awake again in time to see a tearful David Cameron, accompanied by his wife, announcing his resignation as British Prime Minister. It was extraordinary.

As I made my way to work later it became clear that the Irish media, not one of whom had predicted this outcome or provided anything other than pro-'remain' coverage for weeks, were failing utterly to address the real reasons for this result. That morning British voters were insulted by present-ers on Irish national radio stations and patronised by an Irish MEP, while supposedly our markets were falling, our curren-cy plunging, and our parliament had been recalled (they de-cided that they were going to work four days the next week). You would think our country had been subjected to a major natural disaster such was the hue and cry. People like Michael Noonan, Brendan Howlin, Peter Sutherland and even Blairite Alastair Campbell worked themselves into a panic on Irish airwaves.

But if anybody here was worried that this decision by British voters would cause the Irish to question further our relationship with the European Union, nobody told the European Commission. Four days later, while Europe reeled, a spokesman for the Commission confirmed that no matter what Irish voters wanted, and had voted for, that we would be fined if we didn't reinstate domestic water charges. 'Irexit' anyone? If I seem flippant it is not because this situation is not serious. An unelected body from a failing political entity trying to impose its will on the people of a sovereign state against their express wishes? Are we just 'a vassal state'? But the flagrant manner of this behaviour, and the timing and execution, might lead one to ponder whether they actually want the European Union to fail now.

Many in the water movement reacted with horror to this statement from the Commission. The statement that the water charge regime, which had failed utterly and was panned even by Eurostat, is now 'established practice' is utterly lacking in credibility. So too is the decision of an unelected Commission to threaten a nation with fines for not carrying out its will when ultimately this is a matter for the sovereign people of a member state and, if challenged, for the European Court of Justice who has already found for the German people in a similar case. And fines? We live after all in a nation which flagrantly ignores a European Directive on Vehicle Registration Tax (VRT) because successive Ministers for Finance are quite happy to pay fines if abiding by a directive is deemed to be against our national interest.

But this is about democracy now. On the day that the Commission made this ill-judged and ludicrous statement, Right2Water announced that 17 September 2016 would be our next day of action. Why? Because at this point we have to have an honest and open debate about the nature of our membership in the European Union, whether that relationship as currently structured can be sustained.

Right2Change has already called for a referendum on continued membership if the Transatlantic Trade and Investment Partnership (TTIP) is ratified without the consent of the Irish people. Now we have the Commission trying to bully us into the Europeans Union's clearly stated water privatisation agenda. And, as mentioned previously, this small nation with less than 1 per cent of the population of the EU has been saddled with 41 per cent of its banking debt. Whether it's fisheries, natural gas or potentially oil, the stripping of our national assets simply has to stop.

It has been easy since Brexit for the 'consensus' to write off the vote as one of racism and xenophobia. It is true that when Blair's 'New' Labour abandoned working class communities all over Britain that it created a vacuum, some of which has been filled by UKIP, ignorance, racism and even fascism. But only some of it. The truth is that many who voted 'leave' on Brexit did so because they believe that the EU had now cast their communities and their children's futures aside on the altar of financial capital and greed, that it has sacrificed them to lives of inequality, deprivation and hopelessness.

Sound familiar?

# 16

# 17 September 2016 – 'Abolition Not Suspension'

The usual plans for Right2Water Day 8 were put in place and the usual finances, press conference, leafletting and postering were delivered. The usual problem with a location was also present and, having tried without success to get availability in Smithfield and with O'Connell Street still in rubble, we decided the long wide open street on St. Stephen's Green south would be suitable. We were unsure of the numbers on this one. More unsure than usual. With water charges suspended and a commission looking at them – albeit with a deliberately rigged terms of reference and remit – people are not getting bills anymore. Would this provide the space for the Government and Fianna Fáil to wriggle off the hook, or would tens of thousands once more demonstrate that a people's movement would be having none of it?

Right2Water made a submission to the Commission and other submissions and papers were made by the European Water Movement and Maude Barlow's Blue Planet Project. All three submissions are available on www.right2water.ie but for those reading this book who may not have fully absorbed our position yet, the Right2Water submission is set out in full at the end of this chapter. The closing date for submissions was on 9 September but, in addition, just two weeks before the dem-onstration the European Commission made the unsurprising announcement that Apple Corporation had been facilitated by the Irish Government in avoiding taxes here to the tune of €13 billion, or about €19 billion with interest. This was described by the Commission as 'state aid' and Apple were told to pay their dues to the Irish people. Unlike the opinion of the Commission on water charges, this followed a rigorous investigation spanning several years with all sides being allowed to have an input into the deliberations. This meant that, when the determination came, if took the form of a formal decision. Not surprisingly, Apple immediately announced that they would be appealing this decision, as is their right, to the European Court of Justice, but how would the Irish establishment react?

Well what a masterclass in spin and baseless rhetoric we got in the aftermath of that decision. The very people who had used Europe and the EC like a battering ram to push through a water privatisation agenda (not to mention an attack on the people of Greece) were suddenly donning the rhetoric of 100 years ago of 'defending small nations'. Michael Noonan, the greatest Europhile politician we have possibly ever had, argued with a straight face that the Commission was bullying us by trying to force us to take €13 billion in tax from the richest corporation on the planet. It was revealed that Apple had paid just 0.05 per cent in tax in the years under review, and this was widely deemed acceptable. 'How dare the Commission tell how to give free passes to capital while our people suffer excruciating austerity' was the refrain all round. It was very hard to find a voice, anywhere, who was given airtime to advance the alternative view.

Here is an alternative view. Remember the serious, fundamental and challenging statement I made on page 183? It said:

> The services that a society needs to function are in decline because those who can most afford to fund them refuse to, and are allowed to so refuse.

We all know what those services are by now – a home, an education, a hospital bed when you are sick, affordable childcare, transport, water and sanitation. Apple can afford €13 billion. To them it is a drop in the ocean. Almost nothing actually. But they simply refuse to pay their share here or anywhere else.

And they are allowed to so refuse. Apple might not give a toss about the lives of the people who use their products in Ireland, so long as we consume them, but we elect a Government to give a toss, to care for us, to represent us and to do our bidding.

When our Government, including to their shame the so called 'Independent' Alliance, made a decision to appeal the Commission determination they not only took the side of soulless corporate greed over the sovereign states of the European Union, but they put the interests of the most wealthy above the interests of our citizens. Again!

And so a giant inflatable black rotting apple with 13 billion written on it headed a massive demonstration from Connolly and Heuston stations on 17 September. I walked this one in its entirety. I witnessed its scale, its good humour and its colour all the way. I witnessed the people coming out of shops and bars along the route applauding and showing support, even spontaneously joining in. I watched in awe as the throng along the South Quays met a throng on the North Quays at Capel Street bridge, both stretching back as far as the eye could see. And when we got to Harcourt Street and they had to turn off the Luas power so our rotting apple didn't blow up I spoke to stewards on the phone and watched on social media as confirmation came through that the march was stretching back to Wellington Quay. RTÉ said there were 15,000 there, which was a full five times what that morning's *Irish Independent* had predicted. But the RTÉ pictures on the Six One News that night told another story. We put the crowds at 80,000. In any event it was, once again, gigantic and liberating.

On stage I was angry. There had been another scurrilous effort in the papers the previous day to brand this mass people's movement as 'dissident'. As Joan Burton prepared to give evidence against a young lad in the Children's Court two days later, a boy who was only 15 when Jobstown happened and who identified himself to gardaí along with his Mum as carrying a phone that day, some within the media (only some by this point) were trying to again to tie this popular uprising on water to fringe elements in order to discredit it. So I took the word 'dissidents' and stated that none of the people I saw before me were dissident. What I saw were the ordinary people of Ireland fighting for their country. For politicians to govern with the support of less than one in five of the voters was 'dissident'; for politicians to lie through their teeth promising 'abolition' and to then fail to deliver on their democratic mandate was 'dissident'; for a tiny country to be stuck with the banking debts of the wreckers while the people who did nothing are impoverished and made homeless was 'dissident'; and for the media to ignore, misreport or pillory the largest and most peaceful protest movement anywhere in the world today was also 'dissident'.

Others spoke in a similar view. A genuine non-aligned speaker and his daughter from Jobstown read a statement from a community that continues to be under attack to strong and deserved applause. We had Micheal Kelliher talking to the crowd on behalf of the 6,000 users of Irish sign language (ISL), a crucial support for people with hearing difficulties, which apparently is too expensive for successive Governments to designate as an 'official language'. Stephen Murphy was his brilliant self with a poem about mental illness titled 'Before You Push the Chair', and then came Christy O'Neill.

Christy is from Dunleer in County Louth and is married to Kim and has three young children. On stage Christy offered a tale that could be told in every town and village in 'recovery Ireland' today. Christy outlined the story of the 'working poor'. Despite having a job Christy cannot afford a home for his family. This means that as he leaves for work every day Kim is left behind with their three children in the home of Christy's Mum and Dad where they all live. He had a car to get to work but tax and insurance hikes meant he had to give it up. Christy feels for Kim and is genuinely hurt when his kids ask him when they will be getting their own house. This tale had me in tears because of Christy's bravery, honesty, clear love for his family and because it is so typical. This is Ireland in 2016.

Two days later I was on the *Tonight with Vincent Browne* show with a Fine Gael Representative from Meath, Damien English TD, who lives just down the road from Christy. My head nearly exploded to hear this man talk about the recovery and to challenge the statement of Michael D. Higgins in reported in the newspaper the day before that there was no point celebrating personal success in a country surrounded by misery.

This has to change. This country and the hegemony of the those who perpetuate such inequality must change. And it is up to us, the people who aspire to better, to change it. In order to do so we need, above anything else, 'Unity'. But before that here is the Right2Water submission to Simon Coveney's 'Expert Water Commission':

## Right2Water submission to the Expert Commission on Domestic Public Water Services 1. Right2Water: Background and policy

Established in 2014, Right2Water is a public campaign of activists, citizens, community groups, political parties/

individuals and trade unionists which is calling for the Irish government to recognise and legislate for access to water as a human right.

"[The UN] recognizes the right to safe and clean drinking water and sanitation as a human right that is essential for the full enjoyment of life and all human rights."

Concerned that private ownership of water and sanitation introduces the profit motive to this fundamental human right, Right2Water holds as a fundamental principle that water privatisation should not be considered or facilitated in any way. To this end, Right2Water has hosted seven national demonstrations, the largest of which attracted upwards of 120,000 people onto the streets of Dublin. Right2Water's call for the abolition of water charges is supported by a large majority of TDs returned to the Dáil in 2016. We believe that the government's refusal to accept the express wishes of Irish citizens and abolish domestic water charges exposes the anti-democratic nature of Ireland's political system and has given rise to the necessity of an eighth national demonstration against water charges on 17 September.

Right2Water is in favour of protecting our water and sanitation services from privatisation and the profit motive by enshrining public ownership of our entire water system in the Irish Constitution. On legal advice we have commissioned the drafting of a wording and enumeration of a new Article 28 Section 4:2.1, which reads:

"The Government shall be collectively responsible for the protection, management and maintenance of the public water system. The Government shall ensure in the public interest that this resource remains in public ownership and management."

The Right2Water campaign will continue to seek political, trade union and wider public support for a referendum asking Irish citizens if they wish to guarantee, within Bunreacht na hÉireann, the ownership and management of the public water system.

2. Expert Commission on Domestic Public Water Services: Terms of Reference

Right2Water welcomes the opportunity to submit the enclosed evidence to the

Expert Commission on Domestic Public Water Services, whose remit as set out in the Terms of Reference is "to assess and make recommendation upon the funding of domestic public water services in Ireland and improvements in water quality, taking into account:

• The maintenance and investment needs of the public water and waste water system on a short, medium and long-term basis;

• Proposals on how the national utility in State ownership would be able to borrow to invest in water infrastructure;

• The need to encourage water conservation, including through reviewing information campaigns on water conservation in other countries;

• Ireland's domestic and international environmental standards and obligations;

• The role of the Regulator; and

• Submissions from all interested parties.

The Commission will be empowered to commission relevant research and hear evidence to assist this work. The Commission shall endeavour to complete its work within five months of its establishment."

At the outset, we wish to record our concern that the Terms of Reference are restrictive and cynically disposed towards a system of domestic water charges. Specifically, the invitation for "Proposals on how the national utility in State ownership would be able borrow to invest in water infrastructure" is predicated on the existence of a revenue stream to fund repayments of the resulting debt. Unless the Government are disposed to doing this through general taxation, it can be strongly argued that the Terms of

Reference for the Expert Commission imply an outcome favouring the retention of domestic water charges.

Furthermore in relation to the Terms of Reference Right-2Water wrote to the Minister seeking the inclusion of the following paragraph in the Terms of Reference but unfortunately it was denied: "The social implications of funding water services in the short, medium and long term – including water poverty, future privatisation and potential water shut offs for low income families."

The exclusion of this or any similar provision in the Terms of Reference indicates that the Minister takes no cognisance whatever of the costs in terms of the social damage that domestic water charges cause and the cost to the exchequer when tackling these inevitable problems in the future. Ideally, for a balanced and informed debate, the Terms of Reference should include the economic, environmental and social implications of funding water services. To completely exclude from the remit of the Commission any reference to the social implications of this vital human rights issue indicates the ideological perspective behind the Irish Water project from the outset which is solely aimed at water commodification and privatisation.

3. Water charges infringe human rights

Over 2.6 billion people worldwide have no access to proper sanitation, while almost one billion still drink untreated drinking water. Until the introduction of domestic water charges in October 2014, Ireland could boast of being one of the very few OECD countries with guaranteed zero water poverty – i.e. no one would be deprived access to clean, safe water and proper sanitation because on an inability to pay an 'end user' charge. This was due to the funding of water and wastewater services through general taxation with additional contributions from commercial rates, a practice underpinned by the progressive principle of universalism: everyone pays their fair share in order that no one falls through the net.

Right2Water is concerned that, based on international evidence and experience, domestic water charges will lead in due course to water shut-offs and a spike in water poverty, regardless of whether they are administered through a state utility or a private sector entity. This view is borne out by a number of international precedents:

• In the city of Detroit, Michigan, an estimated 70,000 families have been affected by a mass water shut-off conducted by the Detroit Water and Sewerage Department – which is a public owned water system. The UN has described this practice as "contrary to human rights." This practice has also recently been introduced to the city of Philadelphia, where the impact on residents has yet to be felt on the ground.

• Following the privatisation of the municipal water supply Cochabamba, Bolivia's third largest city, Aguas de Tunari, the company which had been granted a monopoly over all water resources threatened to turn off people's water if they did not pay their bills. Rate hikes and water shut-offs ensued, leading to a series of mass protests that culminated in the emergence of a mass social movement and the reversal of privatisation by the government.

• In February 2011, just three months after being taken over by Veolia, the company's local subsidiary, Sofiyska Voda, increased water rates by 9 per cent in Sofia and threatened to shut off the water service of customers who failed to pay their bills. Sofiyska Voda had operated the water system in the Bulgarian capital since 2000 when it received the country's only water service concession.

• In cities in Hungary and Cyprus, where privatisation and the introduction of domestic water charges has taken place, non-paying, poor citizens in the suburbs have been cut off from their water supply. Similar examples are to be found in Paris, Rome, Bucharest and parts of the Czech Republic.

• The price of water in five US cities – Austin, Charlotte, Chicago, San Francisco and Tucson – ballooned by more than 50 per cent over the last five years –five times higher than inflation.

The phenomenon of shutting off citizens' water supply based on their inability to pay is increasingly prevalent across Europe and further afield. It is because this is an established practice worldwide that the introduction of domestic water charges poses such a fundamental threat to the human right to clean drinking water and sanitation.

4. Privatisation and profiteering

4.1 Profiteering in the water industry

Water is fast becoming one of the most profitable industries in the world, with the privatisation market now worth in excess of $1 trillion.

"Water is a focus for those in the know about global strategic commodities. As with oil, the supply is finite but demand is growing by leaps and unlike oil there is no alternative." – Credit Suisse.

"Water as an asset class will, in my view, become eventually the single most important physical-commodity based asset class, dwarfing oil, copper, agriculture commodities and precious metals."–Citigroup Chief Economist Willem Buiter.

"Investments in water offer opportunities: Rising oil prices obscure our view of an even more serious scarcity: water. The global water economy is faced with a multi-billion dollar need for capital expenditure and modernization. Dresdner Bank sees this as offering attractive opportunities for returns for investors with a long-term investment horizon." – Allianz SE's Dresdner Bank.

With the industry expanding at an exponential rate, publications such as Fortune Magazine are advising investors how to maximise their profits from betting on the price of water through emerging futures markets. Meanwhile the list of multinational corporations with water-related investments or water-targeted hedge funds is endless. Household names such as Goldman Sachs, JP Morgan Chase, Citigroup, Credit Suisse, Allianz, Deutche Bank and HSBC have joined companies such as Nestlé in securing a stake in the privatisation of water. Others firms such as Veolia Water, a company intimately linked with Irish Water, form part of a conglomerate known as the Global Water Summit, whose domain name (www.watermeets-money.com) tells us everything we need to know about the agenda being pursued by those involved.

A review of existing case study evidence gives some indication of the exorbitant profits to be made from the privatisation of water. In Britain, for example, the 19 private water firms made profits of more than £2.05 billion in 2013 and paid £1.86 billion to shareholders, but only £74 million in tax. The largest, Thames Water, has made more than £1.8billion between 2008 and 2013, paying more than £1.4billion to its shareholders and paying an effective tax rate of 0.128 per cent for that period. In 2013 it was one of seven firms not to pay any corporation tax at all.

Meanwhile average water bills have rocketed by 313 per cent since the water industry was privatised by the Tory government twenty-five years ago – which is almost double the average price increase of all other goods. An investigation by Westminster's Public Accounts Committee has recently concluded that Britain's privatised water companies made windfall gains of at least £1.2 billion between 2010 and 2015 from bills being higher than necessary.

As one important element of the contract to privatise Berlin's water system, a process that began when the city entered into a public-private partnership with RWE/Vivendi (now Veolia), it was agreed that water and wastewater fees would remain stable until the end of 2003. By 1 April 2004, however, fees were raised by 15.1 per cent, with the company announcing a further 5 per cent increase in 2005 followed by a 2-3 per cent increase in subsequent years. Faced with these steep increases in water prices, Berliners successfully organised a popular referendum in 2011 for the remunicipalisation of the city's water services, with an overwhelming majority voting in favour forcing Veolia out of Berlin.

Finally, a comprehensive survey of water companies across the US, by the Food & Water Watch, has found that privatisation invariably leads to excessive rate increases. This is, by its very definition, profiteering on the back of something that the UN regards as "a human right that is essential for the full enjoyment of life and all human rights."

It must be noted that when dividends are paid to shareholders this results in valuable resources that could be used for investment in necessary infrastructure being lost.

4.2 The privatisation logic of domestic water charges

Privatisation leads to profiteering, and it is our strongly held view that domestic water charges opens the door to privatisation and does so deliberately. Despite the wishes of peoples across Europe (see submission to Commission from the

European Water Movement) the European Commission and other institutions continue to push an ideological commodification and privatisation agenda:

"The Commission believes that the privatisation of public utilities, including water supply firms, can deliver benefits to the society when carefully made. To this end, privatisation should take place once the appropriate regulatory framework has been prepared to avoid abuses by private monopolies." – European Commission response to Parliamentary question, 2 October 2012. "Privatisation of Irish Water is ultimately envisaged." – Eurostat, 2015.

Proposals to introduce domestic water charges first appeared in the Irish government's National Recovery Plan 2011-2014, published in November 2010, and subsequently re-appeared in the Memorandum of Understanding agreed with the Troika in December of that year. It has been suggested on the basis of Cabinet papers that the impetus for domestic water charges came from Fianna Fáil, independent of external pressure and before the Troika bailout.

The EU/European Commission is one of the main driving forces behind the privatisation agenda. The logic of privatisation under the thin veil of "liberalisation" or "competitiveness" is enshrined in the Nice and Lisbon Treaties, and forms a central pillar of the Transatlantic Trade and Investment Partnership (TTIP) currently being negotiated between the US and EU.

The European Commission together with the European Central Bank has imposed some of the harshest discipline, including privatisation conditions, on the European states that sought debt relief in the wake of the 2008 financial crisis. The existence of water charges in Greece and Portugal, for example, has meant that the water utilities there are ripe for privatisation, offering a ready-made income stream for investors. The European Commission (as part of the Troika) has attempted to impose the privatisation of water utilities on Greece, Portugal and other member states by making it a condition of their bailouts.

In response to a question from Irish MEP Marian Harkin in June of this year, the European Commission stated that:

"Ireland made a clear commitment to set up water charges to comply with the provisions of Article 9(1) [of the Water Framework Directive] … Ireland subsequently applied water charges and the commission considers that the directive does not provide for a situation whereby it can revert to any previous practice."

However, the Commission is also on record as stating that it considers "established practices" to be those practices which were "an established practice at the time of adoption of the directive". This Directive was adopted on October 23rd, 2000, and transposed into Irish law in 2003, when it is beyond doubt that Ireland used general taxation as its established practice. Indeed, this was the established practice right up until the introduction of domestic water charges in October 2012 in a project which has now been resoundly rejected by the majority of Irish citizens.

On this basis, Right2Water believes it is the Irish government's duty to use its derogation, justify its approach to river basin management and, if necessary, challenge the Commission through the EU courts. If the political will is there this could be done with reference to the 2014 landmark case on EU water recovery rules whereby the European Court of Justice found in favour of Germany, after the European Commission tried unsuccessfully to take that state to court for, in its opinion, failing to fulfil its Water Framework Directive obligations. This judgment conclusively stated that it cannot be inferred that the absence of pricing for water service activities will necessarily jeopardise the attainment of the Water Framework Directive.

The EU's fiscal rules also have a major bearing on the transition from domestic water charges to privatisation in that the Fiscal Compact Treaty enables water funding to be moved off balance sheet providing the government can prove that over half of Irish Water's revenue comes from customers. By effectively demanding that 51 per cent of funding must come through water charges before it can be discounted from the government balance sheet this rule encourages states to firstly implement water charges in order to offload water from government accounts, and secondly, as we argue above, to privatise the water system.

5. The economics of water charges

Funding water services through domestic water charges is economically inefficient.

"The proposed expenditure on water metering would mean spending more than €1 billion which we don't have on something we don't need!" – Engineers Ireland, 2011.

"Senior Executive Engineer for Water, Gerry Concannon, estimated that the cost of unmetered water is currently about €350.00 p.a. per domestic unit. When all of the costs of metering involving installation, maintenance, administration and replacement are considered he pointed out that this cost almost doubles." – SIPTU, Water... A resource for the people, 2011. Other costs:

• Advertising expenditure (TOTAL €2.85m and €717,000 to RTE alone - FOI)

• Consultants (€90m)

• Call center staff

• Billing cycle (6m letters in 6m envelopes with 6m deliveries) (FOI request showed €5.6m spent in 10 months)

• IBEC fees (six figure sum – Sindo report).

• Metering – as already mentioned - €500m

• Borrowing repayments – interest, etc.

All of the above expenditure comes to approximately €600m which is double the government spend on water services in 2013 – and this is before any investment is spent on fixing pipes or upgrading infrastructure. It is waste that could be completely avoided if water continues to be funded through general taxation. A proportion of the spend could be utilised to encourage water conservation through financially incentivising water saving devices and a nationwide conservation education campaign. This would also allow Ireland to achieve the objectives of the Water Framework Directive.

The government's aim of treating water like any other utility (gas, electricity, etc.) should be a concern for all. Firstly, water is not like any other good in that you cannot live without it and there is no alternative. But with Ireland having the highest fuel poverty levels in the EU, it should be a worry for all low income households as to the future direction of water services. The spend that Ireland currently has in terms of fuel allowance – which tackles fuel poverty – would be necessary to compensate for water poverty should charges proceed. This should be factored into any economic forecasts for Irish Water. 6. Environmentalism and conservation

"International research shows that installing domestic water meters is unlikely to make any real difference to the amount of water used by families. For example in the UK, Germany, and the Netherlands it has been found that metering each home makes little difference to the amount of water used by families." – SIPTU, Water… A resource for the people, 2011.

There is currently no evidence that Irish households are profligate or wasteful with their water. In fact, Irish Water estimates that Irish individuals use 54,750 litres per day. The average usage for a single person medium usage household in the UK is 68,405 per year, approximately 20 per cent more, and the UK has had water meters since the late 1980s.

Astonishingly the government itself has admitted that it did not conduct any research into the environmental impact of introducing domestic water charges and the water metering programme. Given the massive costs and waste involved the failure of the government and the department of the environment to produce any evidence that domestic water charges reduce consumption is itself a worry and, again, exposes the purely ideological privatisation focused nature of the project. The failure to conduct any investigation into whether

introducing domestic water charges have a negative consequence for the environment exposes that the policy is not based on good environmental practice but instead on the commodification of a basic human right. For instance, Irish Water posts more than 6,000,000 letters per year which includes at least six million pages and six million envelopes. The metering programme has hundreds of vans driving throughout Ireland drilling holes in the ground and installing plastic meters that will need regular maintenance and repair, as well as replacement. This all has a cost, both economic and a substantial environmental cost and carbon footprint.

In conclusion, the people the Government says it wants to pay the highest bills are those, apparently, with swimming pools and those constantly washing their cars or watering their gardens. While the seriousness of this matter does not lend itself to flippancy making arguments about swimming pools and pools of cars in Ireland is systematic of the impoverished nature of the debate on this vital human rights issue in Ireland to date. In fact the international evidence shows that the higher a person's income, the less they are likely to conserve in water. This is because domestic water charges are so small in terms of a proportion of income for high-income earners while, for those lower down the earnings brackets the situation gets progressively more serious. While water charges as proposed by Irish Water when applied to a retail worker would reach approximately 3 per cent of their total incomes, a higher earner is expected to pay approximately 0.5 per cent or even more for the more wealthy. There is therefore no incentive for higher earners to conserve water arising from charges. Domestic water charges are extremely regressive in nature.

The situation would be significantly worse if, as proposed by some, 'allowances' were included as part of the package. Because the Irish Water model is based on economics and not social impacts, and because the terms of reference of this Commission continues in that vein, Irish Water is constructed to raise a set amount per annum circa €500 per annum. If allowances are allocated this set amount of income demanded does not reduce and so the allowances simply add to the cost of every litre of water over the allowance threshold, whatever it might be.

Those at home most, usually the most vulnerable, will generally use the most water. Unemployed, under employed, pensioners and those with disabilities will, in that scenario, be hardest hit with increasing bills calculated to reach a determined amount of income over that requires to be raised over and above allowances. The EU insistence that in order to be 'off balance sheet' bill payers must pay 51 per centcosts simply acerbates this problem and makes the entire project unsustainable. In summary including allowances makes an already regressive method of paying for water and sanitation even more so. SUMMARY

Ireland's established practice of paying for water and sanitation is through progressive general taxation. This method is the most environmentally sustainable, economically efficient and equitable manner of doing so. It is also the clearest, possibly only, method which is assured of vindicating the human right to water.

That the EU have refused to follow the United Nations in ascribing water and sanitation as a human right points to the EU's wish to have water turned into a commodity and privatised. This is confirmed by the nature and workings of the EU institutions themselves.

Ireland leads the way in having the most sustainable and efficient way of vindicating for our citizens water and sanitation rights and the Commission must view the international evidence and submissions from Europe and North America in this regard.

Insofar as investment is required this can be raised more cheaply by a sovereign nation than a private or semi-state entity and a funding stream to support such investment should be 'red circled' from progressive taxation.

The Commission is flawed in not being permitted to assess a fundamental issue of human rights in light of social impacts and is prevented, deliberately and by design, by its Terms of Reference, from doing so. In this regard it is impossible to hope that the Commission can help solve this issue of vital national importance.

Right2Water will continue to ensure that Ireland leads the world in refusing to engage in a structured effort to privatise and commodify our water and sanitation rights. Right2Water deplores the waste of vital public money on meters, billing systems, public relations, consultants, legal advisors, and offices in the pursuit of privatisation.

Right2Water demands a referendum as outlined above to allow the Irish people to choose whether to enshrine public ownership and management of our water and sanitation in our Constitution.

Right2Water urges the 32nd Dáil to act on its mandate to abolish domestic water charges and to desist in its efforts to subvert that democratic mandate.

Right2Water notes the recent ability of the Irish Government to face down the will of the EU Commission in the European Court of Justice and insists that this newfound defense of what the Government argue is the Irish interest is extended to defending, should it become necessary, our long established and much envied practice of paying for water and sanitation through progressive general taxation. This completes our submission.

Brendan Ogle
Dave Gibney
Right2Water Campaign Co-ordinators
9 September 2016

# 17

# So Where Will Our Progressive Government Come From?

Earlier I set out a tale of how a political party (Renua) was launched without policies, members or movement and how, in its first election, it fell flat on its face. At last in Irish politics we might be arriving at a stage of political evolution where personality and spin are not enough.

I fundamentally believe that the Right2Change policy principles that have evolved from the ground up and are contained in these pages would, if implemented, benefit every single person in this country. They would bring fairness where there is inequity and suffering, and they would also herald a much needed change to how our tax base is constructed. Progressive, secular and devoid of religious interference they could form the bedrock, the founding principles, of a new egalitarian Republic – at last. But how can they be delivered? I am not going to repeat here my critique of the various political elements that make up the 'political pillar' of Right2Change other than to say, at the moment, the existing players provide no real hope of delivering a broad progressive Government around these principles.

Yet it is clearly my view, and the view of many, that the need is urgent and the time is now. Fine Gael will continue to be the party of the 'monied class', the 20 to 30 per cent who have always held on to the real wealth in this country by only looking inwards and playing, even controlling, the system. Fianna Fáil, on the other hand, play the populist card much more effectively but it was Fianna Fáil who has been in Government most, it was Fianna Fáil who let this nation down most and it was Fianna Fáil who drove us over a cliff through a combination of idiocy, dishonesty, corruption and chicanery that would do the Sicilian mafia proud. That's too far, Brendan, you say? Nobody died, Brendan, you say? Think again about that one!

Sinn Féin see themselves as a future party of Government and that in itself is okay with me. But, in my view, Election 2016 could best be described as 'progress' for them in the South; it certainly couldn't be described as 'a success'. For reasons already expounded upon many who care deeply about the unequal nature of Ireland will never vote for Sinn Féin. I do not state that to offend, I simply state it because to me it appears to be an unarguable fact.

The next Government here, maybe all future Governments, will be a coalition one and, unless something different happens, unless there is a new, broad, popular political evolution I foresee Fianna Fáil and Sinn Féin in talks sometime down the line. When – and I believe it is a 'when' and not an 'if'– that happens Sinn Féin will quite reasonably look at the rest of this movement and point out that no alternative potential partner exists.

Labour? I'm finished with Labour. There is no more to be said. For those who still hope for progressive change Labour are not part of the solution; indeed, they have been a massive part of the problem. They are now so low, however, deservedly almost irrelevant, that they are best ignored. And before Comrade Stalin or Trotsky are thrown at me as the answer, let me say that I'm not sure we can wait for world revolution to make real and important changes in how Ireland is shaped for future generations. There are good and thoughtful people in many of the smaller left parties, but Trotskyist ideology married to hectoring and bullying of any opponent will not help the people of this country anytime soon.

When Connolly, Larkin and O'Brien formed the Irish Labour Party they were right about the need for a political arm to the industrial struggle, as it was framed then. But events took over them and that arm got left to the politicians and, free from democratic accountability to workers and communities, they turned that political arm into a weapon to be pointed at their own people, their own class. And so it has been for decade after decade, getting increasingly worse until the Republic went off a cliff in 2008 and the people with little were forced to bail out the establishment, the purveyors of risk, finance capital, fiscal recklessness and ineptitude. Inequality rules okay?

No it isn't bloody okay! From despair comes opportunity and from a people's movement fighting water commodification and theft, comes a force for change that must be used to enable the citizens themselves, in all 40 constituencies, to take democratic control of their lives. Of their *society*!

Unions and their members, workers, have a role to play. At least those who see their work as extending into every facet of their members' economic existences, 'beyond the factory gate, beyond the shop floor'. 'Union' means working together, nothing more and nothing less, and by working together in 'unity' we can bring resources, skills, planning and numbers to bear in our protests, campaigns and votes. We can reshape a destiny that, right now, will be bleak if we don't deliver 'a game changer'.

What I am saying is that unless the citizens who are now more alert, organised, educated and capable of taking control of their own destiny develop, or are helped to develop, a broad progressive positive movement for change, then the opportunity will be lost and the forces of century-old 'conservative consensus' will recover the ground they have lost. Once we allow them to do that they will then inflict even worse damage in the next century than they did to our dreams in the last.

'Broad' as opposed to 'narrow' or 'sectarian'. 'Progressive' as opposed to 'regressive and 'inequitious'. Can we do it?

We have the policy platform – popular, egalitarian and founded democratically by the people who support it themselves. We have massive, mobilised and determined movement. We have the opportunity, and as Fianna Fáil and Fine Gael contract, as the young and the dispossessed look for something that is hopeful and fair, that window of opportunity is wide open. We have the support from unions and union members including Unite and others. And we have the vision.

We can bloody do it alright. And we must.

'From Dublin to Detroit – Water is a Human Right'

But as Stephen Murphy eloquently explained:

### This Isn't Just About the Water

*By Stephen Murphy*

This isn't just about the water

It's about the prostitution of our island and the clients who have bought her

It's about how they bought and sold us like we're cattle at a mart

As we swallowed what they told us and tore ourselves apart.

It's not meant to be divisive, this is not just us and them

Instead we should unite ourselves again to stand as men, women and children, whose time has come to say

That the system isn't working, there must be another way-

There must be a future where our children won't be forced to leave

To find a better way of life in which they can believe

A future where this island will belong to us once more

And not the corporations that have risen to the fore

But for all that we march, we need to keep this in perspective

That the privatisation of water is an IMF directive

And the IMF themselves, for those who can't yet see

Are trying to write the manuscript for modern history

So it's not as simple as just demanding that water charges are abolished

Because in my understanding it's their objective to demolish

The notion of the nation state, for all that it once stood

Was abandoned there behind the gates those days in Breton Woods

When economists assembled in July of '44

As the whole world shook and trembled in the mire of the war

They were busy sewing seeds for the future of the planet

And the way that we've proceeded is exactly how they planned it

And for those who don't believe me, look up Harry Dexter White

And John Maynard Keynes when you get back home tonight –

Because I'm not some conspiracy theorist, sometimes I wish that was the case

But one thing I really fear is that the problems we all face

Are so entrenched with what we do and how we live our lives

That we'd no longer have a clue of how to just survive

If they took away our iPhones, our Facebook and our Twitter

The way they've taken people's homes and look I know I'm being bitter

But unless we stand united at the bottom to shout stop

You can be certain now of one thing that it won't come from the top

Because the trickle down economy has been dammed up now for years

And the one per cent have no intent to pay back the arrears

So it's time to leave our differences, and learn to come together

Or the freedoms people fought for will be lost and gone forever

'Cause now our ideas of unity and the nature of society

Have abandoned the community and pushed the impropriety

On the people who are making calls for all out revolution

Without any real ideas of a cognisant solution

But in every revolution where the wheels remain the same

The bicycle will only travel further down the lane

No matter who pushes the pedals, the nature of the game,

Just becomes the hunt for medals and the quest to lay the blame

So we look to blame society, and we cite a lack of trust

But in the cold light of sobriety, this all comes back to us –

Because Ireland is the prototype of globalist ambition

We bought the hype and sold the rights to all our old traditions

And those we didn't sell, we just gave away for free

To the cronies and the phonies in this modern dynasty

Who see success as something measured by the others they put down

Just to elevate themselves to the status of the clown.

But it's easy to just stand here and go on about what's wrong

We've elected politicians just for singing that same song

But without a clear direction it's just whistling in the wind

So it's time for introspection, and time that we begin

To decide what way the future is, while that choice is ours to make;

Do we lie back down and take it, or do we stand for what's at stake?

And I know that what I do isn't going to change the world

But if I can make a difference to one person with my words

I would hope that it would be to say that mutual respect

Should be the very least that we as people can expect –

'Cause since these protests started, I've seen hope grow exponential

With people realising the true nature of their potential

Is not to bitch in kitchens wondering what there might have been

If only they'd done this or that or dared to live their dream

But we owe it to each other to be decent when we can

To be kind to one another and to see that while we stand

We're all in this together, every woman and every man

Drawn from all the corners of this rich and fertile land

So I ask the people marching, not to see the guards as others

They're our fathers and our mothers, our sisters and our brothers

And I ask the gardaí likewise, to see us as the same

'Cause to see the bigger picture we must step outside the frame

And to those who see mass protest as a waste of time at best

It's only 'cause of protest that these charges were addressed

And to those who sit there wondering, what it is that they can do

Well, we're trying to shape the future, all we're waiting for is you.

– *December 2014*

# Index

Adams, Gerry, 106, 203
Ahern, Bertie, 50, 175, 233
Allende, Salvador, 33
Amalgamated Transport &
  General Workers Union
  (ATGWU), 35, 44, 60
Anti-Austerity Alliance (AAA),
  61–2, 143, 146, 200, 203,
  205–7, 219–20
Apple Corporation, 244
Archontopoluos, Yiorgos, 131–5
austerity, 55–8, 65, 80, 83, 85,
  94, 109, 127, 149–50, 170, 176,
  188, 221, 223, 244

Baker, Don, 198
Barlow, Maude, 22, 27, 225, 243
Barrett, Richard Boyd, 61, 203,
  205, 226
Beades, Gerry, 78, 109
Blair, Tony, 47–8
*Blue Future*, 22
Boylan, Lynn, 137
Brand, Russell, 97–8
Bree, Declan, 223
Brexit, 140, 238–42
Browne, Richie, 59–60, 193
Bruton, John, 41
Buiter, Willem, 23, 25
Building and Allied Trades'
  Union (BATU), 70–1

Burton, Joan, 41, 50, 85, 89–93,
  191, 218, 233, 246
Bush, George (Sr.), 45
Byrne, Derek, 73
Byrne, Thomas, 77

Campbell, Evelyn, 66, 198
Chambers, Jack, 217
*Change News*, 220, 222
Chicago School of Economics,
  33
Chilcot, Sir John, 48
Civil and Public Service Union
  (CPSU), 64, 174, 192
*Claire Byrne Live*, 123
Clancy, Audrey, 65, 67
Clinton, Bill, 48
'Cobh Says No', 126–7
Collins, Joan, 62, 90, 202, 203
Communications Workers
  Union (CWU), 64, 189, 202
Communist Party, 202
Comprehensive Economic and
  Trade Agreement (CETA), 28,
  169, 225
Connolly, James, 41, 43, 48, 56,
  151, 264
Connor, Anthony, 77
Coonan, Noel, 89
Coppinger, Ruth, 61–2, 218
Corbyn, Jeremy, 221
Coveney, Simon, 18, 237–8

Cowen, Brian, 50
Creighton, Lucinda, 176–8
Crick, Michael, 212
Cuba, 57–9
    healthcare in, 10–11
Curtis, Maeve, 149–50
Curtis, Terry, 195

Daly, Clare, 106, 292, 202–3, 226
Deeter, Karl, 178
Democratic Socialism, 41, 43, 45
Dempsey, Brendan (Wacky),
    65–6
Dempsey, Damien, 106, 198
Detroit Water Brigade, 2, 79, 96
Doherty, Gary, 214
Doherty, Pearse, 214
Doolin, Daithi, 62
Douglas, John, 148, 189, 193,
    202, 204, 211, 224
Doyle, Karen, 126–9
Drennan, John, 6, 178
'Dublin Says No', 72–3, 75, 78
Dunphy, Eamon, 118

Election 2011, 48–56
Electricity Supply Board (ESB), 6
    pension crisis in, 35–9, 57–8
English, Damien, 247
European Central Bank (ECB),
    20, 35, 50
European Citizens Initiative
    (ECI), 138
European Commission, 28
European Public Services
    Union (EPSU), 130
European Water Movement
    (EWM), 130, 137–8, 243

Fagan, Des, 105
Farage, Nigel, 239
Farrell, Alan, 123
Farrell, Vivienne, 195
Fianna Fáil, 41–2, 44, 48–54, 70,
    75, 77–8, 83, 85, 107, 109, 114,

175, 206, 208, 217–18, 232–7,
    243, 255, 263, 265
Fine Gael, 2, 9, 18, 41, 44,
    48–52, 54, 56–7, 72, 80, 82–5,
    89, 102, 124,136, 175, 177, 206,
    208, 232–6, 262, 265
Finucane, Marian, 76
Fitzpatrick, Stevie, 181, 200
Flannery, Frank, 124
Forcades, Sr Teresa, 114
Friedman, Milton, 14, 33–5, 46,
    52

Galvin, Andrew, 198
Gibney, Dave, 62–3, 68, 105,
    141, 148, 181, 196, 202, 204,
    210, 213
Gilligan, Keith, 223
Gilmore, Eamon, 41, 50–3, 55,
    85, 229, 233
Gleick, Dr Peter, 21
Good Friday Agreement, 60,
    205
Gorbachev, Mikhail, 45
Green Party, 85, 175

Halligan, John, 61, 106
Hansard, Glen, 106, 198
Haughey, Charles, 233
healthcare, 10–12, 161–2
Healy, Seamus, 61
Higgins, Joe, 175
Higgins, Michael D., 74
Hilary, John, 225
Hobbs, Eddie, 123, 177–8
Hogan, Phil, 2, 79–82
Hogan, Tom, 190
homelessness, 12–16, 18–19,
    102, 230
Howlin, Brendan, 40, 53, 56, 73,
    136, 235
Hughes, Bernie, 68, 94, 218, 223

International Monetary Fund
    (IMF), 20, 34

Irish Congress of Trade Unions (ICTU), 188–94

Irish Municipal Public & Civil Trade union (IMPACT), 189–92

Irish Water, 2, 25, 29, 64, 80–9, 97, 101, 106, 127, 130, 152, 230, 234, 236–7, 253

Jennings, Gavin, 121–2
Jobstown, 89–95, 246

Kavanagh, Anne, 195
Kavanagh, Pat, 209
Keaveney, Colm, 217
Kelleher, Terry, 192
Kelly, Alan, 81–2, 84–9, 109, 235
Kelly, Declan, 81–2
Kelly, Jimmy, 61–2, 67, 69, 107, 190, 202
Kennerk, Gerry, 70–1
Kenny, Enda, 50, 72, 102, 107, 136, 227
Kenny, Pat, 125
Keynes, John Maynard, 32
King, Gerry, 192
King, Patricia, 193
Kinnock, Neil, 212
Klein, Naomi, 34, 225
Klemm, Alex, 78

Labour Party, 40–56, 72, 80–9, 102–3, 109, 122–3, 136–7, 175, 188, 190–3, 208, 218, 233, 235, 263–4
Labour Party (UK), 47–8, 212
Larkin, James, 41, 43, 56, 151
Lyons, John, 68–9

MacLochlainn, Padraig, 214
Maloney, Pat, 72
Mandate, 62, 202
McCoille, Cathal, 122
McDonagh, Seamus, 76
McDonald, Mary Lou, 203, 226

McGrath, Eamonn, 94
McGrath, Mattie, 107
media, 113–25, 221
  and democracy, 113–15
  Irish, 76, 116–25, 221, 240
Militant Tendency, 212
Monbiot, George, 30
Montague, Pat, 235
Moore, Paul, 94
*Morning Ireland*, 120–3
Murphy, Noreen, 75, 195, 214
Murphy, Paul, 62, 91–4, 204, 211
Murphy, Stephen, 198–9, 226, 246

Nash, Ged, 217
neoliberalism, 27, 30–39, 41, 45, 47–8, 54–6, 61, 83, 93, 103, 133, 138, 154–5, 221, 228, 232, 234
'No Privatisation, Irish Water, Irish Nation', 107
Noonan, Michael, 50, 136, 185, 226–7, 244

O'Brien, Denis, 117, 119–20
O'Brien, Keith, 195
O'Connor, Jack, 192
O'Duffy, Eoin, 232
*Off the Rails: The Story of ILDA*, 6, 76, 116
O'Flynn, Diarmuid, 72
OFWAT (UK), 25–6
O'Gorman, Michael, 223
O'Neill, Christy, 247
O'Neill, Damien, 94, 223
O'Neill, Fran, 59
OPATSI union, 64, 189, 202
O'Rourke, Padraig, 195, 197, 229
O'Rourke, Sean, 103, 119, 123
O'Sullivan, Jeremiah, 109
O'Toole, Joe, 238
*Out of Water*, 22

People Before Profit, 61, 68, 73, 143, 146, 200, 205, 217, 219–20
Pinochet, Augusto, 33
Podemos, 180
Pringle, Thomas, 62, 214
privatisation, 2, 8, 24–9, 33–4, 37, 46, 64, 77, 79, 82, 87–8, 94, 130–42, 153–5, 170, 192, 241, 244, 250–60
Progressive Democrats, 85

Quinn, Ruairi, 57

Rabbitte, Pat, 39, 41, 57, 102–3, 119, 176
Reagan, Ronald, 33
Renua, 123, 176–8, 262
Right2Change, 120, 124, 155, 197, 202, 206–11, 215, 217–20, 223, 230, 241, 262
    policy platform of, 156–87, 189, 195, 200, 202, 208, 214
Right2Water
    three pillars of, 64, 75, 179, 181, 202
Right2Water Day 1, 65–7, 124–5
Right2Water Day 2, 75–9
Right2Water Day 3, 80, 96–113
Right2Water Day 4, 142–4, 147–50
Right2Water Day 5, 195–9
Right2Water Day 6, 224–27
Right2Water Day 7, 228–30
Roche, Dick, 118
Rolling Tav Revue, 3
Romer, Jorge Rodriguez, 139–40
Ronayne, Eoin, 202

Scurry, Dean, 198, 226
Sinn Féin, 106, 137, 175, 200, 202–7. 217, 223
SIPTU, 189
Smith, Brid, 62, 66
social democracy, 41, 43, 47, 54, 56

Social Democrats (party), 175, 202, 207–9
social partnership, 7, 70
Socialist Party, 144, 200, 204–6, 212
Socialist Workers Party, 144, 200
Stewart, Sinead, 148–9, 195, 214
Syriza, 129, 136, 180

Taft, Michael, 185–6
Teneo Holdings, 81–2
Thatcher, Margaret, 8, 14, 32–3, 35, 46, 127
*The Last Word*, 118
Thessaloniki, 79, 129–34
*This Changes Everything*, 225
Today FM, 118–19
Trademark Belfast, 152–3
Transatlantic Trade and Investment Partnership (TTIP), 169, 225, 241
Trichet, Jean-Claude, 34, 49
Troika, 49, 77, 83–5, 130, 132–6, 254–5

Unite union, 35, 57, 59–65, 67, 69–71, 78, 97, 103, 107, 122–4, 153–4, 174, 185, 189–92, 200, 202, 206, 212, 219, 223, 265
United Nations (UN), 9–10, 27, 137, 225

Varadkar, Leo, 217
Varoufakis, Yanis, 226–7

Wall, Billy, 197
Wallace, Mick, 202
Wedes, Justin, 3
Weldon, Garrett, 217
Whelan, Andy, 78
White, Alex, 92
*Whose Water Is It Anyway*, 23

Young, Brendan, 62